AMC'S BEST DAY HIKES IN THE CATSKILLS AND HUDSON VALLEY

D1245442

WELCOME TO THE AMC

Welcome to the Appalachian Mountain Club! Founded in 1876, we are America's oldest conservation and recreation organization. We promote the protection, enjoyment, and wise use of the mountains, rivers, and trails of the Appalachian region. The AMC has twelve chapters from Maine to Washington, D.C., comprised of tens of thousands of outdoor enthusiasts like you.

By purchasing this book you have contributed to our efforts to protect the Appalachian region. Proceeds from the sales of AMC Books and Maps support our regional land conservation efforts; trail building and maintenance; air- and water-quality research; search and rescue; and environmental education programs for school age children, at-risk youth, and outdoor enthusiasts.

The AMC encourages everyone to enjoy and appreciate the natural world because we believe that successful conservation depends on such experiences. So join us in the outdoors! We offer hiking, paddling, biking, skiing, and mountaineering activities throughout the Appalachian region for outdoor adventurers of every age and ability. Our lodging destinations, such as our state-of-the-art Highland Center, are Model Environmental Education Facilities, demonstrating our stewardship ethic and providing a place for you to relax off-trail and learn more about local ecosystems and habitats, regional environmental issues, and mountain history and culture.

For more information about AMC membership, destinations, and conservation and education programs, turn to the back of this book or visit the AMC website at www.outdoors.org.

CATSKILLS & HUDSON VALLEY

Four-Season Guide to 60 of the Best Trails
From New York City to Albany

Including Shawangunks • Taconics • Hudson Highlands

PETER W. KICK

Appalachian Mountain Club Books
Boston, Massachusetts

The AMC is a non-profit organization and sales of AMC books fund our mission of protecting the Northeast outdoors. If you appreciate our efforts and would like to make a donation to the AMC, contact us at Appalachian Mountain Club, 5 Joy Street, Boston, MA 02108.

http://www.outdoors.org/publications/books/

Cover and Interior Design: Eric Edstam
Cartography: Ken Dumas
Front Cover Photographs: *Couple at an overlook above a lake while hiking in the Catskills* © Scott McDermott/IPN Stock, www.ipnstock.com; *Winter hiking* © Jerry and Marcy Monkman, www.ecophotography.com.
Back Cover Photographs: Peter W. Kick
All interior photographs by the author unless otherwise noted.

Distributed by The Globe Pequot Press, Guilford, Conn.

LIBRARY OF CONGRESS CATALOGING-IN-PUBLICATION DATA
Kick, Peter, 1951–
    AMC's best day hikes in the Catskills & Hudson Valley : four-season guide to 60 of the best trails from New York City to Albany / Peter W. Kick.
        p. cm.
    Includes index.
    ISBN-13: 978-1-929173-84-6 (alk. paper)
    1. Hiking—New York (State)—Catskill Mountains—Guidebooks. 2. Hiking—Hudson River Valley (N.Y. and N.J.)—Guidebooks. 3. Trails—New York (State)—Catskill Mountains—Guidebooks. 4. Trails—Hudson River Valley (N.Y. and N.J.)—Guidebooks. 5. Catskill Mountains (N.Y.)—Guidebooks. 6. Hudson River Valley (N.Y. and N.J.)—Guidebooks. I. Title: Best day hikes in the Catskills & Hudson Valley. II. Title: AMC's best day hikes in the Catskills and Hudson Valley. III. Appalachian Mountain Club. IV. Title.

    GV199.42.N652C3736 2006
    917.47'380444—dc22

                                                                                2006004758

The paper used in this publication meets the minimum requirements of the American National Standard for Information Sciences—Permanence of Paper for Printed Library Materials, ANSI Z39.48–1984.∞

Outdoor recreation activities by their very nature are potentially hazardous. This book is not a substitute for good personal judgment and training in outdoor skills. Due to changes in conditions, use of the information in this book is at the sole risk of the user. The author and the Appalachian Mountain Club assume no liability for accidents happening to, or injuries sustained by, readers who engage in the activities described in this book.

Interior pages contain 30% post-consumer recycled fiber.
Cover contains 10% post-consumer recycled fiber.
Printed in the United States of America,
using vegetable-based inks.

10 9 8 7 6 5 4 3   09 10 11 12 13

Mixed Sources
Product group from well-managed forests and recycled wood or fibre
www.fsc.org Cert no. SCS-COC-002464
© 1996 Forest Stewardship Council
FSC

For my mother and father, who introduced
me to the outdoors at a tender age.

ACKNOWLEDGMENTS

You may not want to believe this, but very often, the job of a guidebook writer (*especially* when the subject is hiking) is a harsh, solitary, and tedious one. I am still of the mind, of course, that a "bad day hiking is better than a good day at work." There were many long days of travail and research; however, friends and acquaintances along the trail helped make this an entirely enjoyable if not fascinating bipedal experience—from tip-to-toe.

In view of that I'd like to recognize those who supported me through the creation of this book. Foremost among them is the Catskill Center for Conservation and Development's (CCCD) vibrant Inverna Lockpez. For several successive summers, Inverna selected me as an artist in residence at the Platte Clove Preserve cabin, a woodsy retreat of waterfalls and old-growth forest abutting the Indian Head Wilderness Area, where I worked on this book. I'd also like to thank the CCCD's unwavering Executive Director, Tom Alworth, as well as his hard-working Director of Conservation, Chris Olney, and Watershed Coordinator, Aaron Bennett. My thanks and appreciation also goes to the rest of the CCCD staff, who manage the Catskills' only environmental watchdog agency.

My indebtedness extends to the many hiking companions who joined me on the trails, among them my good friends Barry Knight and Rita Berman,

Dori O'Connell, Nick and Erika Minglis, Ann Chinrella, and Susan Mawr. I also thank Bleecker's Creepers Hiking Club, including Alice Boomhower, Paula Ratliff, Judy Dupont, Larry Montalto, Bill Schwab, Gordon Ingles, Ben Morelli, Marlene Alexander, Marty Higgins, Peter Staats, Bill Tucker, Bob Santoro, Ed McCullough, and Ed Coombs, among others.

Thanks go to Chris Dicintio, the forest ranger covering the Harvey Mountain State Forest and to rangers and foresters who've helped me with this and other books, including the Rudges (Pat and Bill), Dennis Martin, Steve Preston, Stephen Scherry, Fred Dearstyne, Pete Evans and George Profous. Thank you as well, Drew Jones, manager, Hopkins Memorial Forest; Bob Spear, Rough Mountain fire warden, Sterling Forest State Park; Dr. John C. Dwyer, historian; Jim Morton, life-long Platte Clove resident; Dr. Mike Kudish, botanist, author of Catskill-related books and dissertations, and professor of forest history; AMC leaders John Frankfurt, Gary Skura, and Ed Goldstein; and solo hiker George Barrett who has climbed Bear Mountain more than 2,000 times in his lifetime.

Gratitude also goes to my woods-roving neighbors from the Hutterian Bruderhof's Catskill Community, especially the peripatetic Emmy, Lizzy, Abigail, and Eirlys, for their humble and lighthearted company on the trail and their sustained, cordial invitations to visit the community.

I am compelled to recognize, albeit posthumously, my old friend and one-time mentor Barbara McMartin, who died in the fall of 2005 at the age of 73, after a long struggle with cancer. Barbara was one of the Adirondacks' most dedicated preservationists and writers. Together, we co-authored *50 Hikes in the Hudson Valley* (1984), now out of print.

Of course, my endless appreciation goes to all of my readers. It's always such a pleasure to find people carrying your book in the woods (especially if they're not lost), or leaving it on the dashboard of their car, parked at a trailhead, where I might see it.

At last, my appreciation goes to Eric Edstam, who designed this book, and Ken Dumas, who created all of the featured maps. Several current and former members of the AMC staff managed to push this project along through several hardships—Sarah Jane Shangraw; Belinda Thresher; Laurie O'Reilly, senior marketing manager; and Vanessa Torrado, senior editor.

AUTHOR'S NOTE

The nature of guidebooks is that they directly affect the shape and development of recreational resources. The state's Department of Environmental Conservation (DEC) welcomes these publications from the private sector, because it has been able to cut back substantially on costly in-house guide and map production as a result. During the 25 years or so that I have written outdoor material about specific destinations, I have watched some areas change through increased public use. The state has responded by designating trails on such areas and adding signage, as well as including them on maps and pamphlets. Such "pressure" increases as more books are written and more trails are built, a fact that some people lament. To complicate matters is the tendency of guidebooks to clone one another, as each successive author uses (and sometimes "cannibalizes") the existing guides they consult for reference. But I do not feel this increased pressure has resulted in any serious or harmful impacts, especially in light of the fact that education fosters appreciation and thus, preservation. (With few exceptions, the trails of the region have not exceeded their "carrying capacity.") Nor do I offer any apologies for their divulgence; in fact, revealing what I feel are the most desirable places to hike is my explicit promise to my readers.

Finally, our natural environment is the single largest human resource, and it's there to be used and enjoyed. It is my sincere wish that this book and its carefully selected inventory of special, scenic places, will help you to do that. Just be prepared to rub up against the world a bit. Get wet, get dirty, get hungry and get sore. But whatever you do, get out there.

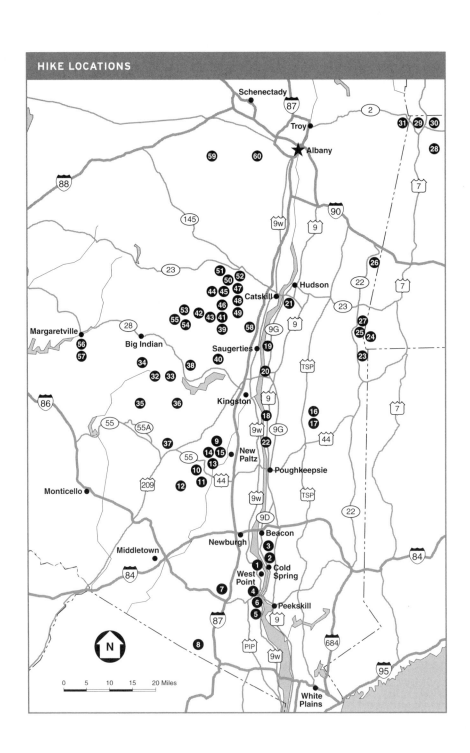

CONTENTS

AT-A-GLANCE TRIP PLANNER

#	Trip	Page	Difficulty	Distance	Elevation Gain	Estimated Time
	THE HUDSON HIGHLANDS					
1	Storm King	4	Moderate	2.3 mi	400 ft	2 hrs
2	Mount Taurus	9	Moderate	6.0 mi	1,400 ft	5 hrs
3	Breakneck Ridge to South Beacon Mountain	12	Strenuous	9.0 mi	1,400 ft	6 hrs
4	Bear Mountain	16	Strenuous	4.0 mi	1,000 ft	3.5 hrs
5	Dunderberg and the Timp	20	Strenuous	6.0 mi	1,600 ft	4.5 hrs
6	Anthony's Nose	24	Moderate	4.0 mi	700 ft	4 hrs
7	Schunemunk Mountain	29	Moderate	12 mi	1,364 ft	6 hrs
8	Sterling Forest Ridge	33	Moderate	7.5 mi	750 ft	4.5 hrs
	THE SHAWANGUNKS					
9	Bonticou Crag	43	Moderate	3.0 mi	500 ft	2.5 hrs

Snow-shoeing	Xcountry Skiing	Trip Highlights
		The Highlands' signature hike, beginning with a steep ascent, then easing up. This is among the shorter and easier Highlands hikes, with a scenic destination looking up and down the Hudson River.
		A fairly relaxed outing with a few steep pitches through deep woods to a scenic viewpoint, and descending along a creek.
		A demanding hike up the steepest and most exposed scenic trail in the Highlands, with sustained views from open ridges and returning through quiet forests.
		A pretty hike from the famous Bear Mountain Inn and state park along Hessian Lake, to Perkins Memorial Tower and its 360-degree views, descending on the Appalachian Trail.
	•	A backcountry ramble through the interior Highlands' historic trails and remote forests, with many scenic lookout points.
		A fairly steep ascent to an easy woods road, leading to Engagement Rock, where you look straight down on the Hudson River and Bear Mountain Bridge. A fairly easy hike with a memorable scenic payoff.
		A steep approach to a long, even ridge hike across a geologically distinctive landmass with far-reaching views across open ridge tops.
		A beautiful outing from Sterling Lake to the fire tower and back along the lake.
		A carriage road walk followed by a short introduction to rock scrambling on the Shawangunks' white quartz conglomerate talus fields, arriving at a bare summit with vertical cliffs and excellent views.

Snow-shoeing	Xcountry Skiing	Trip Highlights
•	•	An easy, but long, hike past two sky lakes along the old Shawangunk carriage roads, with swimming in Lake Awosting and far-reaching valley views from Castle Point.
•		A long and fascinating hike through the glacial cobble fields and pitch pine balds next to the sheer cliffs of Millbrook Mountain.
•		A long and remote scenic hike through the southwestern Shawangunks' oceanic dwarf pitch pine barrens, past Verkeerder Kill Falls and the Ice Caves.
•	•	An easy, enchanting hike along carriage roads under high cliffs, where rock climbing is very popular.
		A boulder scramble from Mohonk Mountain House through a deep and exciting crevice to a 360-degree view from Sky Top tower, and an easy walk back.
		A carriage road walk from Mohonk Mountain House to the gazebos and cliffs overlooking the Shawangunks and Catskills, with a walk around Mohonk Lake.
		A steep ascent to a fire tower overlooking the mid-Hudson Valley's agricultural lands, with views of the Southern Taconic Plateau and the Catskills.
•	•	The pond and surrounding wetlands are a national natural landmark where golden eagles and king rails nest. Excellent family hike.
•	•	A shoreline hike along the Hudson River, and a fine example of a Hudson River mansion and estate. A great family outing.
		A more secluded hike along the Hudson's marshy eastern shore, through the largest of the Hudson River National Estuarine Research Reserves.
•		A scenic river walk among open fields and stone walls with rustic gazebos and unforgettable views of the Catskills. Great family outing.
•	•	A stroll-like hike amid the grounds of Frederic Church's Persian-style castle home and through the picturesque landscapes of pond, gardens and woods created by this second-generation member of the Hudson River school of landscape painting.
•	•	A shore and forest walk on easy carriage roads to points along the Hudson River, from the museum, library, and home of Franklin D. Roosevelt.
		A short, very steep climb followed by a ridge walk across the scenic southern Taconic Plateau, featuring valley and mountain views.
		A gradual climb to the central Taconic Ridge, with views east over the Hudson Valley and Catskills, with free camping.

#	Trip	Page	Difficulty	Distance	Elevation Gain	Estimated Time
25	Bash Bish Mountain	111	Moderate	3.0 mi	1,200 ft	3 hrs
26	Harvey Mountain	114	Moderate	3.0 mi	480 ft	2.5 hrs
27	Sunset Rock	117	Moderate	3.5 mi	740 ft	3 hrs
	THE NORTHERN TACONICS					
28	Mount Greylock	124	Strenuous	8.2 mi	2,300 ft	7 hrs
29	Hopkins Memorial Forest	128	Moderate	4.3 mi	450 ft	2 hrs
30	Pine Cobble	131	Moderate	3.2 mi	1,000 ft	2.5 hrs
31	White Rock	135	Moderate	5.5 mi	300 ft	3.5 hrs
	THE CATSKILLS					
32	Slide Mountain	145	Strenuous	7.0 mi	1,700 ft	5.5 hrs
33	Wittenberg and Cornell Mountains	150	Strenuous	9.4 mi	2,480 ft	7 hrs
34	Giant Ledge	154	Moderate	3.0 mi	1,000 ft	2.5 hrs
35	Peekamoose and Table Mountains	157	Strenuous	10 mi	2,200 ft	5 hrs
36	Ashokan High Point	161	Moderate	7.5 mi	1,980 ft	5.5 hrs
37	Red Hill	165	Moderate	2.2 mi	890 ft	2 hrs
38	Mount Tremper	168	Strenuous	5.6 mi	1,960 ft	4 hrs
39	Codfish Point	171	Moderate	3.5 mi	680 ft	3 hrs
40	Overlook Mountain	176	Strenuous	5.0 mi	1,440 ft	3-4 hrs
41	Indian Head Mountain	180	Strenuous	6.0 mi	1,573 ft	4.5 hrs
42	Twin Mountain	185	Strenuous	4.4 mi	1,740 ft	5 hrs

Snow-shoeing	Xcountry Skiing	Trip Highlights
		Rugged, rocky and steep with a stream crossing and a spur trail to Bash Bish Falls.
•		Little-known trail with views of the southern Taconics from a blueberry knoll and free camping.
•		A walk along a creek and upland ridge environment, amid pinxter blossoms, mountain laurel, evergreen plantations with an optional spur to Bash Bish Falls.
		A long hike showcasing the Greylock massif, Bascom Lodge and the memorial tower, following a section of the Appalachian Trail and descending through a sugar-maple forest.
•	•	A quiet, easy hike through an old settlement area now managed as a research forest and a cross-country ski trail.
•		Williamstown's most popular short hike to a quartzite limestone summit overlooking the Hoosic Valley and the Greylock Range.
•		An easy, east-facing, scenic ridge hike along the Taconic Crest to the Snow Hole, a deep, icebound crevice.
		A day-long hike up the Catskills highest peak in the Slide Mountain Wilderness area. Very scenic.
		A steep climb from the rustic Woodland Valley to an area that is the favorite of many Catskill hikers.
		A short and rewarding hike to the scenic cliffs of a glacial cirque in the epicenter of an ancient meteorite impact zone.
		A remote wilderness hike to a pair of quiet boreal summits with southwesterly views.
		A gradual climb to a scenic and extensive blueberry heath with intimate views of the high peaks.
•		A short, steep hike to the last fire tower that operated in the Catskills. Great for family outings.
•		An interesting hike past a quarry and two lean-tos to the summit fire tower.
•		An historic hike to an old quarry with views overlooking the Hudson River, with a spur to Plattekill Falls.
•		A steep hike to the old hotel ruins and the fire tower and Eagle Cliff from Meads, above the town of Woodstock.
		An interior forest hike to a boreal summit with exciting views.
		A double-peaked mountain with superior views of the Hudson Valley and the Indian Head Wilderness Area.

Snow-shoeing	Xcountry Skiing	Trip Highlights
		A very steep rise out of Stony Clove Notch to a long, level plateau with isolated views.
		A long, remote hike into the isolated Kaaterskill Wild Forest Area, with spectacular views from Hurricane Ledge.
		A steep hike to a quiet ledge overlooking Kaaterskill Clove, the vantage for Sanford R. Gifford's *October in the Catskills* (1845).
•		A short walk through hemlock and pitch pine woods to a scenic overlook above Platte Clove and the Hudson Valley.
		A popular outing along the Escarpment Trail's cliffs to the favorite haunts of the Hudson River school of landscape painters.
		A cliff-edge hike above Kaaterskill Clove to the North/South Lake public campsite, returning along the lakes.
		The most popular short hike in the Catskills, to the state's highest waterfall, great for families.
		A steep climb into Lockwood Gap to the Escarpment Trail.
•		A charming, but strenuous, walk through mature spruce plantations to the northern escarpment with sweeping views to the north.
•		A short hike to an isolated lookout above the Black Dome Valley.
•		A long, gradual climb to the Catskills' second-highest peak and fire tower, with a quiet westerly ledge viewpoint.
•		A hike across the Schoharie-Esopus watershed divide to West Kill Falls.
		A demanding hike across the elongated West Kill plateau, to the scenic Buck Ridge Lookout.
		A remote hike in the western Catskills in a first-growth forest little changed since the Ice Age.
•		This spruce-fir summit would be viewless without its fire tower, which offers 360-degree views of the western Catskills.
•		An historic carriage road to a pair of peaceful lookouts over lower Kaaterskill clove and the Hudson Valley.
•		A beautiful walk offering sweeping views of the Schoharie floodplain and the northern Catskills. An ideal family outing.
•	•	A narrow catwalk trail beneath the cliffs of the world's oldest exposed surface limestone, with extending trails along the Helderberg escarpment. Excellent for families.

INTRODUCTION

I thank God I was born on the banks of the Hudson.

—Washington Irving

WELCOME TO THE HUDSON VALLEY AND CATSKILL REGION, birthplace of a nation. The Hudson River begins at the Adirondacks' Lake Tear of the Clouds at 4,300 feet in elevation, making its way 315 miles to the Battery at sea level as it drains an area of over 13,000 square miles. Next to the Saint Lawrence, it is the only river that provides such a deep and cordial invitation into the North American continent—a fact that has had the largest single influence on the growth and development of the United States. Geologically the Hudson River is a fjord, a long, narrow coastal inlet, its steep slopes formed by glacial action. It is one of only two water gaps that penetrate the Appalachian Mountain chain at a point that is actually below sea level (the other is Maine's Somes Sound). Its deepest point is 216 feet, near West Point; its widest is 3.5 miles, at Haverstraw Bay, and its narrowest is at the Hudson Highlands, where it is constricted into the notorious throat of often rough and windy water dubbed the "Devil's Horse Race" by early mariners.

The history of the region is a study in evolutionary and historical change. After the herd-following Paleo Indians left the Hudson Valley 12,000 years ago, following the retreating glaciers, the hunter-gatherer people of the Woodland Period arrived, leaving evidence in the form of oyster middens, fishing weirs, camps, and villages. By 1000 B.C.E. they began to cultivate crops, a practice that required permanent villages and seasonal encampments, many of them positioned at the mouths of Hudson River tributaries. As a means of crop rotation and soil revitalization, these villages were moved every 8 to 12 years. This ancestral lifestyle was altered permanently with the onset of the Contact Period. Like its rival English Hudson Bay Company, the major interest of the Dutch East India Company (which employed Henry Hudson) was fur. Lured by the false promise of progress and prosperity, the Indians entered the business of commercial trapping and trade practices that, along with broken treaties (particularly under Stuyvesant) would ultimately destroy a traditional lifestyle that was subjected to sustained conflict, disease, and ultimately, displacement.

Realizing that whomever controlled the Hudson River also controlled the American frontier and its rich promise for trade, the British took control of New Amsterdam (New York) by force in 1664. Peter Stuyvesant had become so unpopular as the result of his high taxation policies and his religious intolerance toward Jews and Quakers that he was unable to raise a militia. Following the Dutch, the French and the English fought over the region in the interest of establishing and maintaining their own trading interests, using various Mohawk and Algonquian mercenary factions as their allies. The French and Indian Wars put an end to French aspirations south of the Great Lakes. The British, focusing on the Hudson Valley, were finally defeated in the 1777 Saratoga campaign. The great empire-building period was about to begin.

By this time, writers and artists began to praise the region's scenic character, as part of an international romantic movement that envisaged the world as a place both picturesque and sublime. This enhanced the valley's appeal as a living place as well as a scenic tourist attraction—for both American and Europeans by the early 1820s—and resulted in the valley becoming the first American tourist destination, a rural retreat that focused on the river and the Catskills in celebration of the aesthetic conventions of the time. At the same time, a period of tremendous industrial growth was taking place, bolstered by the nationalistic pride created by the Revolution. In the next century, the valley would be intensively commercially developed for fishing, logging, agriculture, shipping, and power generation, becoming widely settled residentially. By the twenty-first century, these conditions would bring about habitat destruction, the depreciation of scenic resources, continual alterations of the natural shoreline of the river, and diminished public access. One of the major contributing factors to the preservation of open space through this development period were the farms and patronships, and in the Catskills, the tenant farming system of the Hardenburgh Patent.

Today, 70 percent of the Hudson's shores are inaccessible due to rail corridors and private property. The river is also home to a 35-foot shipping channel maintained from New York Harbor to the Port of Albany, between which the river drops only about 5 feet, making it an ideal in route for heavy shipping and a recreational route connecting the Atlantic to the Great Lakes. At the same time, improvements in the river's water quality, a heightened, positive public perception of the river, and an increasing population have created demands for more public access and more open space. Of the 3.9 million acres in the Hudson River Valley National Heritage Area, only 5 percent (203,000 acres) are protected open space. Fortunately, early in its history, sentiments for the preservation of open space were strong, and this led to hard-fought battles in the environmental movement that resulted in the preservation of today's Hudson Valley as we see it.

Below Troy, the Hudson River is a rich and productive tidal estuary inhabited by ospreys, eagles, harbor seals, muskrats, beavers, herons, rails, deer, foxes, turkeys, coyotes, fishers, and even bears, its diverse habitat the result of a broad salinity gradient determined by the mixing of the Atlantic's sea water with the river's fresh water. The Hudson is home to 185 species of fish, and is the last estuary on the east coast to retain self-sustaining spawning stocks of its original native fish species, such as the once commercially important shad and sturgeon, and the very popular game fish, the striped bass. Under the Federal Clean Water Act, the EPA designated these resources as the Hudson River National Estuarine Research Reserve (HRNERR), containing 2,400 designated acres of tidal freshwater fish and wildlife habitat, with an additional 1,500 acres undesignated. The Tivoli Bays hike in this book will introduce you to the largest of the HRNERR communities, a world of tidal marshlands, subtidal shallows, intertidal flats, wetlands, and swamps. Each of the reserves in the Hudson River estuary are protected and managed as field laboratories for research and education.

Beyond the river are a seemingly endless assortment of mountains, lakes and ponds, valleys, and geological intrusions that give the Hudson Valley its character and appeal. The valley's historical development is almost as diverse as its habitat. The region is so unique, early Palatine settlers called it the "American Rhineland," and the first European witnesses, the members of Henry Hudson's crew (who were looking for China), called it "as fine a place as we have ever seen . . . so pleasant with grass and flowers, and goodly trees." Klara Sauer, the former director of Scenic Hudson put the river's scenic resources into another perspective, remarking, "Had this continent been settled west-to-east, the Hudson Valley would be a national park today." It is interesting to reflect on Sauer's comment now that the National Park Service has designated the Hudson Valley a National Heritage Area (1998). Because the Hudson River valley is so large, and its resources so diffuse, the NPS realized it could not create a National Park Unit in the traditional sense, such as a Yellowstone or Yosemite, but it did recognize the region's cultural and natural attributes worthy of federal protection, preservation, and interpretation for the benefit of the nation. Congressman Maurice Hinchey drafted the legislation that created the Hudson River Valley National Heritage Area, based on the region's Revolutionary War history, its role as a living canvas for the first American school of art (the Hudson River school of landscape painting, whose celebration of nature led directly to the creation of our national parks system), the river's function as the nation's principal artery of commerce, and the fact that the Hudson Valley was the birthplace of the modern environmental movement. In fact, the basis of environmental law began with a fight that took place here in the Hudson Valley.

This book will lead you to the Hudson's greatest scenic landscapes: the Highlands, the isolated lump of Schunemunk, the white cliffs of the Shawangunks, and the recesses of the distant Catskills. It reaches west to the Delaware watershed, east to the Taconics, and north to the fortress of the Helderbergs. It penetrates the Southern and Northern Taconics and the Greylock Range. It brings you to the tops of this series of ranges, allowing you the best views of their succession and of the Hudson Valley. The drama of the Hudson Valley landscape has a second story in the very rocks themselves. From the resistant limestone of the Helderberg Escarpment, to the dissected plateau of the Catskills, and into the crystalline Hudson Highlands lying beside the younger folded rocks of the Appalachians, you can see the parts of the puzzle that make up the region's geological history, and have earned the Hudson River its place as one of America's premier scenic and recreational assets.

HIKING THE TRAILS

There are many ways to enjoy these walks. Social hikers will find many outdoor groups that offer regularly scheduled hikes and trips. Appalachian Mountain Club (AMC) members will receive hiking schedules from their respective chapters. The New York–New Jersey Trail Conference (NY-NJTC) will put you in touch with many other groups. Organizations such as the Catskill 3500 Club, the Sierra Club, the Catskill Mountain Club, and chapters of the Adirondack Mountain Club all offer outing schedules for a variety of hikers. Each organization also fills a second role by providing mechanisms for hikers to return something to the land. With programs of trail maintenance, conservation, and education to promote wise use, these organizations help not only to protect our wild lands, but to acquire more of them.

Those who seek quiet in the wild lands also can find that here. Some of these routes are never heavily used. Others are; these trails may best be hiked in early spring, late fall, or on weekdays, when solitude can be mixed with expanded vistas in ways sure to please any wilderness seeker.

There are relatively few hikes on the east side of the Hudson Valley. Its gentler hills were settled early, and although the farms are shrinking, the settlements have grown to fill most of the open land. In contrast, the forests on the west side of the Hudson have been preserved as the valley's water source and as part of the New York State Forest Preserve, whose unique state constitutional protection ensures they will remain "forever wild." Lands within the Blue Line of the Catskill Park offer the largest group of hikes in this guide.

Almost all the lands traversed by today's trails were once settled and used by armies, farmers, miners, loggers, and romantics. Their presence inevitably is reflected in the lore that surrounds the trails. While this guide serves as an invitation to the mountain ranges and valleys of the southern part of the state (as well as a few Hudson Valley watershed hikes in neighboring states), it cannot even begin to probe the vast history that enlivens each route. For further information, consult the reading list at the end of this book.

HOW TO USE THIS BOOK

SUMMARIES AT THE BEGINNING OF EACH HIKE list hiking distance, vertical rise, time on the trail, and United States Geological Survey (USGS) topographic map (or maps) or the local state park or preserve map for the area the hike traverses. Unless otherwise noted, distances are for the round-trip or circuit. Distances are given from state markers where available and correct (incorrect signs are noted in some instances). Where measured mileage information has not been available, distances have been computed from electronically rendered USGS topographic maps and are correct to within 10 percent.

Vertical rise refers to the total change in cumulative elevation for the hike. Hiking time is given for the total time at a leisurely pace, but it is simply the minimum needed to walk the trail as described. The text often suggests that you allow more time for sightseeing.

Rather than relying simply on the map in the book, take the recommended maps too. These maps give the larger picture, and you will have more fun on a mountaintop if you can identify surrounding countryside. A cautionary note on USGS maps: While contours and elevations are by and large reliable, some of the manufactured features, including trails, are seriously out-of-date. All of the supplementary maps mentioned in the hike headings are more convenient and up-to-date than the USGS quads, and I recommend acquiring them. In particular, I recommend the *Appalachian Mountain Club Catskill Mountains* map that was designed to accompany my book *Catskill Mountain Guide*, published by the AMC in 2002. That book is sold with a paper-printed map, but a Tyvek version of the map can also be purchased separately and could prove helpful for the Catskills-related trips in this book. It is also very useful to have the *DeLorme Atlas and Gazetteer for New York State* and *DeLorme Atlas and Gazetteer for Massachusetts* in your car, or the corresponding county map for your area of travel. Don't rely on finding small preserve maps and other handouts at kiosks. Often the supplies are exhausted. Try to find the map you need online, as many of them are these days.

If you do not know how to read a map, you should learn to do so before hiking all but about a dozen of the simplest trails in this guide. Spend time walking with someone who does know how to read a map, such as your friendly chapter hikers from the Appalachian Mountain Club. The same instructions are appropriate for the use of a compass. You may not need either on the easiest of this guide's trails, but walking the easier routes with map and compass will allow you to become comfortable with their use so you can extend your hikes beyond the ones described, or to more difficult hikes. Get the best compass you can afford. I've had the same Silva Ranger for 30 years, and highly recommend a similar type of orienteering compass with a flip-up sight that will also be useful in identifying far-away peaks or triangulating your position from a set of known peaks.

GPS

You don't need a heavy, battery-hungry GPS on any of these hikes. In fact, those new to GPS may encounter a learning curve that could be an obstacle to way-finding instead of an aid. However, I sometimes carry a very small, lightweight GPS unit, a Garmin Geko 201, that is available for under $100 and that you can learn to use in your backyard or neighborhood in a matter of hours. The obvious advantage to the GPS system is its use for emergencies. If you have a phone, you can tell your rescuer your exact location—accurate to about six feet—using your GPS. Ultimately, a GPS will give you a better understanding of position, altitude, direction, and distance—and will help you to better understand, map, compass, and geography.

THE WEATHER

Whenever possible, wait for a sunny day—the pleasures are much greater and the problems more predictable. But even on sunny days you should be prepared for changes and extremes. It can be 20 degrees colder or more on the mountaintops of the Catskills than down in the valley, close to the river. Storms can appear on short warning. It often can be too hot in summer for strenuous hikes. There are many who prefer walking in southern New York State during fall and spring, and these are the most changeable times. Extremes from heat waves to snowstorms can occur. But the rewards of fewer people and expanded distant vistas in the leafless season make hiking at such times worthwhile.

PREPARATIONS

Even with the best of forecasts, your watchword should be plan for the unexpected. Possible changes in temperature mean you should take extra clothing, especially rain gear. Experiment with layers of light, waterproof gear. In the mountains, you will want a layer of pile or wool even in summer, so carry a sweater in your daypack. Many of the trails are as smooth as a sidewalk; some are as rubble-filled as a rock pile. For most of these hikes a sturdy pair of well-broken-in, over-the-ankle boots is essential. Lightweight Gore-Tex or similar-material boots are ideal; they give good traction and support, and they are all you need, except when hiking on the higher mountain trails in early spring or winter. When wearing a backpack, a heavier, perhaps more waterproof boot is desirable. In even the worst winter conditions, I have never needed crampons, even in the Catskills, but a pair of studded ice creepers is a good thing to bring along on winter/spring hikes. You will also be more sure-footed with a pair of trekking poles or a staff, and these will take some weight off your knees, too.

Carry a sturdy daypack, large enough to hold your lunch and a few necessities. I usually leave a few things in my pack such as a whistle, matches, a small jackknife, lip balm or Dermatome, and a headlamp—and have used them all.

Always carry a map and compass and a watch so you do not panic if you get "turned around." You also need a small first-aid kit containing a few bandages, first-aid cream, and moleskin for the unexpected blister. Don't forget your Epipen if you have a bee-sting allergy. Take along a small squeeze bottle of insect repellent. There are black flies in early spring, although not the legions that endure so long in the Adirondacks. Fill a plastic bag with toilet paper and throw in a few toiletries to use before lunch on those dry mountaintops. I like to bring an extra T-shirt to change into when the one I'm wearing becomes sweat-soaked. What a luxury after a hard ascent! On summer hikes, it's nice to have a cooler with a few cold drinks in it waiting for you when you get back to your car.

It is strongly recommended that you wear a pair of unbreakable glasses—light, tinted sunglasses even if you require no prescription. It is all too easy to run into an overhanging branch or twig.

You will enjoy the hikes more if you carry binoculars and learn to identify distant peaks and birds. You may even enjoy carrying a small, lightweight altimeter that works according to barometric pressure if you don't have a GPS. Knowing your altitude is a good clue to progress on a mountain, and will help you know where you are.

Of course, you should always carry water when you hike. These mountains are dry much of the year, and few springs exist. It is becoming increasingly dangerous to trust open water sources because of the spread of Giardia. And, remember to take *enough* water. Dehydration on summer days is always possible; it can even happen on a sunny, leafless spring day or in winter. Trip leaders with the Appalachian Mounatin Club usually require that participants on their hikes carry 2 liters of water, and not until you are caught short will you realize the wisdom of this policy.

Remember, hiking should be fun. If you are uncomfortable with the weather or are tired, turn back and make the complete hike another day. Don't create a situation where you risk yourself or your companions. And, try not to walk alone. Be sure someone knows your intended route and expected return time. Always sign in at the New York State Department of Environmental Conservation (DEC) trailhead registers where they are available. The unexpected can occur. Weather can change, trail markings can become obscured, you can fall, and you can get lost. But, you will not be in real danger if you have anticipated the unexpected. Carry extra food, too—even if it is just a few energy bars you can leave in your pack between hikes and forget about until your hunger reminds you.

CELL PHONES

Don't listen to purists: carry your phone. Even if it doesn't work when you need it, almost all phones will work from summits. There are exceptions of course. If your phone does not work where you are at the moment, it may work if you move even a few dozen feet in elevation or over the next hill. Cell phones are a terrific safety item and they weigh almost nothing. Give your unit a good charge on your drive to the trailhead.

LYME DISEASE

Lyme disease is caused by a tick-borne spirochete that may produce a rash, flulike symptoms, and pain in joints. If untreated it may cause chronic arthritis and nervous-system disorders. It is difficult to diagnose but treatable if diagnosed early. The deer ticks that transmit Lyme disease are now found north and west of Westchester County, where the problem has reached epidemic proportions. Their range is expanding rapidly north and west, and you should take a few preventive measures.

There is no foolproof way to protect yourself from these minute ticks. Check yourself frequently; tuck pants into socks and boots; put insect repellent containing DEET on your pants, shoes, and socks or use tick spray (note that DEET does weaken elastics and "melts" plastic products); and wear tightly woven and light-colored clothing (making it easier to see the ticks). Above all else, shower and change clothes at the end of your hike; this is the best time to make a complete body check. Change out of your hiking clothes to prevent any ticks present from biting you. If you suspect you have contracted Lyme disease, call your physician right away, since early detection is important. (During the approximately 80 outings I made in preparation for this guide—many of them involving overnight bivouacs—I did not get a single tick bite.)

BEHAVIOR IN THE WOODS

So, now you are safe in the woods, but what about the woods? The environment that may threaten you can be just as fragile as you are, and you are the only one who can protect it.

Trail erosion is becoming a serious problem in many areas. Please stay on the main trail at all times to minimize damage to soils, tree roots, and vegetation. Use stepping-stones whenever possible to cross wet areas of the trail. Don't pick wildflowers or dig woodland plants, which is in many cases illegal anyway.

Practice the rules of Leave No Trace. Leave no sign of your presence. Use pit privies when available. If not, bury your wastes at least 150 feet from water or from a trail or path. When you camp, do not bathe with soap in lakes or streams; when picnicking or camping, carry wash water and dishwater back from the shore. If you are camping, carry a stove for cooking, and do not build fires unless they are needed. In most parks, fires are prohibited. These are very fire-prone areas. If you need to build a fire on a Catskill hike, for instance, build it on dry stones, gravel, or sandy soil surfaces, away from duff, leaf mold, or organic soils that will burn. Remember, only dead and down wood can be used. Respect the rights of others and help preserve natural areas for future hikers.

1

THE HUDSON HIGHLANDS

PERHAPS NO OTHER LANDMARK characterizes the Hudson Valley as does its Highlands, the scenic and rugged group of Appalachian hills that rises between Dunderberg Mountain and the Fishkill Ridge. Here, where the river is deep and narrow, the mountains rise steeply from its shores, creating the topography that determined the military, cultural, and environmental history of the region.

Geologically known as the Highlands Province, its rocks are crystalline in structure, originated from Precambrian and early Paleozoic igneous and metamorphic action rather than by the kinds of sedimentation that define a great deal of the surrounding region's surface rock. Hikers will see marble, schist, and gneiss embedded, ribboned, and sprinkled throughout the open outcrops and exposed ridges, along with the surface scars of Pleistocene glacial activity, and they will walk across solidified, granitic magma chambers that were once buried deep in the Earth (such as Bear Mountain). Stripped of their overburden of softer geology, the hard, weather-resistant crystalline rocks remain exposed. The upper elevation ridges are dry and relatively open, with frequent, sweeping views. Today's Highlands are geologically equivalent to and scenically comparable with the Blue Ridge Mountains of North Carolina and Virginia.

Beyond its significance as a commercial trade route, the Highlands' topography determined the settlement of the continent in other ways. Military leaders considered it the most important strategic location in the American colonies. It was here in 1778 that the great Hudson River Chain—wrought in the forges of Sterling Forest (Stirling Iron Works) and floated on log booms—was stretched across the river to stop the British from advancing northward.

Looking south along the Hudson River from Breakneck Ridge.

Already in control of Canada and the Atlantic coast, the British sought to control the Hudson in order to frustrate military transport and travel between the north and south. Although several chains would span the river between New York City and Fort Montgomery, the West Point Chain, built after the defeat of the north-lying forts Montgomery and Clinton, was the most notable in terms of its engineering—its 2-foot-long links weighed in excess of 125 pounds each and the whole 1,500-foot span weighed nearly 200 tons. Defended from both sides of the river, the chain was never challenged or penetrated. Only the treasonous Benedict Arnold would attempt to help the British subdue it, though he never put his plan into action. The existence of the chain changed the course of the war, shortening it substantially. Thirteen links of the original chain can still be seen at West Point, but the remainder was re-smelted for armament at the West Point Foundry in Cold Spring, near the point that the east end of the chain was anchored on Constitution Island. Today the island is an Audubon nature preserve and popular canoeing destination.

A few decades after independence, the picturesque and sublime landscapes of the Hudson Valley—first focusing on the Highlands area and north—gave rise to the Hudson River school of landscape painting. Most of the era's painters worked from New York City studios and painted to please European audiences until, in the early 1820s, Thomas Cole burst upon the scene, issuing among his Catskill scenes several of the Highlands. Inspired by Cole's nearly instant fame, and the existence of a new audience of prosperous patrons and admirers with widening tastes, other artists began to emulate and train under Cole, among them John Frederick Kensett, Sanford R. Gifford, George Inness, Jasper Cropsey, and Frederic Church, who was Cole's star student.

Developing alongside this new artistic revolution, which broke from tradition in terms of conventions and European taste, were the New York literati known as the Knickerbockers, who shared a similar popularity and romantic vision with their counterparts in the art world. These included Washington Irving, Nathaniel Parker Willis, William Cullen Bryant, and James Fenimore Cooper (when his Tory sympathies could be overlooked), among others.

These artists and writers, using the Highlands as their canvasses and as settings for their satire and humor, celebrated a grandeur and beauty that may have been otherwise inexpressible in the rising public conscience of a new and unique America, one that could stand on its own in the world of art and letters, with its own new pedigree and its fierce stamp of individuality. What is certain was the creation of a kind of pride that would later be called into play to protect these same resources from ruin.

TRIP 1
STORM KING

RATING: Moderate
DISTANCE: 2.3 miles
ELEVATION GAIN: 400 feet
ESTIMATED TIME: 2 hours
MAPS: USGS Cornwall; USGS West Point; NY-NJTC West Hudson
Trails

The Highlands' signature hike, beginning with a steep ascent, then easing up. This is among the shorter and easier Highlands hikes, with a scenic destination looking up and down the Hudson River.

DIRECTIONS
Getting to the scenic parking area where the yellow trail begins is tricky, since it's located on a "no turns" section of US 9W in the northbound lane. Accordingly, if you are traveling south (from Cornwall), this requires you to travel past the parking area and make a U-turn at the intersection of US 9W and NY 293/218 at the West Point Reservation, 3.0 miles south. Driving south from Cornwall on US 9W, you will see the parking turnout at the top of the pass (approximately 1,000 feet) 1.5 miles beyond the Angola Road overpass.

TRAIL DESCRIPTION
Storm King is among the most popular hikes in the Hudson Highlands, and a mountain that has had a decisive influence on the national environmental movement. If there is a solitary symbol representing the struggle to preserve scenic open space, this is it. Dramatic views and open rock ledges characterize the trails in Storm King State Park, which is managed by the Palisades Interstate Park Commission (PIPC). Until recently, some interesting destinations in the park were inaccessible, but proactive trail advocacy by the New York-New Jersey Trail Conference (NY-NJTC), has provided more access, particularly in the southern area bordering the West Point Military Reservation.

This prominent little mountain draws its name from its tendency to bottleneck storms at the head of the Highland Gap. It is among the easiest walks in the region, ideal for a day when a moderate, half-day's scenic outing is your goal. If you want to add distance and elevation, there are several choices—the

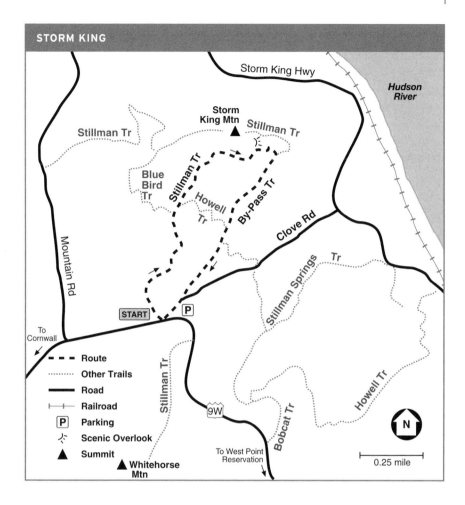

STORM KING

Storm King Hwy

Hudson River

Storm King Mtn

Stillman Tr

Stillman Tr

Stillman Tr

Blue Bird Tr

By-Pass Tr

Howell Tr

Clove Rd

Mountain Rd

Stillman Springs Tr

START

P

To Cornwall

- - - Route
········· Other Trails
—— Road
+—+— Railroad
P Parking
Scenic Overlook
▲ Summit

Stillman Tr

9W

Bobcat Tr

Stillman Springs Tr

Howell Tr

N

To West Point Reservation

0.25 mile

▲ Whitehorse Mtn

Highlands may not be as lofty as surrounding mountain groups, but the trails are extensive and as steep as many in the Catskills.

Of all the approaches to Storm King, the Stillman Trail (which makes up most of that portion of the Highlands Trail running from the Sutherland Pond area of adjacent Black Rock Forest to Cornwall) is the most popular with casual day-hikers. This is largely because the trailhead lies in the upper elevations west of the mountain, making it a fairly easy hike. Many seasoned hikers choose to begin from the east, at the lower elevations along the river, where trailheads can be accessed from NY 218 (Storm King Highway), an approach requiring significant climbing to reach Storm King's summit. The southerly Howell Trail provides part of a very popular, longer loop hike that connects Pitching Point, on the eastern flank of the beautiful Crow's Nest, to Storm King via the Bobcat Trail and the Stillman Springs Trail, the latter climbing through the steep valley of Mother Cronk's Clove (a.k.a. Storm King Clove) beginning at 200 feet above sea level.

Park at the turnout and walk west (to the edge of the turnout) to access the Stillman trailhead. Marking is inconspicuous from the parking lot, but is consistent throughout the hike. Look for yellow (square) and blue (diamond) paint blazes. The only signage here (aside from an historic plaque describing the return route of the Iran Crisis hostages) is the "UXO" (unexploded ordinance) notice that draws the public's attention to the possible existence of left-over (live) artillery rounds that may still remain on the mountain. Used as an artillery range from the 1840s through the 1960s, the hazard of UXO was not realized until a 1999 forest fire detonated several rounds, causing the PIPC to close the park's trails for several years. Even though the Army Corps of Engineers has determined that live rounds may in fact remain in the 400-acre area south of the trail system, the trails were reopened by mounting public pressure led by the NY-NJTC. The areas immediately surrounding the trails have been scanned and they are now considered safe for public use. You will not find it unusual under these circumstances that hikers are advised to stay on the trails, and that fires are not permitted in the park.

The large, round, rocky hill you see directly north of the parking area is your first objective. This is Butter Hill, or Boterberg, the name the Dutch first assigned to present-day Storm King. Fortunately, the efforts of the Knickerbocker-period writer Nathaniel Parker Willis preserved the name Storm King.

Climb fairly steeply up an open series of shrubby slabs for a few minutes, leveling out at the ruins of the Spy Rock House (open to views of Spy Rock, at 1,461 feet, in the south southwest), and descend into a shady ravine full of talus that has fractured away from the upper ledges of Butter Hill. The trail rises sharply from here, turning northeast past several interesting south-facing vistas. About 20 minutes after leaving the parking lot, you will ascend to the small, open, grassy summit of Butter Hill. Take a moment to look at some of the sights you will not see from the easterly ledges of Storm King. To the west, the long serpentine ridge is the low-lying Schunemunk, over which the Long Path travels for roughly 6.0 miles on its way to the southern Shawangunks. The long trestle to the north of Schunemunk is the Moodna Viaduct, the longest rail trestle east of the Mississippi (built 1906–1908, 3,200 feet long). In the far, low western foreground, you can see (with binoculars) a few of the large, welded-steel sculptures at the Storm King Arts Center. (See if you can identify

THE BIRTH OF THE ENVIRONMENTAL MOVEMENT

When development began in the Hudson Valley in the early twentieth century, the Highlands' valuable rocks—the building blocks of New York's skyline—were heavily quarried. The lack of public ownership and protection allowed these private industries, which began in the southerly Palisades, to dismantle the Highlands piecemeal. In an effort to meet the energy needs of the greater New York population, Consolidated Edison appealed to the Federal Power Commission to build a power-generating plant on Storm King Mountain. People who lived in the Highlands, together with the support of hiking clubs and other groups, organized the Scenic Hudson Preservation Conference to fight the plan in court. The 1965 ruling in favor of Scenic Hudson was a legal landmark, representing the first time that a conservation group successfully sued on behalf of the public—and on the basis of the aesthetic value of a landmass. The decision in favor of Scenic Hudson created important legal precedents, led to the 1970 National Environmental Policy Act (NEPA) and other important legislation such as the Clean Air Act and the Clean Water Act. During this time, two environmental law firms emerged—the Environmental Defense Fund (EDF) and the National Resources Defense Council (NRDC). As a direct result of the fight to save Storm King, the field of environmental law was born.

bits of Andy Goldsworthy's 2,278-foot "Storm King Wall" on the south end.) Moving through the south and across the Black Rock highlands' Mount Misery (1,268 feet) and the fire tower beyond, your gaze crosses West Point Reservation lands and the Hudson River to Mount Taurus' lower slopes and the open quarry scar above the village of Cold Spring. The entire Shawangunk Ridge is visible in the west northwest, all the way to Sky Top tower in the Mohonk Preserve (5 degrees magnetic). Several major Catskill wilderness areas are also seen (Slide Mountain is at magnetic north). There are three USGS triangulation benchmarks on Butter Hill (1,300 feet).

On a clear day you will most likely encounter several hikers on Butter Hill, a worthy hike in itself. Continue on the trail through an oak forest, dropping in elevation slightly and reaching within 5 minutes or so a T-intersection where the Blue Bird Trail drops off to the left, heading northwest. Bear right (east) continuing on the yellow trail. In a minute or two, a Y-intersection is reached, where you bear left, following yellow blazes. (The right turn is the blue-blazed Howell Trail that descends across the Clove and climbs to meet the Stillman Springs Trail.)

Soon you will encounter hemlock trees, mountain laurel, and little patches of pitch pine as the trail levels for a while, passing two vantage points looking north. It then dips once more into the woods and arrives at Storm King's "summit," an east-facing promontory. Views are spectacular. An ice sheet carved a deep gorge through the Highlands here, one of the few places where a river bisects the Appalachian chain almost to sea level, lending considerably to the savage look of the landscape. Below and east is Constitution Marsh. Taurus is close across the river, and you can see hikers near the stunning vertical drops of Breakneck Ridge. In the northeast, with many towers, is Mount Beacon. Views taper into the endless, verdant flatlands and the dimple hills and mountains to the northeast. To the southeast you can see into Putnam and Westchester counties. In the river below is Bannerman's Castle, on Pollepel Island. Francis Bannerman was an arms dealer who bought the island in 1900 and built the castle to serve as an arsenal for most of the surplus arms from the Spanish-American War. The island is rumored to be haunted by horses and sea captains, goblins, witches, and "spirits." It is known that the Indians and the Dutch genuinely feared the place, probably because of the strong tidal rips and high winds. A fire destroyed all of the buildings in the late 1960s. The island is owned by the state. Efforts are being made by the Bannerman's Island Trust to create a park there.

Continuing on the trail, you now descend to a T-intersection where the yellow-blazed Stillman Trail goes off to the left (east). Here you turn right onto the white-blazed By-Pass Trail that leads southwest and descends along a rock-strewn trail, offering several southerly lookouts. In less than 0.5 mile, the Howell Trail (blue) comes in from the right and soon leaves to the left. The By-Pass Trail then joins Clove Road (a dirt footpath) and begins climbing. Marking is scarce. After a steep, final ascent, bear left as the trail joins the parking area turnout, and you're back at the trailhead.

TRIP 2
MOUNT TAURUS

RATING: Moderate

DISTANCE: 6.0 miles

ELEVATION GAIN: 1,400 feet

ESTIMATED TIME: 5 hours

MAPS: USGS West Point; NY-NJTC East Hudson Trails

A fairly relaxed outing with a few steep pitches through deep woods to a scenic viewpoint, and descending along a creek.

DIRECTIONS

From the intersection of NY 9D and NY 301 in the village of Cold Spring, drive north on NY 9D 0.7 mile to the Little Stony Point parking area. You can park on either side of NY 9D. This parking area is just under 8.0 miles south of I-84 at Beacon.

TRAIL DESCRIPTION

Mount Taurus, or Bull Hill (1,400 feet), sits authoritatively in the eastern High-lands south of Breakneck Ridge, its ravaged frontcountry along the Hudson's shore the result of extensive quarrying in the early 1900s. If you've already climbed Storm King, you've seen the crumbled leftovers of Little Stony Point jutting into the river above Cold Spring, and you've marveled at the devastat-ing crater on Taurus' lower western slopes. Throw in a few dioxin-belching industrial plants and a pumped storage project, and you have an idea of what the Highlands would look like if such extractive resource industries were left to their own devices. Fortunately, as a result of the sustained struggle for the protection of the Highlands and Palisades, the lands involved were protected by the formation of Hudson Highlands State Park in the late 1960s.

From the east side of NY 9D follow the white-blazed Washburn Trail (the blue-blazed Cornish Trail, your return route, begins here also), heading up-hill and passing the flat quarry entrance to your left as you circle around its southerly rim. You will see Storm King and points west as you follow the lip of the mine and draw close to it here and there. The trail is confused with herd paths and shortcuts, some of them leading to southerly views over Constitu-tion Island, others to the mine's edge; but the markers and blazes are consistent

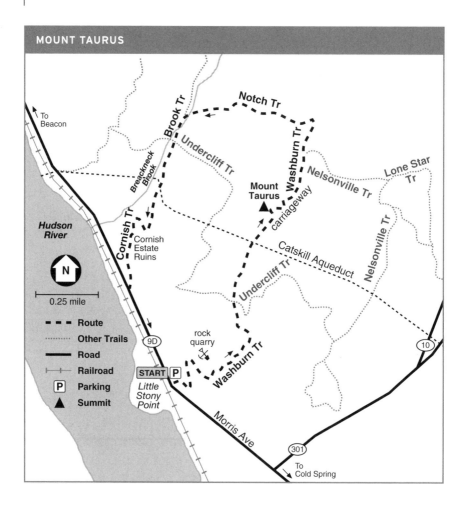

MOUNT TAURUS

although somewhat sparse. Climbing up the southeasterly slopes through the dense hardwoods, you will move generally north as you top a few bare rock lookouts, surveying West Point and the southerly hills. At 1,100 feet in elevation you will intersect with and cross the yellow-blazed Undercliff Trail, a recently undertaken project of the NY-NJTC. Soon you cross a small, wet area and vernal brook where laurel appears, enjoying the first bit of descent since setting out. Several false summits cross open areas where views southward include the New York City skyline. Now an hour plus into the hike, you arrive on Taurus, a flat, treed-in and grassy summit that was once targeted for a hotel. You'll find yourself on an old, reclaimed carriage road that came up the mountain from the east. Follow it to the mountain's eastern shoulder where there are views of the flatlands toward Fahnestock State Park and points southeast. As you continue on the Washburn Trail, it switches into the north where more interesting views to the north include the Catskills and the Shawangunks. In the foreground is Breakneck Ridge, across the near vale of Breakneck Brook and the alluring and remote-looking Schofield Ridge. Now the road switches downhill and loops to the north in sweeping S-curves, while the trail runs straight downhill, bisecting the curves. It's possible to become confused here— just remember to bear north and downhill, looking for blue blazes as you descend. The trail was poorly designed here and needs re-routing—it follows straight downhill rather than using the road and, as a result, is wet and eroded. The carriageway and the trail arrive at the same spot, the four-way intersection of the Washburn Trail, the carriageway, the blue-blazed Notch Trail, and the Nelsonville Trail.

Follow the blue-blazed Notch Trail now, descending easily through a wet depression that forms a tributary of Breakneck Brook. Follow along the edge of a shallow ravine as the brook gains momentum, heading west. Beech, birch, and maple dominate this pretty forest as you enter an old settlement area in a pure sugar maple forest. At the junction with the red-blazed Brook Trail, take a short detour to your right on the Notch Trail (this is Old Lake Surprise Road, a.k.a. Dairy Road), passing an ugly ruined concrete garage on your left to look at the curious 1920s dairy farm ruins of the Edward G. Cornish estate. Cornish was the chairman of the National Lead Company (remember the Dutch Boy logo?) and among the first to point out the dangers of lead-based paints for residential use. Use caution in the ruins and go a bit farther to look at pretty Notch Lake and the interesting long, low dam on its southwest end.

Retrace your steps now to the Brook Trail, and follow it a short distance south along Breakneck Brook; cross the yellow-blazed Undercliff Trail and bear left onto the blue-blazed Cornish Trail. Soon you will cross the Catskill Aqueduct that heads south under (actually through) Mount Taurus. Pass a large, circular cistern. Breakneck Ridge is up to your right (north). Blue markers are less frequent along the road as it makes a long switchback downhill, soon coming upon the gutted-by-fire ruins of the Cornish estate in its silent grandeur, its old hand-laid foundations and greenhouse reclaimed now by mountain laurel, runaway ornamentals, and tangles of grape. Elegant specimens of cedar and Norway spruce stand in the dooryards; second floor fireplaces suspended over nothing hint at the estate's rustic elegance. Continue on the road—now a poured concrete surface—descending still, passing enormous tulip trees south of the estate and drawing close to NY 9D. At a gate near the road, look left and you'll see the blue Cornish Trail, which you follow back to the parking area. Take the time to walk the short loop trail around Little Stony Point, along the scenic shore of the Hudson in full view of Storm King (allow 35 minutes).

TRIP 3
BREAKNECK RIDGE TO SOUTH BEACON MOUNTAIN

RATING: Strenuous
DISTANCE: 9.0 miles
ELEVATION GAIN: 1,400 feet
ESTIMATED TIME: 6 hours
MAPS: USGS West Point; NY-NJTC East Hudson Trails

A demanding hike up the steepest and most exposed scenic trail in the Highlands, with sustained views from open ridges and returning through quiet forests.

DIRECTIONS

From the intersection of Main Street and NY 9D in the village of Cold Spring, drive north on NY 9D, passing the Little Stony Point parking area at 0.8 mile, and continuing north. Just as you pass under the tunnel at 2.1 miles, park immediately on the left (west) side of NY 9D. If this very small lot is full, continue north to find two more parking areas at 0.1 and 0.3 miles. (This hike terminates at the parking area 0.3 mile ahead.)

TRAIL DESCRIPTION

The steep windswept spine of Breakneck Ridge is considered the most difficult and rugged ascent in the Highlands. Rising from nearly sea level on the Hudson at Breakneck Point, to 1,100 feet on Breakneck's summit in less than 0.5 mile, it is a rock scramble requiring an all-fours approach. Because the sheer southerly face of Breakneck draws very close to the trail in spots, this hike is not advisable in wet or icy conditions, or even in periods of high winds—and it's not a good choice for unfit hikers or ones with bad knees. This is an aerobic workout of intense effort, and most hikers will find that they haven't carried enough water (trail leaders for the Appalachian Mountain Club generally require that participants carry 2 liters, minimum, on hikes of this nature). The route described here is a long day hike, but there are several options for shortening the hike if you need to.

Prepare yourself accordingly and locate the white Taconic Region Trailmarkers and white paint blazes of the Breakneck Ridge Trail (BRT) immediately north of the tunnel on NY 9D. The trail's initial ascent brings you to a popular rock ledge over the river, directly facing Storm King Mountain, and

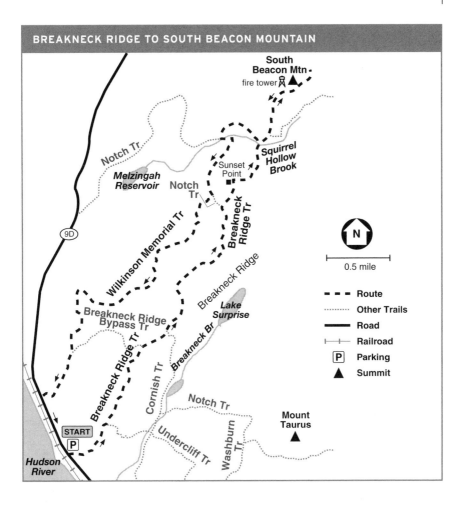

then turns east, crossing over the top of the tunnel and ascending steeply. After 15 minutes of climbing through ledges, over slabs, and around boulders, you'll find yourself on a rock ledge facing west, with fine views up and down the river. At this time an American flag is planted in a steel stand on the precipice. Storm King blocks a good deal of the western skyline. You have a good view of Pollepel Island and Bannerman's Castle just upriver. Resuming the climb, you will follow along the southern cliffs of the ridge, enjoying increasingly good views north to south. If you're lucky, there will be a cooling southwesterly breeze pouring across the ridgetop. You'll see military helicopters from West Point and C5 cargo planes on maneuvers from Stewart Airbase. You'll look down onto the decks of ships moving fuel and freight up- and downriver from the Port of Albany. In fall, many of the large sailing craft you'll see are heading out to the Intracoastal Waterway to wintering places in the Caribbean.

Sometimes the paint blazes may seem confusing, with alternate routes away from the rock ledges presented here and there. Continue climbing (the alternate markings tend to parallel the main trail). The sparse hardwood forest covering most of the ridge gives way to pockets of pitch pine, where sun-starched clutches of violet asters persist late into October. Hawks and vultures, their wingtips trembling on zephyrs, survey the ledges with the rising air. Pine needles make the rocks slippery, so mind your footholds.

Once on top of Breakneck's main summit (the summit ridge is stretched out in a series of domes), you'll be ready for a break. The ground you've covered to this point is probably the most popular "Weekend Warrior" hike in the Highlands, and there is obvious impact. The trail would be in much worse condition if it weren't for the erosion-and-impact-resistant rock surface. From this point, most day hikers turn back, so chances are you will have the ridge to yourself from here.

Get a good look at the views again before you continue, descending to a point where the yellow Undercliff Trail departs to the south. Climb northeast on the BRT again to another scenic crest, where you look across the forests of Breakneck Brook at Mount Taurus (Trip 2). The trail continues through grassy oak woodlands. Nearly 2 hours into the hike, you will pass the red-on-white-blazed Breakneck Bypass Trail on your left (north). You can shorten the hike by taking this trail north to the Wilkinson Memorial Trail (WMT, yellow) and turning southwest to NY 9D. Continue straight ahead on the BRT. In 15 minutes or so, the blue-marked Notch Trail joins the BRT from the south and continues with it. Following blue and white markers now, you're headed for Sunset Point. The trail surface is moderately rocky, but soft; it's mostly self-guiding and marking can be sparse in rocky areas. The trail goes through flat, shady woods for a spell.

Arrive at a T and bear left. Don't make the mistake of going off to the right on the informal, blue-blazed trails you'll see—stick to the blue and white Taconic Region discs for now. As you reach another T, bear right with the white markers as the blue Notch Trail goes left (northwest). This is another place where you may wish to turn around, following the Notch Trail to the WMT, where you would turn left (southwest) with the option of climbing Sugarloaf Mountain on your return. Continue on the BRT, climbing slightly to Sunset Point. Once treeless and scenic, the point is now enclosed by vegetation. A very well-built observation deck appears along the trail, but even it provides little in the way of views, although you can see South Beacon's fire tower if you look northeast. If it seems far away (and it does) you can backtrack from here or bail out ahead. The BRT heads downhill now through an area crisscrossed with old trails and skid roads, to a point where it intersects with the yellow WMT at a four-way intersection (the unmarked trail to the right leads to private property). This is your last bail-out point. If it's late in the day or your energy is ebbing, consider the additional distance and elevation gain required to ascend South Beacon. (To quit here, bear left and follow the WMT out, as described from this point.) Continue straight on a woods road now, following both white and yellow blazes for a few hundred feet and turn left (north) on white to begin the ascent of South Beacon. This is the steepest section of trail since Breakneck. Climb open rock ledges and east-facing flats as the woods turn grassy and sheltered again, and the trail swings gradually into the east. After about four hours of hiking, you will summit South Beacon at 1,400 feet, the highest point in the Highlands. (Your return route is much faster.) You won't

Hiking east along spectacular Breakneck Ridge.

see the fire tower until you're almost at its base. The tower is in a dangerous state of disrepair and is closed to the public. The views are excellent from the summit, however, from points north to the Catskills and the Shawangunks (you can pick out Sky Top in the Mohonk Preserve), south across the river into the Highlands, and east into the low hills of Dutchess and Putnam Counties and Fahnestock State Park. The tower field of North Beacon Mountain stands close to the north. The Newburgh-Beacon Bridge spans the Hudson 3.0 miles to the northwest.

Turn around now and retrace your steps to the WMT following it to the right at both intersections, proceeding downhill to a point where it crosses Squirrel Hollow Brook, turns left (east, then south) and rises (with the Notch Trail) along a pleasant old woods road. Watch carefully to the right as the easily missed, yellow-blazed WMT parts company with the Notch Trail (you've gone too far if you encounter the white-and-blue-marked intersection you crossed earlier). Heading southwest, your route takes you through airy woods with a few herd trails to scenic overlooks, and climbs the northeastern shoulder of Sugarloaf Mountain. Views to the north and south from Sugarloaf are the last you'll get. The yellow WMT markers are complemented by white paint blazes here, so don't get confused. Drop down the south side of the mountain and pass the Breakneck Bypass Trail on your left. The trail is now an old road with a good surface that takes you back to NY 9D.

Be careful as you follow this busy stretch of road back to your car.

TRIP 4
BEAR MOUNTAIN

RATING: Strenuous
DISTANCE: 4.0 miles
ELEVATION GAIN: 1,000 feet
ESTIMATED TIME: 3.5 hours
MAPS: USGS Peekskill; USGS Popolopen Lake; NY-NJTC Northern Harriman Bear Mountain Trails; Bear Mountain and Harriman State Parks, Palisades Interstate Park Commission

A pretty hike from the famous Bear Mountain Inn and state park along Hessian Lake, to Perkins Memorial Tower and its 360-degree views, descending on the Appalachian Trail.

DIRECTIONS
Begin at Bear Mountain State Park, 0.4 mile south of the Bear Mountain traffic circle on US 9W. The traffic circle is located at the northern end of the Palisades Interstate Parkway, at the western entrance to the Bear Mountain Bridge.

TRAIL DESCRIPTION
Since its creation in 1913, millions of people have visited Bear Mountain State Park to indulge in George Perkins' version of "rest and relaxation," but only a fraction of them ever climb its namesake, the scenic "little" mountain lying west of Hessian Lake. Though not especially formidable at a modest 1,305 feet, Bear Mountain "feels" much bigger because of the steep northerly ascent from near sea level to its summit via the Major Welch Trail. Because of the elevation changes, this hike feels longer than it is, and you should prepare accordingly.

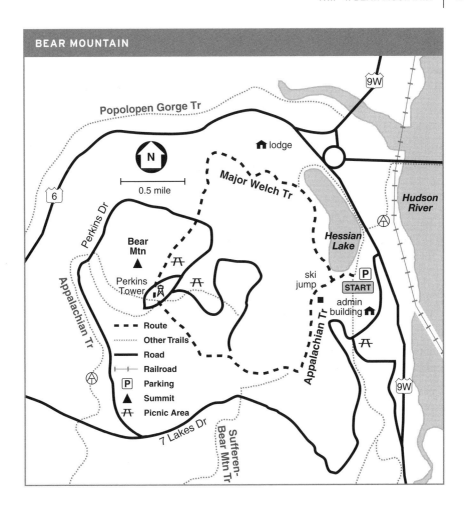

There are several approaches to Bear Mountain, but the Major Welch Trail is the most scenic and interesting of them, sharing its popularity among hikers with the easier southerly approach using the Appalachian Trail (AT). (It is also possible to drive to the summit on Perkins Memorial Drive, so expect to see cars and people at the summit picnic area.) Major Welch was the general manager of Palisades Interstate Park from 1912 to 1940. He organized the completion of the first section of the AT, and designed the trail's distinctive logo. (The AT Conference believes that the Bear Mountain section of the AT is the most heavily used portion of the 2,150-mile trail. It is scheduled for improvement, and some sections may be relocated.)

It seems amazing that in spite of the extremely high day-use figures Bear Mountain State Park sustains, it has been kept so clean and orderly—a result of the park's careful planning, management, and supervision. You will appreciate this as you stroll through the inn complex, where you'll park. Try to take this hike before the pool opens on the first day of summer, or after it closes, when parking is free and visitors are not present in great numbers.

Walk in front of the inn and bear left toward the south end of Hessian Lake. Orient yourself at the southern shore, behind the inn on the paved path. Watch for the red circle on a white background as you follow the shore in the company of friendly geese and squirrels. Head toward the boat rental concession to the west. As you pass a children's playground on your left, the AT joins the paved lake path. That's your return route. Leave the AT to your left and walk along the pretty western shore of Hessian Lake. In 15 minutes or so, look left at the location of a bench, where the Major Welch Trail departs to the left (northwest). If you're daydreaming, you might miss it.

The Major Welch Trail is slow in ascending. The first 0.5 mile is forgiving as the trail rises gently and sidehills along the northeasterly hardwood slopes, passing a water tower on the left and the park's Overlook Lodge, downhill and north. By the time you're wondering where the vertical rise begins, you've turned south and the trail climbs directly upslope over a rocky surface. These rocks have enabled the trail's direct approach, protecting it from the kind of erosion you'll see on the softer southern slopes. You'll appreciate your poles or hiking staff here! Most of the hike's vertical rise is packed into the next half-mile.

The trail climbs through a nearly pure oak/laurel woods, among thick mats of blueberry bushes. Underfoot is the bright limestone of the Greenville Series of Precambrian origins—amongst the oldest surface bedrock of its kind. As you gain elevation, you come upon a long, angled slab with a northern exposure. Things get more interesting now as views of the valley open up. Here you will get a close look at Popolopen Torne with its brown, exposed summit. Ahead, the scenery improves as you are treated to views to the north, west, and east, encompassing a good deal of the northern Highlands and the river. You can identify Sugarloaf, Taurus, Storm King, the Black Rock Forest, the lands of Fahnestock State Park, and down along the river, Garrison Landing. A few pitch pines appear.

The trail cuts across Perkins Memorial Drive and continues to climb, more easily now, flattening out after one more steep pitch. After crossing a gravel road in the picnic area, you will soon pass the true summit, where tower bolts can be seen in the rocks to the right of the trail. Continue straight through the picnic area, following markers past a rest room on your left (with a pair of vending machines outside), and ascending slightly to Perkins Tower. Take a few minutes to see the tower, with its tiled, art deco pictorial history of the park, and each of the four walls detailed with panoramic locator maps of the 360-degree views. The tower was constructed to take advantage of these views, and was such a hit with the touring public that in September and October of 1935, it attracted 9,869 cars from 36 states and two Canadian provinces. Note, in particular, Anthony's Nose to the east and Dunderberg, Bald, and the Timp to the south. The tower commemorates George Perkins, of the banking firm J.P. Morgan, who envisioned a place where the people of New York City could find "rest and relaxation." Perkins was an activist instrumental in the long and important struggle to preserve the Palisades, leading to the effort to preserve and protect the entire Hudson Valley from exploitation and development.

The Major Welch Trail ends here. Just outside the front entrance of the tower and across the drive to the south, your route continues on the AT. In the rocks at the trailside, you'll find the AT between the bronze plaque honoring Joe Bartha, trails chairman from 1940 to 1955, and a vague, weathered carving indicating the AT's distance to Arden and to Vogel State Park in Georgia (1,260 miles; the southern terminus has since been relocated to Springer Mountain). Descend through open hardwoods.

Within 10 minutes or so, you will cross Perkins Memorial Drive, and descending, will again reach it at a point where a trail marker says *Tower, 30 mins.*, and the word *tower* is stenciled on a rock to the left, next to the road. Pay close attention, as the trail turns right and follows the road. (It is evident by herd paths that many hikers unwittingly continue down-hill into the woods once crossing the road.) Follow the road for 10 minutes until reaching a loop. The AT leaves the loop on the right side over a stretch of broken pavement; marking is good. Within 100 feet it turns hard left (east) and descends. The AT switches and drops into the east, passing through a beautiful grove of white pine before continuing through

A hiker along the Major Welch Trail.

hardwoods. At the well-marked junction where the Suffern-Bear Mountain Trail (SBM) comes in, bear left with the SBM and AT. At the head of a gully the trail swings hard to the right, continuing its descent and flattening out at a point where the park complex becomes visible. Avoid the trail to the right, instead continuing on the AT and SBM for a short climb past the old ski jump and tower; piecing together the missing runway and the crowds of spectators, you can imagine what the scene must have looked like.

Now the trail follows the old service road to the ski jump as it switches back and drops to lake level again behind the inn. The SBM trail ends and the AT makes its lonely way along Hessian Lake, across the Hudson toward Maine's Mount Katahdin. You may ponder, for a moment, the vision of Mary Averell Harriman, wife of Edward Harriman, who gave 10,000 acres of land to the state under the condition that they discontinue plans for the construction of Sing Sing prison at the base of Bear Mountain. It was eventually built downriver, in Ossining, north of New York City, giving rise to the old expression, "Sent up the river."

From here, you know the way back.

TRIP 5
DUNDERBERG AND THE TIMP

RATING: Strenuous
DISTANCE: 6.0 miles
ELEVATION GAIN: 1,600 feet
ESTIMATED TIME: 4.5 hours
MAP: USGS Peekskill; USGS Popolopen Lake; NY-NJTC Northern Harriman Bear Mountain Trails; Bear Mountain and Harriman State Parks, Palisades Interstate Park Commission

A backcountry ramble through the interior Highlands' historic trails and remote forests, with many scenic lookout points.

DIRECTIONS

The trailhead is located on US 9W/202, 3.8 miles south of the Bear Mountain Bridge traffic circle. The trailhead parking area lies on the west side of US 9W/202 at its intersection with Jones Point Road, a.k.a. Old Route 9W. (If you go south as far as the Anchor Monument, you've gone too far. Backtrack

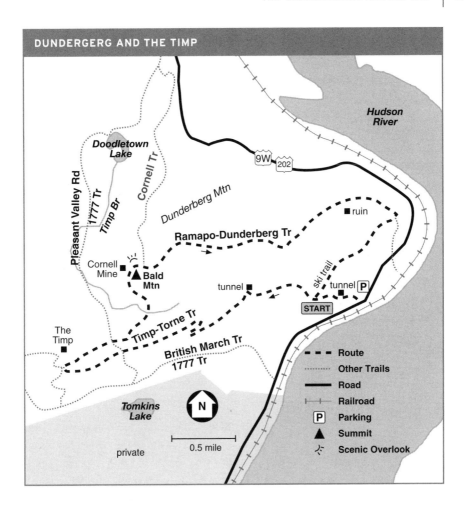

DUNDERGERG AND THE TIMP

0.2 mile.) The trailhead parking area, while sanctioned, is not clearly identified with state park signs. Park in the gravel turnout, walk south along US 9W/202 about 200 feet, and look carefully to the right for the trail as it is easy to walk past it.

TRAIL DESCRIPTION

Ravaged by fire, mining, and failed human ambition, the landscape of the Dunderberg may at first strike you as raw and unappealing. The standing dead snags of bleached, barkless oaks project hauntingly above ravenous pioneer growth. Gaping pits and talus piles indent and litter the hillsides. Vast hand-made berms, dark dead-end tunnels, and an embroidery of lost and forgotten roads are the haunting remains of an abandoned spiral railway to a hotel that would never be built. And it was through here, in 1777, that the British army

View of the Hudson River from the burnt-over Dunderberg summit.

marched upon Fort Clinton and Fort Montgomery, destroying both and killing hundreds of American soldiers in the process.

In addition to the troubled history and visible scars of the mountain itself, your first impressions of the trailhead parking area will raise your suspicion that this area has everything going against it. Across the Hudson River—too close for comfort—you look directly at the reactors and cooling tower of the Indian Point Nuclear Power Plant that has enjoyed the dubious distinction of being a Federal Energy Regulatory Commission "most watched" facility. Traffic is fast and often heavy on this stretch of highway, and the road's wooded margins are heavily littered. By the time you wend your way through the tangled margin of undergrowth below Dunderberg's easterly slopes, you'll breathe a deep sigh of relief as you witness the powers of Mother Nature at work in the slow but inexorable process of healing and reclamation.

This collection of three peaks and the attractions surrounding them—including West Mountain and the ghost town Doodletown—has long been popular with hikers from the Appalachian Mountain Club (AMC). Though the trails have been rerouted time and again, AMC member Bob Marshall pioneered the Timp Torne Trail (TT) in 1987, which is used today. Many variations of this hike exist, but the classic approach is the one described here.

Walk just south of the sanctioned trailhead parking area along US 9W perhaps 200 feet or a one-minute walk looking hard to the right beyond a highway sign, for the fairly obscure trail. Here you will see paint blazes of the red-on-white Ramapo-Dunderberg Trail (RD), your return route, and the blue Timp Torne Trail. Follow the trail through a thick and overgrown wood of locust and cottonwoods, where some of the trees are completely cloaked in grapevines. Follow as the trail heads uphill easily, passing a stone archway of the begotten spiral railway. Switching back above the arch, the trail soon splits. Bear left (southwest) on the TT (the RD heads north) and work your way uphill over rocky terrain. The trail soon flattens and you stride easily heading due west on a section of built-up railroad grade. Watch carefully for markers as the trail leaves and joins again the series of old roads and connecting paths that crisscross the slope as it climbs in pitches. Rise into the northwest. In many places the trail is neither intuitive nor self-guiding, but you can trust the marking. (In the event that you do step off-trail, return to the last blaze and re-orient yourself. Trail markers work together, positioning themselves to ensure that each subsequent blaze is visible from the one before it.) Soon you will pass the unfinished tunnel, thereafter walking a berm with marginal views south over Haverstraw Bay. You will soon find yourself in a grassy, open oak wood as the trail turns northeast. One hour into the hike, at the point where the trail turns southwest, a small rock provides good views to the southeast, including a surprise appearance of the New York City skyline and the close, easterly burnt knob of Dunderberg in the northeast, from which you will descend later on.

The trail is rocky, winding, and heads up and down, over and around rock outcroppings through pretty, parklike forests as it makes its way southwest, descending sharply to cross the 1777 Trail (red numbers on a white disc), the route the British forces used as they marched north from Stony Point. Within 20 minutes of crossing the 1777 Trail, you will intersect with the RD. Take a left on the TT here for the 5-to-10-minute hike up to the Timp (1,080 feet), an airy, open cliff with excellent views south to New York City, west across the un-broken forests of Harriman State Park, and north, upriver, past Bear Mountain and the Perkins Memorial Tower, beyond the Bear Mountain Bridge and into the Highlands. (You can see the West Mountain shelter from here, lying just east off the Appalachian Trail, if you know where to look.)

Resume the hike, backtracking to the RD Trail (Note: Don't turn right on the RD Trail), and following it straight ahead, northeast, and downhill, soon crossing the 1777 Trail a short distance north of where you crossed it earlier on the TT. The RD climbs and levels through open oak woods followed by a laurel tunnel, crosses a stream, and courts an old roadbed as it rises steeply now, up the southeasterly shoulder of Bald Mountain. Continue north as the southern summit offers marginal views to a point in the north, where just off the trail there are excellent views to the north. From this vantage, hikers can easily relate to the Hudson Valley's alternate identity as the "American Rhineland." The river bends north and west behind the Highlands and the hills roll away into the fertile valley beyond. The remains of the Cornell mines lie below the cliff face to the north and in other nearby sites on the mountain; Thomas Cornell was a United States senator, as well as president of the Cornell Steamship Company and the Ulster and Delaware Railroad. (Cornell Mountain, the central peak in the Catskills' Burroughs Range, bears his name.) This vantage point is the scenic highlight of the hike. Return to the RD, as it hairpins around and descends to the blue-blazed Cornell Mine Trail departing to the north. Bearing right on the RD, follow through high, airy woods and climb the rolling ridge of Dunderberg. Soon you will cross the burnt-over ridges of dead oak, where wildflowers and sedges grow in the moist pockets of moss amid vernal pools and wet swales. Ragweed, thistle, milkweed, wild rose, cattails, and speckled alder frame views to the south.

Just when you think Dunderberg's extended ridge will never end, the trail drops off the eastern knob (930 feet) and gradually turns south, leaving the skeletonized open balds for the lush lowlands. A white spur trail leads east to the last of the viewpoints; the trail shares the old railbed along a flat section, and descends to a stone wall ruin, dropping down on the large built-up berm of the cable incline. Beyond, it rejoins the blue Timp Torne Trail and backtracks past the archway and back to the parking area.

TRIP 6
ANTHONY'S NOSE

RATING: Moderate
DISTANCE: 4.0 miles
ELEVATION GAIN: 700 feet
ESTIMATED TIME: 4 hours
MAPS: USGS Peekskill; NY-NJTC East Hudson Trails

A fairly steep ascent to an easy woods road, leading to Engagement Rock, where you look straight down on the Hudson River and Bear Mountain Bridge. A fairly easy hike with a memorable scenic payoff.

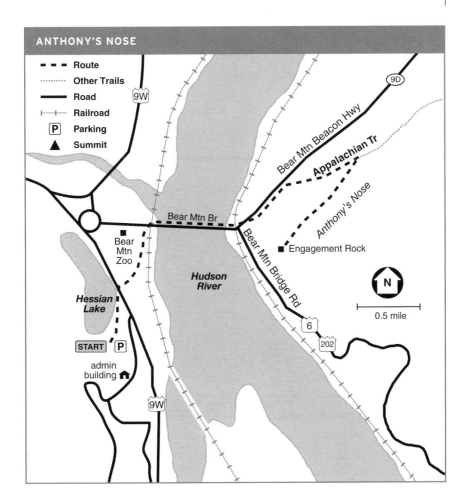

DIRECTIONS

Begin at Bear Mountain State Park, 0.4 mile south of the Bear Mountain traffic circle on US 9W. The traffic circle is located at the northern end of the Palisades Interstate Parkway, at the western entrance to the Bear Mountain Bridge.

TRAIL DESCRIPTION

How about a hike that takes you past a parish green lake, through a zoo, along the lowest stretch of the entire Appalachian Trail (AT), and across the Bear Mountain Bridge to one of the most dramatic scenic destinations in the Hudson Valley? This unforgettable outing begins at Bear Mountain State Park and Inn Complex, where you join the AT as it makes its way across the Hudson River. There are other ways to reach Anthony's Nose (900 feet), but this one is

Looking south from Anthony's Nose (Engagement Rock).

the shortest and most interesting, and easily the most exciting.

You can begin at the Bear Mountain Inn parking lot, but only when the park and zoo are open (generally 365 days a year, 10 A.M. to 6 P.M.). There is a $6 parking fee at this writing, beginning on June 21 when the pool opens. You can also park on NY 9D on the east side of the Hudson River, 0.2 mile north of the Bear Mountain Bridge where there are two very small (and often full) legal pull-offs near the AT signage. This option cuts out the Bear Mountain Zoo and bridge, however. When the zoo and inn are closed, the official route of the AT becomes the shoulder of US 9W.

From the Bear Mountain Inn parking area, walk toward the inn, keeping the main entrance to your left. To the right (east), beyond the flagpole and canon, you are looking directly at Anthony's Nose, 0.7 mile to the east (straight line distance). The highest reach of exposed rock (Engagement Rock) on the western face is your destination.

Two paved paths diverge into the picnic area to the north within 100 feet of the inn. Stay to the left, walking with Hessian Lake to your left, and in a few minutes you will intersect with the white-blazed AT (near the rest rooms). Be alert now as the AT bears right (east) and tunnels under US 9W/202, passing the pool, and entering the wooded paths of the zoo. (There is a $1 fee for adults, but no charge for AT hikers. Handicapped parking is available.) As zoos go, this is a well-kept and interesting one, and you should allow extra time to see it. (It may make you feel better to know that many of these animals are "rescues.") Interpretive trail signs identify the indigenous fauna and flora; the very worthwhile Trailside Museum (a joint effort of the American Museum of Natural History, Mrs. John D. Rockefeller, and the Palisades Park Commission) displays cultural and historical themes.

The zoo marks the lowest elevation of the AT between Maine and Georgia (124 feet above sea level). The AT is consistently well marked and will bring you to the northern exit at the Bear Mountain Bridge administration building. Bear left as you reach the toll plaza and follow blazes left to the pedestrian crossing just west of the tollbooths. Cross carefully here and walk along the north side of the bridge on the protected pedestrian path. As you reach the

THE APPALACHIAN TRAIL

Conceived in 1921 and completed in 1937, the Appalachian Trail (AT) is a 2,169-mile, National Park Service-protected trail corridor stretching from Springer Mountain in Georgia to Maine's Mount Katahdin, passing through fourteen states. The first section of the AT was built in Bear Mountain State Park in an effort led by Major William A. Welch, the general manager of the Palisades Interstate Park from 1912 to 1940 (hikers to Bear Mountain will use the Major Welch Trail). He was the first chairman of the Appalachian Trail Conference, and designed the AT logo. Hikers will see few if any of the original logos marking the trail, however—the AT is marked with rectangular white paint blazes. Hikers bound for Bear Mountain and Anthony's Nose will use sections of the AT, and stand a good chance of meeting a thru-hiker, who has walked nearly 1,400 miles to reach Bear Mountain. The trail is most often hiked from south to north, beginning in April and taking about six months to complete. Using the south to north approach, a hiker who begins in Georgia amid freezing temperatures and often, heavy snow, will be walking toward spring. The Appalachian Trail Conference oversees the trail, and a partner group, the Appalachian Long Distance Hikers Association, promotes the trail. Visit their website at www.aldha.org.

east side of the river, bear left onto the shoulder of NY 9D, and follow the AT markers to the point where the white-blazed trail enters the woods on the east side of the road. Be careful here. Although you have only a 0.2-mile walk, traffic moves briskly through this short road stretch of the AT. Follow the trail uphill as it swings northeast to begin a 700-foot vertical rise. Most of this gain is experienced in the first 0.6 mile of the AT as it climbs a good footway on a well-maintained trail with makeshift steps and heavy rock waterbars.

At an obvious, well-marked T, the trail relaxes and the AT departs left (northeast) to the Hudson Highlands State Park (Osborne Preserve). Congratulations, you're around mile point 1,360 (from Springer Mountain, Georgia) on the AT! Turn right here following the blue-blazed Hudson River Trail onto the lands the New York State Military Reservation (Camp Smith). This gentler, more enjoyable section of the trail follows an old woods road that rises briefly and levels at 700-feet elevation, where it passes through open hardwoods, winds past a vernal pond, and gently rises to a T. This point is not signed, and if you didn't know to turn right here, you'd miss the Nose completely. The blue blazes lead southeast here on a foot trail, but the roadbed you've been walking on continues to the right (west) immediately reaching the open ledges of Anthony's Nose at Engagement Rock. The views are startling. More than the view itself is the breathless sensation you get from standing over the Hudson that lies at your feet nearly 900 feet below. Freighters, plying the river's channel, pass beneath you, their turbid wakes twisting 0.5 mile behind them. The hills of Harriman State Park are displayed, north to south, from the northern torne (Popolopen) to Dunderburg and the Timp. From here, Haverstraw Bay looks like a vast arm of the sea, which it is—and upriver the Central Highlands lay in a pastel haze of multiple horizons beyond World's End. This section of the Hudson is called the Devil's Horse Race, so named for the high winds and strong tides that funnel through its narrowest point. According to legend, the Nose is named for a sea captain's proboscis—one Captain Antony Hogans'— whose crew thought the two had a great deal in common. This section of the Hudson lies below sea level. Here was the location of the famous log boom and chain that was strung across the river to prevent British ships from passing. On the west bank, on either side of Popolopen Creek, were forts Montgomery and Clinton, standing sentinel over the passage with heavy cannon. On October 6, 1777, both forts were overwhelmed from behind by British forces marching over Dunderberg. Three hundred American patriots were killed. Many of their bodies were thrown into Hessian Lake, then called Bloody Pond. You can see Hessian Lake and the park complex. There's Perkins Memorial Tower on Bear Mountain, and Iona Island, nudged against the western shore of the river. This is a popular spot and you're likely to be sharing it with other hikers. There is another, less spectacular outcropping nearby, just a few feet south on the blue trail from the junction where you turned east to the Nose, where you can find more privacy amongst the burnished summit rocks facing the southern valley.

Directly below is the Bear Mountain Bridge, privately built by the Harriman family in 1923. When Earl Shaffer became the first AT hiker to cross the bridge in 1948, it cost a nickel. Today, passage is free for hikers.

Return the way you came.

TRIP 7
SCHUNEMUNK MOUNTAIN

RATING: Moderate
DISTANCE: 12 miles
ELEVATION GAIN: 1,364 feet
ESTIMATED TIME: 6 hours
MAPS: USGS Cornwall; NY-NJTC West Hudson Trails

A steep approach to a long, even ridge hike across a geologically distinctive landmass with far-reaching views across open ridge tops.

DIRECTIONS
From NYS Thruway (I-87) Exit 16, take NY 32 north for 7.4 miles, bearing left after a sign for the Black Rock Fish and Game Club onto Pleasant Hill Road. Go 0.1 mile, then turn left onto Taylor Road. Go 0.3 mile and park on the right (east) side of the road at the trailhead parking area.

TRAIL DESCRIPTION
Isolated in a place and time of its own, the Schunemunk Ridge (pronounced skun-uh-munk, meaning excellent fireplace in the Algonquin language) rises subtly in the rolling Northern Highlands. Even at 1,700 feet, its long, serpentine double ridge seems to elude the gaze of hikers from afar, as it lies neatly tucked between the Central Highlands and the little hills that taper into western flatlands. But once you've experienced the ridge personally, you'll be able to pick it out of the crowd.

Though it may be low and hemmed about by larger east-lying hills such as

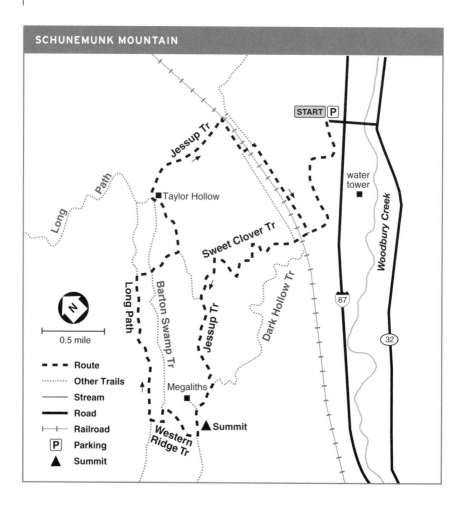

SCHUNEMUNK MOUNTAIN

Jessup Tr

Long Path

Taylor Hollow

Sweet Clover Tr

water tower

Woodbury Creek

Long Path

Barton Swamp Tr

Jessup Tr

Dark Hollow Tr

START P

87

32

N

0.5 mile

- - - Route
.... Other Trails
———— Stream
———— Road
⊢—+—⊣ Railroad
P Parking
▲ Summit

Megaliths

▲ Summit

Western Ridge Tr

Storm King, the views from this uplifted sandstone ridge of Devonian vintage are dramatic and sweeping—particularly to the west and north. And because of the cruelly steep elevation gain required to reach its summit, the ridge seems to frustrate all but the most determined hikers. Come prepared with plenty of water and your best day-hiking gear.

From the parking lot, follow southwest through open meadows on a private (legal) easement, keeping the cornfields to your right. The trail follows a farmer's road through cutover fields, and within 10 minutes of walking enters the woods to the right of a residence, where trail signs are posted. Go right, around a chained gate on the farm road. Marking is excellent. At the first intersection, bear left on the white-blazed Sweet Clover Trail and cross a shallow creek. Cross a large meadow in view of the Ridge to your right, where the easement is kept mowed for hikers and where wild morning glory and bindweed dot

Cairns mark the way along Schunemunk Ridge.

the fields along with brilliant hawkweed, Indian paintbrush, and clutches of asters. You draw unpleasantly close to the NYS Thruway (I-87) now, but soon put it behind you as the trail enters an oak woods turning decisively southwest. Follow the white blazes uphill, crossing the railroad tracks and avoiding the intersecting red trail. The footing is easy as you climb along the northern rim of Dark Hollow, becoming rocky with talus as the ascent is engaged along the route of an old, built-up road amid scrub oak and pine woods. Quarry talus appears uphill where heavy, stone water bars protect the trail, which then levels between pitches so you can catch your breath. As you ascend, impatiently anticipating your scenic payback, a few long, conglomerate outcroppings offer views to the east. Suddenly at 1,500 feet, you're at Sweet Clover Junction, an intersection of the Jessup and Highlands trails signed with no less than magic marker on a piece of tin. Bear left on the yellow-marked Jessup Trail and climb a short distance to finally attain ridge elevation where a dramatic type change to pitch pine and blueberry heath takes place. The colors are what get your attention. The rock is pinkish-purple with hematite—the concretized sands of an ancient tropical beach—inlaid with white quartz pebbles, and the fuchsia berry bushes make a startling contrast against the dark pines. You will be reminded of the much older but similar-looking Shawangunk conglomerate and the pine barrens as you thread your way along the trail between hardwood patches and open heaths. As for views, you will get some now, over the Hudson River into the Highlands, including Storm King, Mount Beacon, Mount Taurus, and the nearer-at-hand Black Rock Forest.

The trail is identified with paint blazes and cairns as it crosses the open rocks. At a tilted slab, the poorly identified, even obscure Dark Hollow Trail (black rectangle on a white background) bears left and descends. This is Dark Hollow Junction. Continue following the yellow blazes (blue will also be present), until, at a little over two hours into the hike, you reach a large open area where white paint blazes mark a spur trail to the right (west), and the site of the Megaliths (not to be missed). The 5-minute walk features expansive views across the Delaware Valley, and north to the Shawangunks and Catskills. You look across the shallow valley of Barton Swamp at the Western Ridge Trail outcroppings, where you'll soon be headed. The Megaliths themselves are large blocks of fissured bedrock, split away from the ridge and separated by deep crevices. Be careful—you can fall into them. This is the natural mid-point and highlight of the hike, although more scenic treats lie ahead.

From the main trail, proceed south again following the Jessup and Highlands trails, quickly reaching the summit (1,664 feet) and additional easterly views. Within minutes of leaving the summit the blue-on-white marked Western Ridge Trail departs to the right (west). Follow it downhill as it descends gradually into lush woods over sloppy, makeshift corduroy to intersect with the Barton Swamp Trail (red on white markers) as it cuts across to the lower western ridge. Go left (south) to suddenly turn west as the red trail ends. (You can save a bit of distance by turning right here, but the trail is often very wet. Either way, the Western Ridge Trail is followed to the Long Path.) Join the Long Path atop the western ridge and follow it to the right (north). Now you walk a narrow ridge, crossing tilted slabs of pitch pine on the eastern slope. At Sweet Clover Junction (not the first one you saw by the same name), by now an hour beyond the Megaliths, bear right (east) onto the white-blazed Sweet Clover Trail, descend across Barton Swamp and climb the eastern ridge again, through thick patches of laurel and red oak. Turn left (north) as you intersect with the Jessup Trail on a prominent spine of the ridge with excellent views to the east (you can see the sculptures at the Storm King Art Center) and of the Catskills and Shawangunks. The Jessup Trail descends into Taylor Hollow and bears right at a four-way intersection with the Barton Swamp Trail and Long Path, then follows Baby Brook downhill through pine and hemlock forest to the railroad tracks. Go right (south), following the yellow markers along the west side of the tracks, within 250 feet crossing them to join a woods road heading south. After passing an arch stone culvert under the tracks to your right, be alert as the Jessup Trail departs the woods road to the left. Follow it across an open meadow where metal posts mark the way into the woods again. Shortly you will arrive at the first intersection with the Sweet Clover Trail, which you'll recognize. Turn left and backtrack your way to the parking area.

TRIP 8
STERLING FOREST RIDGE

RATING: Moderate

DISTANCE: 7.5 miles

ELEVATION GAIN: 750 feet

ESTIMATED TIME: 4.5 hours

MAPS: USGS Greenwood Lake; NY-NJTC, Sterling Forest Trails; Sterling Forest State Park Hiking Map

A beautiful outing from Sterling Lake to the fire tower and back along the lake.

DIRECTIONS
To reach the Visitors Center from the junction of Routes 17 and 17A, take 17A west 1.4 miles and turn left onto Long Meadow Road (Route 84). Go 3.5 miles and take a right onto Old Forge Road. The Visitors Center is on the right.

TRAIL DESCRIPTION
The fight to save Sterling Forest has become one of the most interesting and important success stories in the continuing saga of the Hudson Valley's open-space preservation movement. Publicly acquired after a decade or more of effort on behalf of various conservation groups including the Appalachian Mountain Club, this 20,000-acre tract just 40 miles from New York City was destined for intensive development by the multinational Sterling Forest Corporation. Their plan—to build 13,000 homes, a golf course, and a series of industrial and commercial buildings—was abandoned when the Trust for Public Land and the Open Space Institute raised the owners' $55 million asking price. The acquisition effort gained momentum with the 1996 senate approval of a parks bill that gave $17.5 million to the cause. But the procurement of Sterling

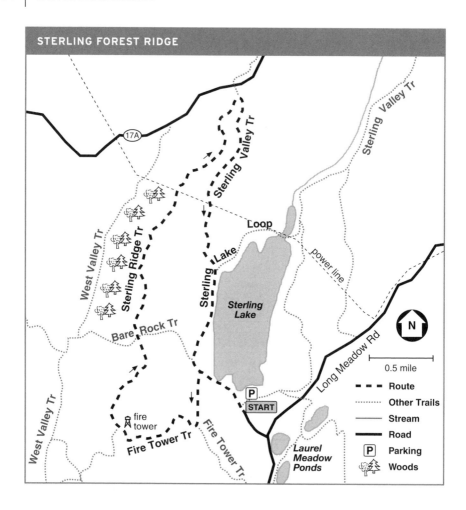

STERLING FOREST RIDGE

Forest had additional costs. Political compromises, made to assure the bill's passage, would result in an extension of logging contracts in Alaska's Tongass National Forest, and more relaxed development laws for Florida's barrier island beaches.

One hundred fifty years earlier, John Alexander, the Fifth Earl of Stirling, found all he needed in the gentle terrain, dense forests, and abundant, clean waters of these woods to help build an empire out of iron. He and other producers worked in support of the American quest for independence, carving roadways and footpaths and leaving the remains of mines and ironworks that we see today along Sterling Forest's trails. Before him, Native Americans hunted and fished here, and were able to guide Alexander's agent Cornelius Ford to Tampamopack the "place of deep waters" that would later become Sterling Lake.

At the visitor center you will find all you need for a quick orientation to the park—including the suggested Trail Conference map. There are also displays, a large three-dimensional map, and a small theater where you can see a film about the park's development and research programs.

To begin the hike, step out the front door of the visitor center and turn right, following the Sterling Lake Loop Trail (blue rectangular markers). This trail will lead you across a lawn, past an old stone foundation, and into dense woods. Cross the outlet of Sterling Lake on a wooden bridge and continue through a white pine stand to West Sterling Lake Road. Bear right and follow blue markers (sparse), passing an iron furnace and chimney ruin on your left. Sterling Lake appears on your right.

At the point where the paved road bears right, you're at the junction of several trails. Signage is good. You'll be returning (coming south) on the Sterling Lake Loop Trail that's ahead of you (north) at this point. Take care that you don't take the orange-marked Bare Rock Trail by mistake. Locate the red-marked Fire Tower Connector Trail to your left (south) and follow it uphill along the fire tower road. The dead and dying hemlocks you'll see are victims of the adelgid (the visitor center was built from adelgid-killed hemlocks).

This trail rises gently and is regularly driven by the fire warden. After 10 minutes, the trail flattens and a branch of the red trail goes left, but you bear right. A small wooden sign indicates the direction to the tower. Continue following red markers as the trail turns northwest and renews its ascent, bearing southwest and west again as it rises to the ridge. Soon a trail kiosk appears below the fire tower and observer's cabin, and you join the Sterling Ridge Trail (blue dot on white field) and the Highlands Trail (light blue diamonds). Take a moment to climb the tower that is usually open. This is the only remaining active tower (for the express purpose of fire detection) in New York State. Bob Spear, the 15-year-veteran fire warden and guardian spirit of Rough Mountain, lives in the cabin during the fire months. (He grows tomatoes on the summit.) Bob will invite you to visit the tower's cab, where a functioning alidade identifies the 100-mile-plus views. You will see the Devil's Path Mountains in the Indian Head Wilderness Area, 60 miles to the north, as well as the interior high peaks of the Burroughs Range in the Slide Mountain Wilderness Area. And you can see the Empire State Building, 40 miles to the south, along with a good deal of the New York City skyline. To the east lies Harriman State Park. To the west is the Appalachian Trail corridor and the rolling hills of New Jersey and Pennsylvania. To the south are Ringwood, the Ramapos, and the Southern Torne. The tower, built in 1924, is registered on the National Historic Lookout Registry (firelookout.net) and averages 3,500 visitors each year. When he's not relocating timber rattlers away from the busy summit area, Bob spends the entire day, on a "bad fire day," aloft in the tower.

Continue now, following the trail north as it leads you across the ridge. You're an hour and a half from NY 17A and the yellow trail where you will turn south to complete the loop. The footway is mostly smooth, grassy, and level. It is sometimes vague and appears to be little used. You will pass several open, sunny, east-facing outcroppings as you travel north through otherwise shady woods. After a half hour or so from the tower, you'll cross the orange-marked Bare Rock Trail that falls away on a gentle descent to the east and heads back to the Sterling Lake Loop Trail. (This is your last bailout point if you need to shorten the hike.) Continuing on the Sterling Ridge Trail, you'll pass beneath a power line and eventually drop downhill across an open, north-facing bedrock slab as you approach the hiker's parking area on NY 17A. At a point 200 feet from the parking area (appearing to your left), turn right on the yellow-marked trail, an old, disused woods road. This trail soon ascends slightly to a Y, where it bears left (watch for those yellow markers!) and there-after descends on a grassy, rocky, and sometimes wet surface. After you pass beneath the power line you saw earlier, the trail improves, rises somewhat, and is better drained amid oak and laurel woods as it approaches Sterling Lake, soon appearing on your left (east). At a T, you're at the lake's edge. Bear right on the Sterling Lake Loop Trail, a substantial dirt road in good condition. Follow this along the lake's edge until it bears away from the shore and brings you through a gate and a locked cable barrier, back to the trail junction where you'll recognize the Fire Tower Connector and Bare Rock trailheads. Retrace your steps from here, returning to the visitor center and parking area.

2

THE SHAWANGUNKS

THE ENCHANTING SHAWANGUNK RIDGE (the Shongums or Gunks, a.k.a. the Ridge) is the scenic and recreational mecca of the mid-Hudson Valley. It is amongst the region's most ecologically important landmasses. An extension of the south-lying Kittatinny Ridge of the Appalachian Mountains, the Gunks stretch longitudinally from the town of Rosendale in the north to Cragsmoor in the south, rising between the Wallkill and Rondout valleys. It is a place of high, windswept plateaus and cliffs (average elevation 2,000 feet), remarkably clear "sky" lakes, sheer ledges (the highest vertical drops east of the Mississippi), pelucid streams, robust waterfalls, and diverse natural habitats. The Ridge contains one of the most important and extensive dwarf pitch pine barrens in the world, and has been identified as one of the Earth's "Last Great Places" by the Nature Conservancy, as well as one of the top-40 most important natural resources lying within the North American continent and the Pacific Rim Basin.

The first thing that visitors to the ridge will realize is that the Shawangunk Mountains look a good deal different from the surrounding, younger ranges, such as the Catskills. This is because of the Ridge's prominent, white-quartz conglomerate bedrock of Silurian origin; 450-million-year-old sands, and quartz gravels that were deposited at the base of a shallow sea during the

Taconic Orogeny, and much later uplifted and eroded, faulted, fractured, and smoothed by a million years of glacial action. The glaciers dragged off the tops of ridges, breaking them into talus blocks and leaving behind vertical cliffs such as Sky Top, the Trapps, and Millbrook Mountain (Trips 14, 13, and 11, respectively). The resulting bare rock can be seen from great distances. Folding lifted the sandstone into broad, west-tilted slabs, and retreating ice nearly a mile thick scraped and polished the uplands into bright, open promontories such as Gertrude's Nose and Castle Point (Trips 11 and 10), studded with pitch pine and thick with blueberry heaths. This impervious, nutrient-poor rock held water, resulting in the creation of the five sky lakes that are strung across the top of the ridge. These (in particular Lakes Minnewaska and Awosting, Trip 10) are among the clearest lakes imaginable, because aquatic plants cannot grow in their thin, acidic, nutrient-poor soils. House-sized blocks, multi-tonned pebbles, and cobble-to-sand-sized glacial till are strewn liberally across the tablelands. In addition to decorating the ridge with glacial debris, the ice also dragged erratics—boulders of non-local composition—from the Catskills, depositing them in the Gunks. Underlying the conglomerate, the softer, older layer of Martinsburg shale is of Ordovician origin, a few thousand feet thick. Hikers will see the shale layer spilling out here and there around the ridge, where it was mined for building material as well as crushed and sprinkled on the extensive carriage roads of Mohonk and Minnewaska. This durable surface gives the carriage roads the appearance of narrow dirt roads, and as a result, the words road and drive are often used synonymously with the words carriage road and carriageway throughout the Gunks.

As the glaciers retreated, plants took hold in protected crevices and on the bare rocks, beginning a succession that would ultimately lead to today's varied vegetation profile. Hikers will often see typical oak woods with the mountain laurel understory that is so common in the higher woodlands, along with pockets of hemlock and, less frequently, white pine and red spruce. The northern hardwood group (beech, birch, maple, and associated species) appeared about 8,000 years ago, followed by southern trees (the Carolinian forest types) including oak, chestnut, and hickory. Comprising a good deal of the often dense understory are flowering dogwood, shadbush, striped maple, viburnum, witch hazel, low blueberry, huckleberry, and raspberry.

The southern area of the ridge is dominated by the widely distributed pitch pine (the Badlands, or Pine Plains), for which the Shawangunks are famous. Although there are extensive pitch pine barrens in places such as Long Island and New Jersey, those forests are growing on sand—not rock. Erik Kiviat points out that the Shawangunks contain "the only extensive high-altitude pitch pine barrens, and the only bedrock dwarf pine plains in the world." Hikers will see these forests in patches all around the Gunks, but most intimately in the otherworldly Badlands (Trip 12).

In addition to its alteration by physical forces and soil type, the distribution of the Gunks' vegetation groups was impacted significantly by human intervention. Although the ridge area was not fertile enough to attract anything more than seasonal use by indigenous, valley-dwelling peoples, it is possible that they manipulated the land with fire, opening it up for deer browse and nut trees or berry growth. Resource extractive industries followed when, by the early 1700s, settlers were using the forests for lumber, charcoal production, tanbarking, barrel hoop and furniture making, and for the production of the very desirable Shawangunk millstones. Particularly in the southern Shawangunks, the Ridge was perennially burned to enhance growth (by removing the competing vegetation) during the commercial berry-picking industry that thrived here until the 1930s. Pickers' shacks can still be seen along the trails of the southern ridge. Efforts to protect the Ridge from commercial and residential development have been difficult and ongoing, defeating several potentially ruinous projects, sustaining a broadening plan of protection and acquisition of buffer lands to protect this precious resource.

At this time there are four independent, cooperating management partnerships stewarding the Ridge.

THE MOHONK PRESERVE

The largest member-and-visitor-supported nature preserve in New York State, the Mohonk Preserve protects 6,400 acres of the northern Shawangunk Ridge. Established in 1963, its primary mission to protect and preserve the Ridge includes the fostering of an "understanding of the relationship between people and nature." The preserve is also committed to providing open space for "contemplation and recreation in keeping with the peace and natural beauty of the land."

The Smiley family, who, in 1869, began building what would become today's Mohonk Mountain House resort hotel, initiated the continuing tradition of land stewardship in the Shawangunks. Their holdings grew to 7,500 acres over the next century. The Smileys created the Mohonk Preserve (previously called the Mohonk Trust) to provide a management presence for the public use of preserve lands lying beyond the Mountain House boundaries.

Today the preserve has nearly 10,000 members and 350 volunteers. These financial and human resources support the preserve's four integrated programs of land stewardship, research, education, and land protection.

The preserve's recreational resources include 100 miles of multi-use carriage roads and trails for hiking and jogging, mountain biking, cross-country skiing, snowshoeing, and horseback riding. There are an estimated 1,000 rock-climbing routes on the preserve's lands. All of these resources are heavily used; the greatest challenge the preserve faces next to the preservation of the Ridge itself is the management of human impact. Those with annual memberships constitute most of the user group.

Take the time to stop at the Mohonk Preserve Trapps Gateway visitor center on your trip to the Gunks; you'll go past it on your way to the Trapps trailheads. Here you will find interpretive displays, a gift shop with books and maps of local interest, a kid's corner and butterfly garden, and a self-guiding nature trail. You can purchase day passes and memberships.

Access Fees. You'll find that after a single visit to the Ridge, you will want to purchase an annual membership (purchasing a membership first will ultimately be a savings). What some hikers will consider relatively high, current day-use fees are substantially reduced through the purchase of an annual membership ($55 basic membership for an individual, to which additional adult individuals can be added for $20 each; youths 13–18 an additional $5 each). Thus, a family of four adults will have "broken even" after only three visits. There are additional fees for mountain biking and rock climbing. As a member, you can enjoy additional privileges and access preserve lands from sunrise to sunset, 365 days a year.

Parking. On peak weekends, the preserve parking areas fill up extremely fast—and early. Try to arrive before 10 A.M. to be assured a spot. Parking is limited to 30 minutes at the Scenic Overlook and Hairpin Turn above the visitor center on US 44/NY 55, and tickets are issued. Although the preserve's Wawarsing and West Trapps parking lots fill quickly (the majority of this user group are rock climbers), weekdays are seldom a problem.

Camping and Pets. Pets must be leashed and cleaned up after. No camping or fires are permitted. There is a very small campsite east of Trapps Bridge for use by rock climbers only. The nearest legal camping area can be found at the Shawangunk Multiple Use Area, 0.8 mile east of the intersection of US 44/NY 55 on NY 299.

Directions and Information. Mohonk Preserve Visitor Center: On US 44/NY 55, 0.5 mile west of its intersection with NY 299, Gardiner, New York, 6.0 miles west of New Paltz. Mohonk Preserve, P.O. Box 715, New Paltz, NY 12561; 845-255-0919; mohonkpreserve.org/visit/.

MOHONK MOUNTAIN HOUSE

Named a National Historic Landmark in 1986, this private, nineteenth-century, Victorian-style castle and the beautiful lands, trails, and carriageways surrounding Lake Mohonk is a separate entity from the Mohonk Preserve. The resort began in 1869 with the Smiley brothers' purchase of 280 acres of the Ridge, on which they built a ten-room boarding house. Subsequent purchases and improvements resulted in today's hotel of 250 rooms, 138 of them with working fireplaces, with 238 balconies providing world-class lake and mountain scenery. Room fees vary from $235 to $750 a night!

Day access is similarly pricey. While a membership with the preserve will allow you access to the Mountain House property and trails, additional fees and restrictions apply. At this time there is a members' parking fee of $2 at the Gatehouse lot when space is available (the hotel's main entrance), and hikers are asked not to enter the hotel. Hotel facilities are reserved for hotel guests only. Hikers purchasing day-use passes at the hotel Gatehouse (rather than the Preserve Visitor Center) will be charged a daunting $16 per person on weekends, and $12 on weekdays. A shuttle is available from the Gatehouse to the hotel trailheads for an additional $5, round-trip.

No pets are allowed on the property.

Directions and Information. From Exit 18 of the NYS Thruway (I-87), drive west through the village of New Paltz on NY 299. As you cross the bridge over the Wallkill River, take the first right onto Springtown Road and set to zero. At 0.5 mile, turn left onto Mountain Rest Road (CR 6), where you'll see signs for Mohonk. At 1.7 miles, go through the intersection of Butterville-Canaan Road. Continue up Mountain Rest Road, when at 4.0 miles, you pass the Mohonk Mountain House main gate on the left.

Mohonk Mountain House, Mountain Rest Road, New Paltz, NY 12561: 845-255-1000, 800-772-6646; www.mohonk.com.

SAM'S POINT PRESERVE

This 4,600-acre preserve and interpretive center lies in the southern Shawangunks' historic village of Cragsmoor. Efforts to procure and protect this area of rare plant and animal species (and three rare natural communities) have been ongoing since 1980. Led by a partnership between the Nature Conservancy and the Open Space Institute, the preserve was acquired in 1997 in response to growing development pressure around the sensitive areas of the Ridge. Within the preserve is the most extensive example of a globally rare ridge-top pine barrens—one of the Earth's most endangered ecosystems. Also contained within the preserve are Sam's Point, the Ice Caves, and Verkeerder Kill Falls, its most popular destination hikes.

Several marked trails lead from the interpretive center into the pine "barrens," so-called because of the arid landscape of stunted trees and an understory of shrubs. Hikers must obtain permits to enter some areas of the preserve (none of these areas are included in this book). Hunting is allowed but strictly controlled. This open plateau area is the highest in the Shawangunks, and is exposed to rapid changes in weather. Be prepared as you would in any upper-elevation environment.

The preserve is closed from dusk to dawn. Overnight parking, camping, fires, and swimming in Lake Maratanza are prohibited. Also forbidden are mountain biking, off-road vehicles, and rock climbing. Pets must be leashed.

Directions and Information: Sam's Point Preserve, P.O. Box 86, Cragsmoor, NY 12420; Preserve Manager: 845-647-7989.

The Nature Conservancy, Shawangunk Ridge Program, Eastern New York Chapter, 108 Main St., New Paltz, NY 12561; 845-255-9051.

Open Space Institute, Inc., 1350 Broadway, Rm. 201, New York, NY 10018; 212-629-3981.

MINNEWASKA STATE PARK PRESERVE

Encompassing nearly 12,000 acres of forested land on the Shawangunk Ridge, Minnewaska appears to be just as beautiful as Mohonk—but more remote. Originally owned and developed as a rustic resort area by the Smiley brothers, this day-use park is connected to the Mohonk Preserve by the same extensive trails and carriage roads that were built over a century ago. It contains three lakes—Minnewaska, Awosting, and the remote Mud Pond—as well as the high ledges, cliff-top promontories, and dwarf pitch pine barrens that have made the Ridge one of the world's most unique natural resources.

Recreational use in the park is intensive and includes cycling, hiking, biking, snow-shoeing, cross-country skiing, horseback riding and horse carriages, swimming (accessible to people with disabilities), and scuba diving under permit in Lake Minnewaska. Cartop boats are permitted in Lake Minnewaska by permit. Rock climbing is permitted at the Peterskill Area.

There is a visitor/interpretive center in the park's headquarters building near the upper parking lot, along with the Conservation Education and Research Center (the large stone building above Lake Minnewaska).

TRIP 9
BONTICOU CRAG

RATING: Moderate

DISTANCE: 3.0 miles

ELEVATION GAIN: 500 feet

ESTIMATED TIME: 2.5 hrs

MAP: USGS Mohonk Lake; NY-NJTC Shawangunk Trails, Lake Mohonk Area; Mohonk Preserve Trail Map, Northern Section

A carriage road walk followed by a short introduction to rock scrambling on the Shawangunks' white quartz conglomerate talus fields, arriving at a bare summit with vertical cliffs and excellent views.

DIRECTIONS

The most convenient access to the Crag Trail is from Upper 27 Knolls Road, just west of the Mohonk Mountain House main entrance on Mountain Rest Road in New Paltz. From Exit 18 of the NYS Thruway (I-87), drive west through the village of New Paltz on NY 299. As you cross the bridge over the Wallkill River, take the first right onto Springtown Road and set to zero. At 0.5 mile, turn left onto Mountain Rest Road (CR 6), where you'll see signs for Mohonk. At 1.7 miles, go through the intersection of Butterville-Canaan Road. Continue up Mountain Rest Road, when at 4.0 miles, you pass the Mohonk Mountain House main gate on the left. (You can ask for a map here.) At 5.0 miles, turn right onto Upper 27 Knolls Road and in another 0.3 mile, park in the Spring Farm trailhead parking area. There's a self-pay fee collector ("iron ranger") here for times when the booth is not staffed (during winter and on spring and fall weekdays). There's a kiosk with map and trail information adjacent to the attendant booth.

TRAIL DESCRIPTION

This short but rigorous hike includes a stroll through the northernmost Shawangunk forests, on the foot trails and carriage paths of the Virginia Smiley Preserve, plus an invigorating, short rock scramble through the savage, broken talus of the Gunks' conglomerate cliffs. What you get in exchange for a relatively short half-day hike are sweeping views of the Catskills and the southeastern Hudson Valley lowlands, as well as a "hands-on" feel for a re-

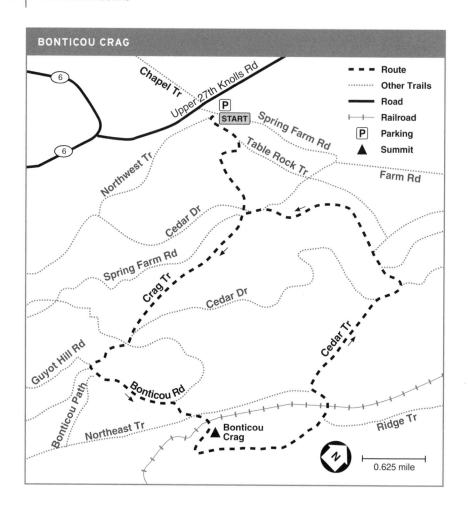

BONTICOU CRAG

markably contrasty cliff-and-talus environment of dark green pitch pine and white, tilted slabs.

Locate the red-marked Crag Trail across the road from the kiosk and follow it through open fields past cedar hedgerows, climbing. Immediately you will be treated to views of the Catskills over the Esopus and Rondout valleys, and these views improve dramatically as you ascend the Crag itself. Cross Cedar Drive and Spring Farm Road, climbing through open hardwoods into the east. At the four-way intersection of Cedar Drive and Bonticou Road, go straight ahead on Cedar Drive. This will bring you to circuitous Bonticou Road again where you turn nearly 180 degrees into the northeast. Stay alert here so that you leave the red-marked Bonticou Path to your right (it descends to the Northeast Trail, out of your way), remaining on Bonticou Road. This level carriageway will soon treat you to open views of Bonticou Crag, looming

The white conglomerate sandstone of Bonticou Crag.

brightly in the north. Within a few minutes you will see the yellow-marked Bonticou Ascent Path, where you turn right toward the cliff face. At the edge of the cliff base, cross the Northeast Trail to find yourself standing at the bottom of the talus field. (Now that you've seen the talus face you're about to climb, note that you can avoid it by following the Northeast Trail to ascend the Crag from the north on the easy section of the Bonticou Ascent Path.)

There's a flat rock to the right of the ascent where you can adjust your pack, tighten your boot laces, and prepare for the climb. You may wish to remove your wristwatch to protect it from scrapes—you're going to be using all fours now as you make your way through the tumult of broken, radically angled slabs that have fallen away from the cliff. As a general rule in scrambling high-angle rock faces, keep your body low and close to the rock. Search for good foot-, hand-, fist-, and fingerholds as you move upward, moving slowly and deliberately. The going is generally easy if you're reasonably agile and fit. Follow the yellow paint blazes. There's one challenging point at the upper end of the climb where you ascend through a narrow crack. Some members of your party may need assistance. Be careful and stick together.

Feel that cold air coming from the deep crevices of the talus? These moist fissures, some of them appearing endless, may well be one of the last known habitats of the endangered eastern woodrat, which, although once common here, has not been seen on the Mohonk Preserve since 1967. Eric Kiviat, author of *The Northern Shawangunks* and a founding ecologist of Hudsonia Limited, observes that the once common woodrat, which resembles an "oversized Norway rat (house rat)…with larger ears and longer whiskers" has been found in the Ice Caves Mountain area of the southern Shawangunks, a locale that may in fact currently be the "most northeastern station in the eastern woodrat's range." Do not be alarmed in the fortunate event that you see one—they are not aggressive. One thing you will notice is how little soil there is in these crevices, and how little vegetation is able to grow in among the shifting (over longer periods of time) blocks of talus. Here and there are trees perhaps 20 years old, and as you ascend, more appear along with mountain laurel and, at last, pitch pine, the most dominant and obvious member of this cliff-and-talus plant community.

Very soon after cresting this narrow ridge, bear right (south) following the yellow paint blazes. The scarp opens up and you walk across the tilted summit rocks. These open slabs provide you with several choices for relaxing and observing the magnificent views to the west and southeast. You'll also be treated to the antics of curious turkey vultures, some of which glided to within 10 feet of our faces as we ate lunch. Note the two-tone wing colors, with the flight feathers being lighter in color. These scavengers, nearly the size of an eagle with up to a 6-foot wingspan, get their names from the bare red heads of the mature birds. They are gregarious, commonly soaring in groups of a dozen or more in search of carrion. Beware of the extremely high vertical drops of the cliffs!

Follow the spine of the Crag north and recover the yellow paint blazes; go past your ascent point and continue north and downhill. Join the obscure blue-marked Northeast Trail (joined here by the Ridge Trail), where the yellow paint blazes of the Ascent Path end. After 15 minutes, you're down to forest level again. Pass beneath one last ledge and bear right onto the Cedar Trail (red blazes), following through reclaimed fields, now ash groves, and join Cedar Drive in a mature oak forest. Follow the carriageway along an even, northerly contour, passing Spring Farm Road, and suddenly you're back at the point at which the Crag Trail is recognized. Go right to the Spring Farm parking area and your point of origin.

BLACK VULTURE

The black vulture, *Coragyps atratus*, is an exciting recent addition to the Shawangunks' bird population (along with the clay-colored sparrow and the peregrine falcon). This large southern scavenger has been expanding its habitat into more rugged areas farther north due to warming trends. The first documented nest in the state appeared near Bonticou Crag in 1997. By 2004, there were three confirmed nesting sites on the Mohonk Preserve, now the bird's northernmost known breeding area in the United States. Eggs, two to a clutch, take from 38 to 41 days to incubate. The birds fledge at around 70 days.

It is likely that the black vulture will do well in the Shawangunks, and in similar areas of moderate to intensive human use, because it is not overly sensitive to human presence during its breeding season. (It is considerably less sensitive, by contrast, to the peregrine falcon.)

From time to time, the Trapps cliffs have been closed to protect both falcon and vulture nesting sites from disturbance by rock climbers. The increasing populations of turkey vultures and now, the smaller black vulture, often confuse observers. Black vultures have a short, square tail, with whitish patches toward the wingtips. They have a black head (as opposed to the adult turkey vultures' easily identified bald, red head) and a smaller wingspan. They tend to flap vigorously and glide in short intervals. The heads of both species are bald to keep them clean of carrion as they consume carcasses. In order to control their core body temperature, vultures defecate on their feet.

TRIP 10
CASTLE POINT, LAKE AWOSTING, AND MARGARET CLIFF

RATING: Moderate

DISTANCE: 10 miles

ELEVATION GAIN: 500 feet

ESTIMATED TIME: 6.5 hours

MAPS: USGS Gardiner; USGS Naponoch; NY-NJTC Southern Shawangunk Trails; Minnewaska State Park Preserve Hiking Map

An easy, but long, hike past two sky lakes along the old Shawangunk carriage roads, with swimming in Lake Awosting and far-reaching valley views from Castle Point.

DIRECTIONS

From Exit 18 of the NYS Thruway (I-87), head west through the village of New Paltz on NY 299 for 7.5 miles. Turn right onto US 44/NY 55 and drive past the Mohonk Gateway Center. Continue up the hill and under Trapps Bridge, and go another 3.0 miles to the Minnewaska State Park entrance on your left (total 11.4 miles from I-87).

TRAIL DESCRIPTION

Many hikers walk the easy, scenic carriage roads of Minnewaska to Castle and Hamilton points, taking a brief side trip to swim in Lake Awosting's saffire waters. But few venture beyond Awosting, the point where this hike turns north to approach Castle Point across the lonely rim rocks of Murray Hill, Spruce Glen, and Margaret Cliff.

Plan for a long day outing and bring your bathing suit. Try to reach Minnewaska State Park before 9:30 A.M. on nice weekends or you may have to park in the Lower Awosting lot, requiring an additional 1.5 miles of hiking and 400 feet in added elevation gain to this already long hike. There's a per-car entry fee of $6 at this writing. From the gate house, drive 0.7 mile to the upper lots.

There are two levels to the upper (Wildmere) parking area. The trail begins at the southwest corner of the higher lot, at the north end of Lake Minnewaska. A map and interpretive kiosk is posted on the picnic area lawn nearby. Walk toward the lake (the view is terrific) and bear right (south) to find the trailhead.

With Lake Minnewaska to your left, bear left at the first fork (don't take

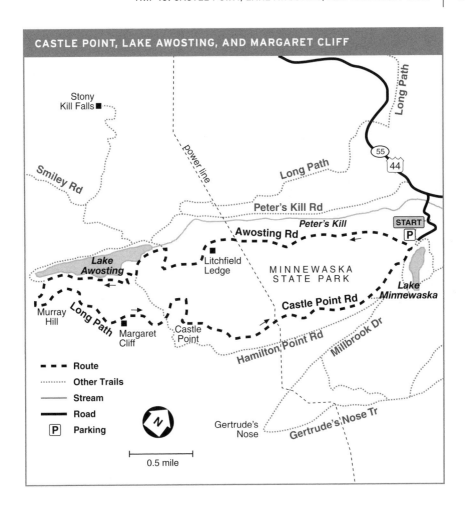

CASTLE POINT, LAKE AWOSTING, AND MARGARET CLIFF

Stony Kill Falls■

Smiley Rd

power line

Long Path

Peter's Kill Rd

Peter's Kill

Awosting Rd

START
P

Lake Awosting

Litchfield Ledge

M I N N E W A S K A
S T A T E   P A R K

Castle Point Rd

Lake Minnewaska

Murray Hill

Long Path

Margaret Cliff

Castle Point

Hamilton Point Rd

Millbrook Dr

Long Path

55

44

- - - Route
.... Other Trails
――― Stream
▬▬▬ Road
P Parking

N

0.5 mile

Gertrude's Nose

Gertrude's Nose Tr

the Sunset Trail!), and walk down to the Lake Minnewaska swimming area where you'll find a map and a battalion of chemical toilets. Bear right onto the green-marked Upper Awosting Carriageway. You will be sharing the path with bikers and equestrians. The surface is hard-packed shale with no rocks—those will come later.

Views of the Catskills will appear intermittently to the right (west) as you travel south on the carriage road. Within a half hour you'll pass a stone stream-bed to the left. Pass under the power line where you get a look at some white conglomerate bedrock. A few ledges offer views of the Peters Kill Valley to the right as Litchfield Ledge begins to build up on your left. Leaving the long ledge behind, you climb easily to the intersection where the Lake Awosting Carriageway goes right; you bear left here, staying on the green Upper Awosting Carriageway.

A mountain biker surveys the view from Castle Point.

Soon, the seemingly long walk (more than 3.0 miles) will begin to pay off as you climb the ramparts of Lake Awosting's north shore. These provide long views of the Catskills to the northwest and south, over the lake. Short spur trails lead to expansive panoramas and vertical pitch pine ledges as you level out on the carriage road.

At the intersection of Hamilton Point Carriageway and Upper Awosting Carriageway, turn right onto the black-marked Lake Awosting Carriageway. You'll pass through a thick hemlock glen before arriving at Awosting's stone beach, where swimming is allowed only when lifeguards are on duty. There's a comfort station here. Continue along the lake's edge, passing two small peninsulas where people frequently sunbathe.

As you approach the south end of the lake, ledges appear across it to your right. Be alert for a left, unmarked turn here. As this trail departs to the south, two rocks lie across the trail next to a *No Bikes* sign. Very old blazes are detectable on the trees. Follow this trail and bear left as the blue-blazed Long Path enters from the right. This will bring you uphill easily to the deeply fractured southerly summit of Murray Hill, a ledge outcropping facing southwest, with sprawling views of the Badlands, including High Point and the lands of the Sam's Point Preserve with the Kittatinnys lying beyond to the south. Peekamoose, in the Catskills, lies due north. As you cross Murray Hill, stay on the Long Path; some spurs lead to dangerous drops that are concealed by low vegetation.

As you work your way north toward Margaret Cliff, views to the northwest and southeast are dramatic, with the Catskills rising beyond the glacially ravaged, pitch pine tablelands. Battlement Terrace, Castle Point, and Lake Awosting appear ahead. The landscape looks raw and weather-beaten; cairns appear to help you stay on course, and blazes appear more frequently on rock. Margaret Cliff lies ahead, identifiable by its two deep cracks. Stay with the blue-marked trail as you pass few established-looking spurs that head east to create a herd connector along the extensive Margaret Cliff. At a third T, bear right. Blue markers are not obvious at this junction until you follow the trail for a moment. This is one of the few areas in the park where red spruce appears in numbers—you can distinguish it from surrounding hemlock and white pine by its pointed, spearlike spires.

Nearly 3 hours into the hike, the trail follows onto an old carriage road. The type change to hemlock is dramatic; at this point watch very carefully for the Long Path as it goes left onto a narrow, slightly eroded laurel path, climbing. As the trail levels, you will pass a small rock balanced upon a cannonball-sized stone adjacent to a high and dangerous fissure. Shortly thereafter the trail heads downhill steeply but soon levels, crossing a talus field among oaks and a moist glen with a few very large hemlocks at the site of a grassy, dead-end carriage road. Climb now, tunneling through the rocks at one point before ascending to meet the intersection of Hamilton Point and Castle Point carriageways. Follow the blue-marked Castle Point Carriageway (0.7 mile) uphill. Walk under the large overhanging ledges of Battlement Terrace, then wind around to cross the top of it, climbing into the east and enjoying far-flung views from east to west across the Badlands. Soon you will reach Castle Point, a high white conglomerate ledge forming the eastern-most cliff of the Terrace. The views are the culmination of most everything you've seen so far, only better; to the southeast, you'll see the fertile, agricultural lands of the Wallkill River floodplain with the Hudson Highlands beyond.

Castle Point Carriageway treats you to fine views to the north and east as you continue following north along the ledges, descending. Perhaps nowhere else is the view of Gertrude's Nose so complete and vivid. The little dimples to the north of it are the backsides of the otherwise dramatic Millbrook Mountain. You can see the white, obelisk-like Patterson's Pellet balanced on the ledge next to Millbrook Carriageway across the Palmaghatt Ravine. In another 45 minutes or so you will arrive at a T, where the Hamilton Point Carriageway goes right. You go left, staying with the Castle Point Carriageway. Lake Minnewaska's high northern ledges appear to the right as you descend, shortly to arrive back at the swimming area and the short climb back to the parking area.

TRIP 11
MILLBROOK MOUNTAIN AND GERTRUDE'S NOSE

RATING: Strenuous

DISTANCE: 9.5 miles

ELEVATION GAIN: 850 feet

ESTIMATED TIME: 5.5 hours

MAPS: USGS Gardiner; USGS Naponoch; NY-NJTC Southern Shawangunks; Minnewaska State Park Preserve

A long and fascinating hike through the glacial cobble fields and pitch pine balds next to the sheer cliffs of Millbrook Mountain.

DIRECTIONS
From Exit 18 of the NYS Thruway (I-87), head west through the village of New Paltz on NY 299 for 7.5 miles. Turn right onto US 44/NY 55 and drive 0.8 mile up the hill to the Mohonk Gateway Center. Just beyond the entrance, turn right into the Wawarsing parking area. Arrive early or you won't get a spot (as a rule of thumb, early means before 9:30 A.M. on a nice weekend). If you can't get a spot here, continue on US 44/NY 55 to the West Trapps parking area (fee) just beyond Trapps Bridge on the right.

TRAIL DESCRIPTION
The hike across Millbrook Mountain to the white conglomerate cliffs of Gertrude's Nose is among the longest and easily the most memorable outings in the Gunks. These landmarks are less frequented than the popular destinations nearer to the Trapps or Lake Minnewaska. Be prepared with plenty of food and water, a good map, and boots with enough support to protect your feet from the rocky trails.

Park at either the Mohonk Preserve's Gateway Center Wawarsing area or the West Trapps parking area and make your way up to Trapps Bridge. (See Trip 13 for details.) Turn west, crossing the bridge onto Trapps Road (carriage road). Watch carefully to the left while still in sight of the bridge, and bear left (southwest) onto the blue-blazed Millbrook Ridge Trail. As you climb, views to the west across the Coxing Kill Valley include the ledges of the High Peter's Kill as well as Dickie Barre and Ronde Barre in Minnewaska State Park.

Signage and blazes are faint at the trailhead. The trail begins by climbing up the low-angle pitch pine slabs of the Near Trapps and continues southwest

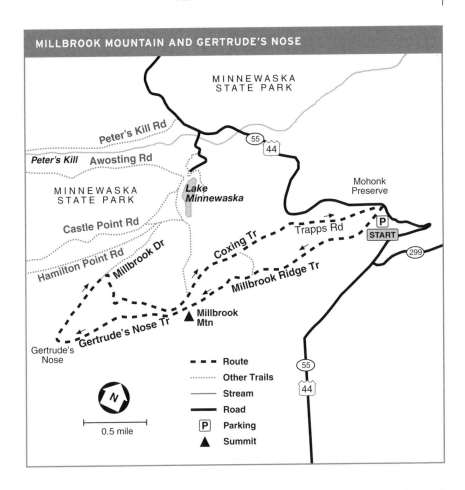

MILLBROOK MOUNTAIN AND GERTRUDE'S NOSE

MINNEWASKA
STATE PARK

Peter's Kill Rd

Peter's Kill   Awosting Rd

55
44

MINNEWASKA
STATE PARK

Lake
Minnewaska

Mohonk
Preserve

Castle Point Rd

Coxing Tr   Trapps Rd

P

START

Hamilton Point Rd   Millbrook Dr

Millbrook Ridge Tr

299

Gertrude's Nose Tr

Millbrook
Mtn

Gertrude's
Nose

▪ ▪ ▪   Route
··········   Other Trails
————   Stream
————   Road
P   Parking
▲   Summit

55
44

N

0.5 mile

along the cliffs. Interesting views develop back across the Trapps as the trail winds in and out of the woods over a variety of surfaces from rocks and soil to pine needles, sometimes coming close to high vertical ledges.

In his ecological survey *The Northern Shawangunks*, Erik Kiviat points out that this area of the Ridge is part of the Appalachian hawk migration route, noting that "during certain weather conditions, updrafts and tail winds allow hawks to soar long distances with little energy expenditure." During the fall of each year, the preserve conducts their annual hawk watch along these slabs and cliffs, where observers can see hawks, harriers, and vultures moving through the flyway. You will almost always see vultures and hawks here, and sometimes a bald or golden eagle.

You will pass the Bayard Path (red blazes) when you are 25 minutes into the hike. Continue through rolling oak and laurel woods into the southwest. Here and there you'll have a glimpse of Millbrook Mountain ahead of you.

An hour or less into the hike, turn left on blue blazes as the red-blazed Millbrook Cross Path departs to the right. (It's easy to absentmindedly bear right here.) Continue left on the Millbrook Ridge Trail, rising into an open area before descending to a little hemlock glen, where the trail crosses an unnamed, mossy creek that dries in the summer months. From this point you will ascend consistently along the northern spine of Millbrook's steep ridge. Dramatic views of the Trapps and Sky Top appear as you progress, and the trail walks the lip of a spine-tingling, 350-foot-high vertical cliff to your left (east). Dr. Kiviat points out that this is one of the highest sheer cliff faces east of the Mississippi River. Be careful!

Walking below the west-tilted knife edge of the ridge, you will see the red-blazed Millbrook Mountain Trail appearing on the right (west). This will be your return route to the Trapps, so fix this spot in your memory. Where the blue trail ends, the vegetation changes from oaks over bedrock and blueberry to the white conglomerate, piney summit of Millbrook—not exactly a "summit" in appearance or feel but the highest point along the ridge. Millbrook Mountain was fractured more or less in two by the Wisconsin ice sheet, so what you're standing on is roughly half its preglacial shape. (The other half of the mountain can be seen lying in chunks below the cliffs.) Here are extensive views of the ridges to the west, the flatlands to the south and east, the Hudson Highlands and Fishkill Ridge beyond them, and the Catskills to the northwest. You can see both Hamilton and Castle points to the west, and the lands of the Mohonk Preserve to the north.

Millbrook Mountain marks the boundary between the Mohonk Preserve and Minnewaska State Park. Adjacent and downhill from the summit of Millbrook Mountain, Millbrook Drive (carriage road) ends in a hairpin turn. Here, the red-blazed Gertrude's Nose Trail begins and the Millbrook Ridge Trail ends. Follow the red blazes, continuing along the ridge into the southwest. For a while the Gertrude's Nose Trail parallels Millbrook Drive. You will have glimpses of Gertrude's Nose ahead, a diminished version of Millbrook without the rocks. The trail traverses variable terrain, crossing a beautiful, flat-rock pitch pine barren before descending steeply past a deep hole near a hemlock ledge to the left of the trail, and continues, walking beneath a power line at 1,500 feet. Now you ascend again, following a level contour along the cliffs. The forest type will change several times, from hardwood to hemlock to pitch pine over blueberry heaths when, with little warning, you're on Gertrude's Nose, about three hours into the hike at this point. The trail curves around into the northeast to cross the wind-punished conglomerate flats.

The southwest-facing promontory of the Nose, though lower in elevation,

A hiker surveys the Badlands from Gertrude's Nose.

is similar in many respects to both Hamilton and Castle points. Each is a high, level plateau of faulted and fractured conglomerate cap rock, the white stone that is the signature geology of the Shawangunks. Long fractures reach from the cliffs' edges back to the woods; some are dangerously deep and can be obscured by a significant snowfall. Signs are posted on the cliffs reminding hikers to move cautiously across the rocks, mindful not to trample the fragile vegetation off-trail. Below the cliffs are large talus blocks and rubble that have fallen away from the cliff face, forming crevices that are old enough and deep enough to support a significant plant and animal habitat. The rock margins are covered in thick mats of blueberries. As you move west, you'll walk in and out of the woods along the upper northerly edge of wild Palmaghatt Ravine and the Kline Kill (pronounced kline-ah-kill). The trail walks next to the cliffs, past scattered erratics (boulders, pebbles) and isolated patches of pitch pine, hemlock, and hardwoods before it rises through an enchanted hemlock forest and up to a high, rocky ledge you can see ahead of you.

Soon you will arrive at Millbrook Carriageway. Turn right and follow the carriageway back to Millbrook Mountain. You'll recognize the summit area soon. Turn left on the blue-blazed Millbrook Ridge Trail, backtracking on your earlier route a short distance to the red-blazed Millbrook Mountain Trail, where you bear left and descend. Within 10 minutes do not fail to turn right on the blue-blazed Coxing Trail, descending from open pitch pine slabs with northerly views into dense woods. These westerly slopes of Millbrook Mountain—the boisterous Coxing Kill's watershed—are often wet. Puncheons have been placed in the wettest areas to protect the soft soils. You will pass the Millbrook Cross Path on your right, remaining on the blue Coxing Trail until you reach Trapps Road. Bear right on Trapps Road and walk northeast, back to Trapps Bridge and your point of origin.

TRIP 12
SAM'S POINT AND THE BADLANDS

RATING: Strenuous

DISTANCE: 8.5 miles

ELEVATION GAIN: 800 feet

ESTIMATED TIME: 5 hours

MAP: USGS Ellenville; USGS Naponoch; NY-NJTC Southern Shawangunks

A long and remote scenic hike through the southwestern Shawangunks' oceanic dwarf pitch pine barrens, past Verkeerder Kill Falls and the Ice Caves.

DIRECTIONS

From Exit 18 off the NYS Thruway (I-87), set to zero, and head west through the village of New Paltz on NY 299. Cross the Wallkill Bridge, and bear left (south) at 2.5 miles onto CR 7 (Libertyville Road). At 15.5 miles, turn right on NY 52. Reset your odometer. At 6.0 miles (or 7.5 if you're coming from NY 302/NY 52 in Pine Bush), turn right onto Cragsmoor Road (not signed) at the Sam's Point Preserve sign, heading for Cragsmoor. (This point is 5.0 miles east of the intersections of NY 52 and US 209 in Ellenville.) At 1.5 miles from NY 52, turn right at the Cragsmoor post office. And continue past the firehouse to the Sam's Point Preserve parking lot (entrance fee).

TRAIL DESCRIPTION

Called a "global treasure" by the Open Space Institute and the Nature Conservancy, the 4,600-acre Sam's Point Preserve protects one of the world's best ex-

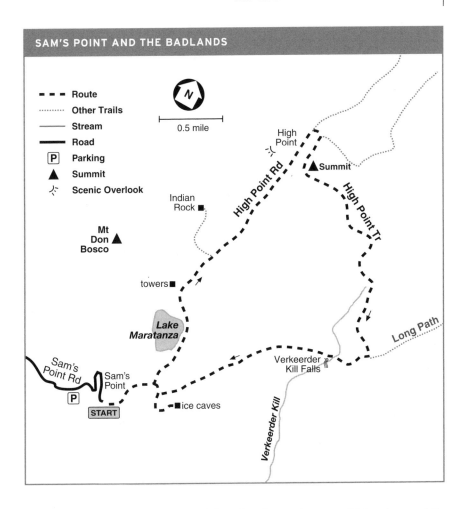

SAM'S POINT AND THE BADLANDS

Route
Other Trails
Stream
Road
P Parking
▲ Summit
⚘ Scenic Overlook

0.5 mile

High Point
Summit
High Point Rd
High Point Tr
Indian Rock ■
Mt Don Bosco ▲
towers ■
Lake Maratanza
Long Path
Sam's Point Rd
Sam's Point
P
START
■ ice caves
Verkeerder Kill Falls
Verkeerder Kill

amples of the globally endangered dwarf pitch pine barrens. This otherworldly ecozone poised high in the remote southern Shawangunk interior will introduce you to yet another dimension of the Ridge's broad ecological diversity. The preserve also contains one of the only accessible ice cave systems on the Ridge, as well as the isolated and picturesque Verkeerder Kill Falls. Plan on an early start so you can visit all three destinations.

The main attraction of this hike is the aptly named Badlands, or pitch pine barrens themselves, an arid plain reminiscent of the western alpine plateaus—the highest lands on the Ridge. A tourist attraction in the 1960s, the Ice Caves and the sadly impacted area around Sam's Point and Lake Maratanza still attract enough casual visitors to sustain a vicarious tourist atmosphere that hikers will escape as they make for the barrens. Most of the preserve's visitors come for the Ice Caves, and, judging by trail impact, do a one-way trip to the falls and back. Perhaps not realizing what they're missing, few visitors venture beyond to experience the lonely pine plains, the heart of the preserve's wilderness experience.

Park at the preserve's beautifully designed, staffed interpretive center (established in 2005), and pay the parking/access fee ($7 per car at this writing). At the trailhead to the north of the lot, bear right toward Sam's Point and the Ice Caves. In 10 minutes or more the old paved road will bring you uphill, beneath sheer cliffs as it curves around a short way off-trail to the scenic overlook of Sam's Point. These extensive views to the southwest are anticlimactic to those you'll experience from High Point. Return to the road, heading left (north) into the barrens. To the right of the road you can see deep into the Hudson Highlands.

One mile from the interpretive center, you will pass the road to the Ice Caves on your right. (This road leads 300 feet to the Verkeerder Kill Falls Trail, from which you will emerge later on.) Continue straight ahead, in the indicated direction of Lake Maratanza and High Point Road. Hike past the lake toward the ugly, lunar landscape of a microwave tower farm. Bear right on High Point Carriageway, leaving the pedestrian loop trail that circles Lake Maratanza, and suddenly it feels as if you are leaving the world behind.

First, you walk on gravel, then a grassy carriage road that turns rocky as it becomes narrow. Blueberries—the constant companion of the pitch pine—line the trail along with dense sweet-fern thickets and sometimes cranberry as the barrens begin to take shape. An hour into the hike you will pass the Indian Rock Trail to your left (west). Views to the west develop from the level terrain of the carriageway. Pass an open area to the right, where you may be lured off-trail by a herd path leading to views of Castle Point. In 10 more minutes, you'll reach the intersection of High Point Road and the High Point Trail. At the junction, bear right on the red-blazed High Point Trail and climb steeply over loose rock, bearing left at a fork, and go a short distance up the southwesterly side of High Point. This northwest-facing ledge has a phenomenal, 70-degree view of the Catskills, from Overlook Mountain through the Burroughs Range to Peekamoose and Table mountains in the Southern Catskills. Here was the site of an old fire tower; its anchor bolts still fixed in the stone. Continue on red markers as the trail turns due south, crossing the open, ledgy heaths of High Point, and arriving at its summit (2,230 feet) in another 0.4 mile, two and a half hours from the start of the hike. From here you survey the Badlands in their entire boreal splendor. Oceanic, dwarf pitch pine plains extend in all directions, thousands of acres of nearly homogeneous, miniature evergreen forest. To the east, you look across the lands of Minnewaska and Mohonk at the prominent landmarks of Castle Point and Sky Top. Hamilton Point lies lower down and to the right of Castle Point. You see the ledge of Battlement Terrace to the left of Castle Point, and the rim rocks around Murray Hill, Spruce Glen, and Margaret Cliff. Views of the Catskills persist, with the Devil's Path showing from Plateau Mountain, east to the Indian Head Wilderness Area and the Overlook Wild Forest. Farther to the west are the low, rolling lands of Forestburgh, Liberty, and Callicoon in the Delaware River watershed. To the east and south across the Wallkill Valley and the Hudson River are the Highlands again, the northern hills of the Fishkill Ridge, and the sprawling woods of Black Rock Forest and the Schunemunk, west of the Hudson. USGS triangulation benchmark number eight is anchored in the summit rock.

On your way again, drop down through the ledges following the red High Point Trail, passing through corridors of pitch pine, winding your way across the northern side of the Verkeerder Kill Valley, heading southeast. The cliffs along the trail (2,135 feet) have a few dangerous vertical drops. You will pass through margins of mixed woods with richer soils supporting soft (red) maple, birch, and black tupelo (a dogwood) with its shiny leaves. You'll get a good look at slick spots on glacially polished conglomerate, where a mile-thick sheet of ice slid southward. These surface marks, created during the Wisconsin advance roughly 15,000 to 27,000 years ago, are still visible today because the ordinarily erosion-resistant rock was protected by soil layers.

It will seem a long (but interesting) walk to the next trail junction, where the High Point Trail ends and the turquoise Verkeerder Kill Trail (Long Path) begins. Go right (southwest) on the Verkeerder Kill Falls Trail, dropping down into a lush, shady woods of sassafras, striped maple, witch hazel, and shadbush; chestnut oak appears and hemlocks hint at what lies ahead. At a bend in the trail you sense the abyss to your left where, taking a closer look, you can see into the vertically walled Verkeerder Kill gorge and the 75-foot falls that run dry in late summer. This vantage provides

A climber scaling High Point.

the only frontal view of the falls. Continue along the trail to cross the Kill, where amid the hemlocks you'll see shiny clusters of primordial-looking great laurels (rosebay rhododendron), an evergreen shrub of the heath family.

Now the trail climbs gradually onto the easterly ridge, exposed to the southwest winds. Pine barrens persist, sometimes interrupted by moist, shady woods and lush, open heaths. The region's best views of the Northern Shawangunk tablelands lie behind you, including some new additions to the viewshed, the formerly hidden Lake Awosting and farther east, Gertrude's Nose.

Within 45 minutes of the Falls, you'll emerge on a dirt road. The Ice Caves are a 5-minute walk downhill to the left (southeast). An interpretive sign kiosk exists at the head of the caves, where ladders take you through the dark (somewhat creepy) passageways, illuminated by (temperamental) solar-powered lights. It's a good idea to carry a flashlight if you go. (I was surprised to find no on-site supervision here.) A tour of the caves takes 20 minutes.

If you don't visit the caves, turn right as you come off the Verkeerder Kill Trail and walk up to the road. You'll recognize the junction. Turn left where the sign indicates the interpretive center at 1.0 mile, and return to Sam's Point, where you might see the sun setting.

TRIP 13
THE TRAPPS

RATING: Easy
DISTANCE: 5.0 miles
ELEVATION GAIN: 400 feet
ESTIMATED TIME: 2 hours
MAPS: USGS Gardiner; USGS Mohonk Lake; NY-NJTC Northern Shawangunk Trails; Mohonk Preserve Trail Map

An easy, enchanting hike along carriage roads under high cliffs, where rock climbing is very popular.

DIRECTIONS
From Exit 18 of the NYS Thruway (I-87), head west through the village of New Paltz on NY 299 for 7.5 miles. Turn right onto US 44/NY 55 and drive 0.8 mile up the hill to the Mohonk Gateway Center. Just beyond the entrance, turn right into the Wawarsing parking area. Arrive early or you won't get a spot (as

a rule of thumb, early means before 9:30 A.M. on a nice weekend). If you can't get a spot here, continue on US 44/NY 55 to the West Trapps parking area (fee) just beyond Trapps Bridge on the right.

TRAIL DESCRIPTION

The century-old Undercliff/Overcliff Carriageways form a loop around the famous cliffs known as the Trapps, creating one of the most popular scenic hikes (and bike rides) in the Shawangunks. The route travels beneath, then above the high vertical cliffs of bright conglomerate that are unique to the Gunks. Here, you will become intimately acquainted with the diverse cliff, talus, and slabrock communities that have made the Trapps not only the most fascinating scenic attraction of the mid-Hudson Valley, but an ecological preserve of global significance.

Both the Undercliff and Overcliff are multi-use carriage roads, so you will encounter many cyclists, hikers, and joggers, as well as the knowledgeable preserve rangers who patrol the cliffs and carriage roads. (You may be asked to show or purchase your day pass at this point.) These carriage roads are also popular cross-country ski routes, their surfaces carved into dual, diagonal striding tracks by local skiers the moment there is a 4-inch snowfall. But by far, the Trapps are most renowned for the world-class rock-climbing routes that have been pioneered along their eastern face. As you hike, you'll get to see climbers in action on the vertical walls, some as high as 250 feet.

Begin at the Mohonk Preserve visitor center (Trapps Gateway Center). Take the short but steep East Trapps Connector Trail from the north end of the Wawarsing parking area up to Undercliff Road (a.k.a. Undercliff Carriageway). (If this lot is full, continue to the West Trapps parking area 1.0 mile ahead and walk east up the gravel path to Trapps Bridge.) Catch your breath after climbing the Connector Trail's 250 stone steps and turn left (southwest) on Undercliff Carriageway. Signage is good. From here, the hike remains fairly level.

In a few minutes, you will arrive at the wooden hut and information kiosk, (with a rest room) in the general meeting area known as the Uberfall. The carriage road continues directly under the sheer cliffs here, where dozens of climbers can be seen top-roping (a method by which an anchor, or protection, is placed above the climber who is then held on belay from below by another person, thereby protecting the climber from a fall). It will amaze you to see how some climbers are able to scale a vertical wall that seems to have no handholds or ledges on it; for a non-climber, difficulty is hard to judge. Some of these very difficult climbs are in many cases adjacent to very easy ones. You'll find yourself enthralled, even eager to give this thrilling sport a try. Although climbers are

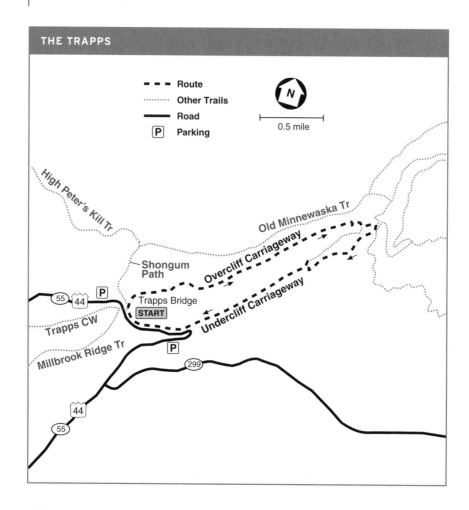

a friendly bunch, many of those who are "on-belay" are in close vocal contact with their partners and can't risk being distracted. The atmosphere is somewhat solemn, and highly focused. The white stains on the rock are from chalk, used by climbers to keep their hands dry and maximize friction.

Continue, ascending slightly past a southerly view, rising to Trapps Bridge. Don't cross the bridge. Turn right here where the Overcliff Carriageway departs to the west. Shortly, the flat carriage road turns northeast, as views to the west appear, slowly revealing the Coxing Valley, and the broad lowlands of the Rondout Valley and the Southern Catskills beyond. The viewshed expands as the carriage road cuts through sunny, low-angle pitch pine and oak-covered slabrocks. The entire east-facing silhouette of the Catskills, from Ashokan High Point in the south to Overlook Mountain in the north, forms the western horizon. Continue into the woods as the road descends slightly and curves past ledges on the left, passing an unmarked connector road on the left (avoid it) to Laurel Ledge Carriageway. Within minutes you'll arrive at Rhododendron Bridge, a shaded five-way intersection in the densely wooded heart of the Mohonk Preserve. Bear right on Undercliff Carriageway, winding around below the massive cliffs of the Trapps as the road turns south. Soon you will enjoy views of the broad, flat Wallkill Valley and its little hamlets and farms, and the Fishkill Ridge and Hudson Highlands beyond the village of New Paltz. On the talus alongside the carriage road, climbers will be "bouldering," practicing overhang holds and relaxing between routes. The yellow spur trails lead through the labyrinths of talus to reach climbing routes. On days that are not busy, it is not unusual to see copperheads sunning themselves in the middle of the road. Give them

A climber on the Trapps.

space. You'll be pleased to know that there have been few if any incidents involving hikers and snakes here.

From time to time, the cliffs may be closed to hikers in order to protect a peregrine falcon or black vulture nest; often you will see observers set up along the carriageway with telescopes trained on the nests. Most of them are volunteers and enthusiasts who help with census and tracking studies. If you've never seen a raptor close up, this is your chance to study the head of a falcon completely filling the view field of a high-power telescope—a surprising and unforgettable image. Soon you will come upon the East Trapps Connector Trail junction you used earlier. Descend to return to your car.

Undercliff Carriageway was built by hand in 1903. The area became a climbing destination when Fritz Wiessner, a climber scaling the cliffs around Breakneck, spotted the white cliffs of the Gunks. He pioneered the first routes on Millbrook Mountain, and then moved to Sky Top. His efforts led to the involvement of the Appalachian Mountain Club, which took measures to regulate climbing in the Gunks. This led to the rise of the autonomous "Vulgarians," a subculture of climbers characterized by a reckless lifestyle and a "live-to-climb" philosophy. Today there are an estimated 1,000 climbing routes in the Shawangunks. To find out more about climbing in the Gunks, visit Rock and Snow on Main Street in New Paltz.

TRIP 14
SKY TOP

RATING: Easy
DISTANCE: 2.5 miles
ELEVATION GAIN: 350 feet
ESTIMATED TIME: 2 hours
MAPS: USGS Mohonk Lake; NY-NJTC Shawangunk Trails, Lake Mohonk Area 10A; Mohonk Preserve Trail Map

A boulder scramble from Mohonk Mountain House through a deep and exciting crevice to a 360-degree view from Sky Top Tower, and an easy walk back.

DIRECTIONS

From Exit 18 of the NYS Thruway (I-87), drive west through the village of New Paltz on NY 299. As you cross the bridge over the Wallkill River, take the first right onto Springtown Road and set to zero. At 0.5 mile, turn left onto Mountain Rest Road (CR 6), where you'll see signs for Mohonk. At 1.7 miles, go through the intersection of Butterville-Canaan Road. Continue up Mountain Rest Road, when at 4.0 miles, you enter the Mohonk Mountain House main gate on the left.

TRAIL DESCRIPTION

This historic, scenic hike to Sky Top is perhaps the Shawangunks' most popular outing; the "signature" hike to the crowning glory of the Mohonk Mountain House property that adjoins the 6,400-acre Mohonk Preserve. Sky Top Tower is the memorial erected for Albert K. Smiley, one of the Quaker brothers who purchased the Mohonk property in 1869 and developed the first boarding house that eventually evolved into the present-day Mountain House.

For casual visitors and Mountain House guests, the main attraction of Sky Top is its views of six states (some will argue seven). Hikers have the added

PEREGRINE FALCON

Probably the most successful wildlife reintroduction effort in the United States was that of the peregrine falcon, *Falco peregrinus*, or duck hawk. Before the 1950s, the birds bred from the southern states as far north as the high arctic islands (status unknown). Peregrines were nearly wiped out by the rampant use of dichloro-diphenyl-trichloroehane (DDT), and were completely extirpated from the area east of the Mississippi River by 1964 (their distribution is worldwide). When DDT was banned in North America in the early 1970s, the birds were reintroduced through a captive breeding program (the Cornell Recovery Program) to places where it was believed they would thrive—especially bridges and skyscrapers. Because of this, and to the surprise of many people, their reappearance occurred around large population centers.

Peregrines are common migrants and can be observed in increasing numbers along the Appalachian Highlands and into the upper Hudson Valley. One of the most popular places to watch them is from the Trapps area of the Shawangunks, where the Mohonk Preserve conducts an annual hawk watch. Often you will meet volunteer observers tracking nesting pairs of falcons along the Undercliff Carriageway. The birds are sensitive to disturbance, and parts of the Trapps have been closed to rock climbing from time to time in order to protect their breeding sites.

bonus of actually tunneling their way through the white conglomerate talus fields below the cliffs, scaling the cliff face itself on rustic ladders and bridges following the cool, dark path known as the Labyrinth. The two most popular approaches to Sky Top are the Labyrinth Path, your ascent route, and Sky Top Path, your descent route. The designated, well-traveled Labyrinth Path is a serious "rock scramble" requiring all-fours agility, a good share of gumption, and in some instances, raw courage. This trail is recommended only to the strong and adventurous, and not to anyone who is unsteady or afraid of heights. Sky Top Path, on the other hand—although like the Labyrinth requires the same ascent (350 feet) from Mohonk Lake to the tower's base—follows a graded, easily managed footway and takes half the time to climb. Many parties split up at the Mountain House's East Porchere and rendezvous at the tower. Make certain that younger children are closely supervised—this is no place to lose track of a child. Both hikes approach and in some cases traverse high vertical ledges

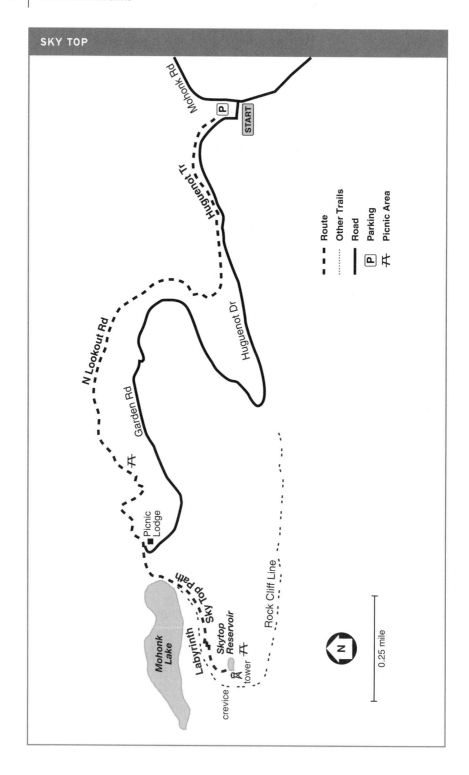

and crevices. The Labyrinth is not recommended as a descent route. It's a good idea to carry as small a pack as possible. Bring a first-aid kit.

One thing you'll want to be sure to do while your party is getting organized is to have a look at the huge, stocked rainbow trout that swirl around Mohonk Lake under the East Porchere, waiting for food pellets that you can buy from dispensers near the archway. (Fishing is reserved for Mountain House guests only.) With the the East Porchere at your back, follow the path along the edge of the lake (Lake Shore Road), go under a foot bridge, through a crevice, and join Sky Top Path. (Follow Sky Top Path if you do not wish to take the Labyrinth Path). Cross a boardwalk and go a short distance to Sentinel Rock, where the Labyrinth Path to the Crevice (a.k.a. Lemon Squeezer)

Sky Top Tower.

and Sky Top appears to your left. Signage is good. Follow the red paint blazes into the Labyrinth.

Immediately you will make your way through holes and crevices, stooping, crab-walking, and crawling under house-sized boulders. You'll climb ladders, cross catwalks, and scale the tops of tilted slabs. You will pass connector trails to both Spring Path and Sky Top Path, where you continue straight ahead toward the Crevice. Within a half hour of beginning your hike, the trail breaks out onto the sunny, treeless scree slopes west of Sky Top, with rugged views of the Hudson Valley to the south, the Trapps, Millbrook Mountain, and Eagle Cliff.

Follow the paint blazes carefully now as you rock-hop your way below the cliffs toward the Crevice. (Stay alert so that you do not continue past the Crevice onto the Staircliff Path.) The Crevice appears in the cliff on your left as a high, narrow fissure. A series of wooden stairways ascends through several dark, damp pitches. The final climb out of the Crevice is a challenging, 10-foot vertical wall (be sure of your foot- and handholds, and assist younger hikers here) that brings you out to a flat slab with high, vertical drops, overlooking the preserve lands. (You can see the top of Sky Top Tower from here if you look up and north.) Now you walk back over the top of the Crevice on a wooden bridge, following the blazes for a short distance up to Sky Top Road. Go left, pass the Armstrong Seat, and turn right onto the tar-paved walkway (note that Sky Top Path meets Sky Top Road here—this is your descent route), and walk a short distance to Sky Top Tower. The tower is open and you can climb to the observation deck, where you'll enjoy 360-degree views, from the Green Mountains of Vermont over to New York's Taconics, the Catskills, the Hudson Highlands, and New Jersey's Kittatinnys. Below is the Mountain House and Mohonk Lake. The tower stands over Sky Top Reservoir, originally constructed for fire control. There is a picnic table next to the map kiosk on Sky Top. Return via the Sky Top Path for the fastest descent (25 minutes) to the Mountain House.

There are several choices for return routes to the Mountain House. Many hikers opt for the longer, gentler Sky Top Road, or the Reservoir, Pinkster, or Bruin paths. Often, Sky Top hikers who have parked at the Gatehouse return by way of Sky Top Road and the Fox Path, crossing Garden Road onto the Glen Anna Path, North Lookout Road, Whitney Road, and the Huguenot Path.

EASTERN WOOD RAT

The friendly and curious bushy-tailed eastern wood rat was last seen on Storm King Mountain in 1980. Because they proliferate in the kind of rocky slopes found in the Shawangunks, an attempt was made to reintroduce them into the ideal cliff talus habitat of Bonticou Crag in 1991. The rats, introduced from Virginia and equipped with radio transmitters, all perished as a result of the raccoon nematode, an insidious roundworm parasite that can survive for more than 10 years in dens and still be virulent. Biologists are puzzled by this evidence, since raccoons and wood rats have been sharing the same habitat for thousands of years. At this time the only active population of the eastern wood rat in New York State is in the Palisades—and it has been extirpated from the northern part of even this range.

Daniel and Keith Smiley of Mohonk gave vivid accounts of baiting and hand-feeding these vegetarian pack rats on Sky Top in 1931. A common species and resident of the cliff and talus community, the disappearance of the wood rat acts more as an indicator of negative change in the local environment than as the potential endangerment of the species in general. Healthy, reproducing populations of the wood rat survive throughout the south.

TRIP 15
EAGLE CLIFF AND MOHONK LAKE

RATING: Easy

DISTANCE: 6.0 miles (2.0 miles if you begin at the Mountain House)

ELEVATION GAIN: 625 feet

ESTIMATED TIME: 3.5 hours

MAPS: USGS Mohonk Lake; NY-NJTC Shawangunk Trails, Lake Mohonk Area; Mohonk Preserve Trail Map

A carriage road walk from Mohonk Mountain House to the gazebos and cliffs overlooking the Shawangunks and Catskills, with a walk around Mohonk Lake.

DIRECTIONS

From Exit 18 of the NYS Thruway (I-87), drive west through the village of New Paltz on NY 299. As you cross the bridge over the Wallkill River, take the first right onto Springtown Road and set to zero. At 0.5 mile, turn left onto Mountain Rest Road (CR 6), where you'll see signs for Mohonk. At 1.7 miles, go through the intersection of Butterville-Canaan Road. Continue up Mountain Rest Road, when at 4.0 miles, you enter the Mohonk Mountain House main gate on the left.

TRAIL DESCRIPTION

Rivaled only by Sky Top for its dramatic views, this short, easy hike reveals the kind of bewitching and far-reaching landscapes for which Mohonk is famous. It ranks as a Mountain House "favorite," and perhaps because of its gentle, easy grades and scenic "payoffs," it may be the most popular hike on the hotel property. Suffice it to say that the easy jaunt to Eagle Cliff with the views of Sky Top, the southlands, and the Victorian "castle" of the Mountain House along the shores of Mohonk Lake will be among the stateliest and alluring easy hikes you'll have ever taken.

Eagle Cliff is an east- and south-facing escarpment of vertical white conglomerate. Its rugged beauty is due in part to the jumbled tonnage of talus that has broken away from Eagle Cliff and lies glistening among moss- and tree-clad pockets below. The serpentine route of the carriage road will introduce you to an awe-inspiring series of panoramic surprises, from the Catskills in the west, through the southerly rolling hills of western New Jersey, Minnewaska

State Park, and the Hudson Valley Highlands. In the foreground, the jagged rocks of the Mohonk Preserve form a fitting picture frame for some of the east's most startling vistas, and one of the world's most enchanting carriage roads, created by the Smiley brothers to delight their guests.

Hikers who are not guests at the Mountain House must begin at the Gatehouse parking lot. Members will be required to pay the additional parking fee of $2 for each hiker over the age of twelve. A seasonal shuttle bus is available for those who wish to begin their hike from the Mountain House (inquire at Gatehouse). The walk, as described here, begins at the Gatehouse parking lot (maps are available here). Follow the footpath at the southwest corner of the parking lot to Whitney Road (these are carriage roads). Follow scenic North Lookout Road to a point at which you will see signs for Picnic Lodge (food, rest rooms, phone). From Picnic Lodge, walk across Garden Road, past the greenhouses, and up through the gardens to the Mountain House. (Estimated time from Gatehouse, 40 minutes.)

Begin at the front entrance of the hotel and turn left onto the main service road (Garden Road). Follow the road a few hundred feet to the apex of the hairpin turn. Here you will find Eagle Cliff Road. Follow this cinder carriage road, leaving the tennis courts to your right. Entering the forest, you're surrounded by moss-frocked boulders sticking out of the ground like fuzzy emeralds. Amid the hemlock and laurels, ascend easily, passing a small bench on a slab of stone to your right, yielding only limited views to the west. Keep climbing, and soon you will come upon a small pair of gazebos with views of the Trapps and Millbrook Mountain. The trail turns through the south now, passing another west-facing gazebo with views of the Catskills.

Soon you will reach an H intersection. Bear right now, and, although you can't sense it just yet, you're climbing the tilted northwest slopes of Eagle Cliff and Huntington Ledge. Red and white oak appears through here, along with hemlock, white pine, and pitch pine. Suddenly, you arrive at Huntington Lookout, a stunning tableau across the preserve lands and beyond. Here, beneath you, are the pristine lands of the Trapps and Millbrook Mountain, and rising to the west, the retreating folds of hills that reach up across the Rondout Valley to Ashokan High Point. The south is enveloped in the scrubby pitch pines of the Badlands. Right at your feet is the thin valley of Rhododendron Brook, which if you cannot see you can "locate" by pouring an imaginary torrent of water between you and the Trapps, and following its course eastward, downhill. Humpty Dumpty Road is there, just below you, amid the dizzying, bright chunks of talus rock. Continuing the hike, the next gazebo is the magical Artist's Rock, and more follow as you turn toward the south. Pass Eagle Cliff Descent

EAGLE CLIFF AND MOHONK LAKE

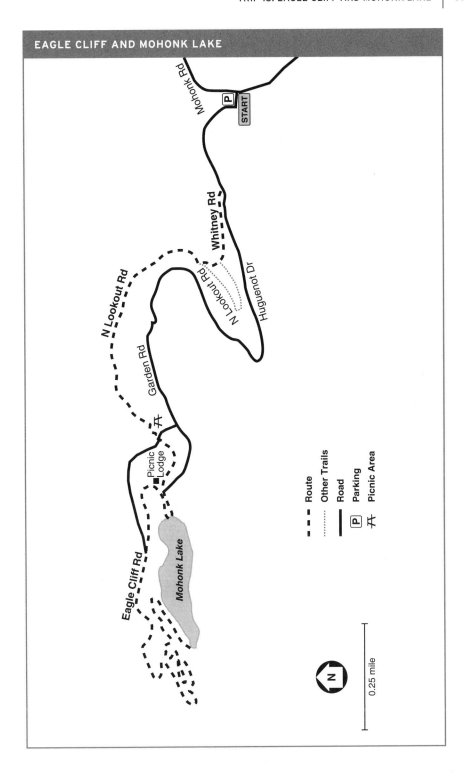

Mohonk Rd

P

START

Whitney Rd

N Lookout Rd

N Lookout Rd

Huguenot Dr

Garden Rd

Picnic Lodge

Eagle Cliff Rd

Mohonk Lake

Route
Other Trails
Road
P   Parking
⊼   Picnic Area

N

0.25 mile

Hikers ascend a Mohonk path.

on your right, a rough path that short-cuts down to Short Woodland Drive and Humpty Dumpty Road.

Eagle Cliff Road now heads north, and suddenly the vertical cone of Sky Top comes into view. The carriage road now threads in and out of the woods, walking the cliff's edge past a collection of the world's finest hand-made cedar gazebos, constructed by the Mountain House's rustic builders. From here are sweeping valley views, and close-ups of the Mountain House and its terra cotta roof, with Sky Top on your right, perched on its mono-lith of bright conglomerate. Mohonk Lake, shimmering in deep shades of viridian, lies beneath you. Views to the northeast are striking, with the hotel imposed before the northern lowlands of the Hudson Valley.

From Arthur's Seat gazebo, the views don't get much better, anywhere, and surely you will think that this stretch of carriageway ranks as one of the finest short walks in the world. The carriage road curls into the forest again, passing Cuyler Castle gazebo. Pass the H intersection you saw earlier, bearing right toward the Mountain House, and just after crossing a wooden bridge, turn right and descend Lambdins Path, turning left under the bridge and de-scending a three-pitched flight of stairs to join the Undercliff Path. Bear right, walk around the southwest shore of Mohonk Lake, and follow along the lake's edge on the Shore Path, joining Lake Shore Road (east) back along the water's edge to the Mountain House.

Return to the Gatehouse the way you came, or navigate the return using your map.

3

THE EASTERN MID-HUDSON REGION

THE HUDSON VALLEY DEVELOPED SLOWLY in comparison with the English settlements of New England and Virginia. The Dutch East India Company lost interest after Henry Hudson determined that the Hudson River was not the sea route to the Orient. (On his return to the Netherlands, the British seized the *Half Moon*; Hudson's last expedition to the Northwest Passage in 1610 would be under the British flag in the ship *Discovery*.) Hudson did, however, interest a powerful group of private investors in the region's lucrative fur trade, and this group formed the Dutch West India Company, chartered in 1621 with a 21-year trading monopoly.

The company established trade connections with the colonies, built forts in Albany and New York City, and introduced the system of patroonships as an inexpensive means of encouraging colonization. These were, in essence, land grants, given to a patroon (a lord or feudal master) who could establish a colony of 50 settlers within a 4-year period. Because the patroonships were so large (8.0 miles long), and its farmers' tenants could not own the land, this system prevented permanent settlement on both the east and west sides of the river. Ultimately the patroonships failed. Most farmers found that life was better in the Netherlands, where the land could be privately owned. The most popular patron was Peter Minuit, who is remembered for the purchase of Manhattan Island from the Canarsie tribe. Only one patroonship survived the

Stissing Mountain rises above Thompson Pond.

transition to British rule intact (Rensselaerwyck).

Much of the open lands surviving from the patroonships remained unsettled by the time the Palatines arrived in 1710. Fleeing persecution in their homeland, 3,000 of the refugees relocated to America after seeking asylum in Britain. Robert Hunter, appointed as the first governor of the New York province, undertook this task. They were "encamped" in the vicinity of Germantown, on both sides of the river (East Camp and West Camp), and employed by the crown for the manufacture of naval stores. The lands on the east bank were purchased from Robert Livingston; the west banks were the queen's lands. In spite of a concentrated effort, the production of naval stores (such as tar), which were so desperately needed by the navy, was unsuccessful, and the Palatines disbanded, most of them remaining in the region to take up farming. Later, marble, slate, and iron mining would contribute to the region's prosperity. Eventually, the area contributed to the lucrative world trade that was made accessible by the proximity of the Hudson River.

The eastern mid-Hudson Valley is bounded in the east by the Taconic Range, to the south by the Fishkill Ridge, and to the west by the Hudson. A substantial quantity of open space exists along the river's edge in the eastern mid-Hudson region, where most of the hikes in this guide are located.

TRIP 16
STISSING MOUNTAIN

RATING: Moderate

DISTANCE: 3.0 miles

ELEVATION GAIN: 1,000 feet

ESTIMATED TIME: 2 hours

MAP: USGS Pine Plains

A steep ascent to a fire tower overlooking the mid-Hudson Valley's agricultural lands, with views of the Southern Taconic Plateau and the Catskills.

DIRECTIONS

To reach Pine Plains from the Taconic State Parkway, take Exit 44 to NY 82 north. Watch carefully for the firehouse on the left, and turn left here onto Lake Road, where you will see Stissing Mountain and its fire tower ahead. (From the center of Pine Plains, go south on CR 82 for 0.4 mile, and turn right on Lake Road.) At 1.6 miles, pass the Thompson Pond Preserve trailheads (there's one on each side of the Stissing Pond outlet). At 2.2 miles, park at the Stissing Mountain trailhead, on the right. The trail begins across the street. This parking area is also a Friends of Stissing Landmarks (FOSL) trailhead that you can take to reach the Thompson Pond trailhead, rather than walking the road.

TRAIL DESCRIPTION

Choose a clear, sunny day for this short hike to Stissing's summit (1,403 feet) and fire tower, leaving time to hike the loop trail around Thompson Pond. Together, they make an unforgettable outing to a surprisingly diverse 507-acre preserve, located midway between the Hudson River and the Southern Taconic Mountains.

Legend has it that Stissing is named for Tishasink (folk typonomized to "Stissing"), a Mahican who lived in the notch between Stissing and Little Stissing mountains. The area's natural value was recognized by a group of local citizens whose dedication led to the involvement of The Nature Conservancy (TNC) in 1957, and finally the preserve's designation as a registered National Natural Landmark in 1973. FOSL continues to act as liaison to the conservancy today.

The trail to Stissing summit, although short, is steep and rocky. Especially

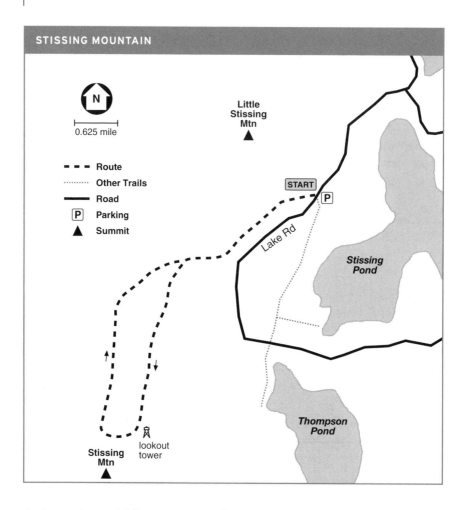

during spring and fall, come prepared to experience high winds and their corresponding chill factor if you plan to climb the fire tower, which is not on the true summit of Stissing, but on its northerly slope. From the FOSL trailhead, cross the street to the Stissing trailhead, identified with a preserve sign and diamond/oak leaf TNC arrow markers. (These markers may differ from those you are used to—the arrow is not an icon but a navigation symbol that is positioned to indicate your direction of travel.) Climb immediately up the rocky, steep trail as it bears left onto an old fire access road that's posted to the right (north). A seasonal brook sometimes shares this old roadway that served the fire tower, but soon you will climb above it. At a Y, where at this writing there is a pile of stones but no trail markers, bear left for the most direct and steepest route to the summit. (The trail forms a loop, so you may go either way.) The incline relaxes only slightly as the trail cuts east across the northerly side of the mountain, then it climbs stiffly as it turns south toward the summit. Now you will begin to see the open farmlands to the east, through a second-growth hardwood forest that was originally clear cut for charcoal production. Just as you're wondering where the tower could be, it appears. As you top out on the summit, there's the foundation of an old observer's cabin. Now, the tower is 200 feet to your left. It is open and maintained by FOSL at this time. This fire tower is very tall, enough so that the squeamish may be content with the limited views from below. It has a cab (a waist-high steel enclosure) and roof but no windows, so you're going to feel the full force of the wind here.

Stissing Mountain is isolated within a relatively flat, peripheral plain of softer sandstones. Its Precambrian gneiss is erosion resistant, representing some of the Earth's oldest surface rock.

Stissing Fire Tower.

The views from Stissing's heights are expansive, taking in a 360-degree panorama of the north and east farmlands of Columbia and Dutchess counties, the southern Taconic Ridge stretching from North Egremont and Mount Washington State Forest in Massachusetts, to Bash Bish, Alander, and Brace Mountain as the ridge tapers down to the flatlands around Millerton, New York. At your feet, north to south, are Twin Island Lake, Stissing Pond, and Thompson Pond. To the southwest, you see the long Shawangunk Ridge, sweeping across Minnewaska State Park from Sam's Point all the way to Sky Top Tower in the Mohonk Preserve. You can see High Point tower in northwestern New Jersey with binoculars, and the jagged Kittatinnys. In the west, the entire Catskill Range takes your gaze from Peekamoose and Table through the Burroughs Range (the high peaks area of Slide, Wittenberg, and Cornell mountains) and into the vast northerly wilderness areas, to the northerly "Big Three"—Thomas Cole, Black Dome, and Blackhead mountains. Beyond these are the Helderbergs, and to the north and east on a good day you may see the southern Adirondacks, and the Green Mountains of Vermont. Your compass will not function in the steel tower, so map orientation and peak identification present a challenge.

For the return trip, you may elect to follow the longer but more relaxed trail that completes the loop. To do so, proceed past the tower on the trail, which the tower straddles, following downhill into the west, where you'll soon see the arrow markers. Pay attention to the arrows on these markers, which indicate the trail's many switches. Don't get discouraged with the apparent herd trails and washed-out gullies; the marking is sufficient if you're patient and observant. Generally, however, the trail is poorly marked and needs maintenance. Winding your way around and down, bearing right, note that the trail widens and improves as it turns east through the notch between Stissing and Little Stissing mountains in a healthy oak forest. Bear right at a Y where postings appear, and soon you will have reached the first Y and rock pile where you went left up the mountain. Bear left now, returning to the FOSL trailhead parking area, marked with plain yellow disks. This trail will lead you to the Thompson Pond trailhead. (See Trip 17 for details.)

THE GOLDEN EAGLE

Visitors to Stissing Mountain and Thompson Pond are likely to get a glimpse of the majestic golden eagle, *Aquila chrysaetos*, wheeling overhead in search of food. This large bird is capable of taking game as large as house cats, foxes, turkeys, geese, and similar game. Considered a threat to livestock in the western states, at one time there was a bounty issued on them.

Although these majestic birds have lived here for many years, they are threatened by habitat degradation and reduction. They need as much as 35 square miles of uninterrupted hunting and breeding ground, and even under ideal circumstances, juvenile mortality can be as high as 75 percent. Golden eagles are distinguishable from bald eagles (though they look very similar at a distance) by the darker, obscurely banded tail. Confusing for distant observers, the immature birds have a white tail, similar to the bald eagles'. The hindneck appears copperish or "golden," but don't expect to get that close.

The golden eagle's range in New York is shrinking. Once a common breeder in the Adirondacks, its range has moved south. These endangered birds are now protected under the Migratory Bird Treaty Act.

TRIP 17
THOMPSON POND

RATING: Easy

DISTANCE: 3.0 miles

ELEVATION GAIN: 50 feet

ESTIMATED TIME: 2 hours

MAPS: USGS Pine Plains; Nature Conservancy, Thompson Pond Nature Preserve

The pond and surrounding wetlands are a national natural landmark where golden eagles and king rails nest. Excellent family hike.

DIRECTIONS

To reach Pine Plains from the Taconic State Parkway, take Exit 44 to NY 82 north. Watch carefully for the firehouse on the left, and turn left here onto Lake Road, where you will see Stissing Mountain and its fire tower ahead. (From the center of Pine Plains, go south on CR 82 for 0.4 mile, and turn right on Lake Road.) At 1.6 miles, pass the Thompson Pond Preserve trailheads (there's one on each side of the Stissing Pond outlet). At 2.2 miles, park at the Stissing Mountain trailhead, on the right. The trail begins across the street. This parking area is also a Friends of Stissing Landmarks (FOSL) trailhead that you can take to reach the Thompson Pond trailhead, rather than walking the road.

TRAIL DESCRIPTION

Thompson Pond lies east and directly beneath Stissing Mountain in the town of Pine Plains. You can hike both destinations for a scenic day outing if you plan ahead a bit. The pond was named for Amos Thompson, who in 1746 was among the earliest white settlers in Dutchess County. Around this time, during King George's War (1744–1748, French and Indian wars), a Moravian mission also existed nearby, ministering to the Mahican group that was soon disbanded by settlement, aided by the King's dissolution of the mission.

The trailhead is reached from the same parking lot as the Stissing Mountain trailhead. Ideally, you should change into waterproof boots for the hike around Thompson Pond, which forms the soggy headwaters of Wappingers Creek. If the water table is high, you might find yourself ankle-deep or more in standing water at the pond's south end, where a series of boardwalks are sometimes submerged. These conditions exist mostly in early spring, usually the

Thompson Pond is a popular snowshoeing destination.

best time to observe the bird life for which this area is known. Many naturalists consider Thompson Pond to be the best location for viewing water birds in the entire central Hudson Valley area. Something that is not mentioned in much of the literature concerning the preserve are the nesting golden eagles that are found here; you'll have a very good chance of seeing them if you arrive in the early season before hikers have appeared in numbers.

If you're parked at the Stissing Mountain trailhead (FOSL trailhead) and want to leave your car there, you can either walk 0.2 mile south along the road to the Thompson Pond trailhead (where there's also a small parking lot), or walk the FOSL Trail (yellow discs) that begins opposite the Stissing Mountain trailhead. If you do take the FOSL Trail, bear right at the first junction you reach (unmarked); this will bring you directly to the Thompson Pond trailhead. (The left turn is a short spur leading to the edge of Stissing Pond.)

Equipped with your bird guide and binoculars (you might appreciate a staff to help you safely ford the high water), set out along the preserve's yellow-marked trail. This is a road-wide dirt path. Up to your right are the steep eastern slopes of Stissing. To the left is Thompson Pond. The forest is full of sweet birch here (a.k.a. black or cherry birch), identifiable by the thin, horizontal lines on its trunk. This "aromatic" tree was is the traditional source of birch beer, fermented from its sap, and was the source of oil of wintergreen,

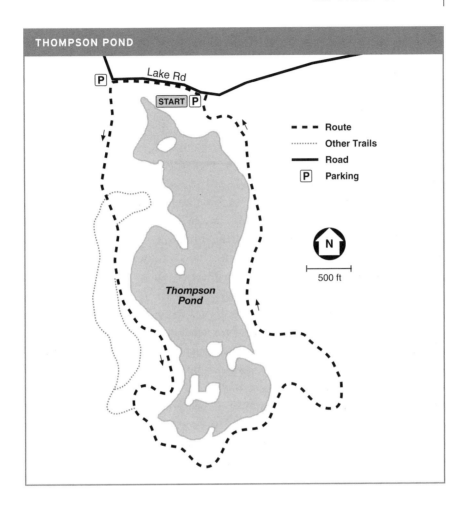

THOMPSON POND

Lake Rd

START

- - - Route
.... Other Trails
——— Road
P Parking

N

500 ft

Thompson
Pond

now chemically manufactured. The buds and seeds of this tree provide browse for rabbits, deer, and ruffed grouse.

Soon you will arrive at a kiosk with maps and information, describing the details of this calcareous limestone wetland. What makes the preserve so unusual is the high biological diversity found in the relatively small space of 507 acres: 300 species of plants, 160 of birds, and 20 of mammals. The exquisite, small orchidlike milkwort, fringed polygala (a.k.a. gaywings) is also found here in the damp woods, blooming in late spring. There is another trail (blue markers) that approaches the pond at this point and forms a loop around the main trail. Remain on the yellow trail, continuing south through pockets of hemlocks, passing a pair of stone commemorative benches. Follow along the pond's western fringes, passing a cornfield and descending to a swampy section of trail with a long boardwalk at the south end. Here, my companion and I were quite surprised to get very close to two golden eagles, neither of them in a hurry to avoid us as they dropped lazily from the treetops to finally ascend toward Stissing. Although these majestic birds have lived here for many years, they are threatened by habitat degradation and reduction.

As you turn north to cross the Wappingers' headwaters, you walk adjacent to a farm over several sections of boardwalk. Some are covered with chicken wire to provide traction. Walk carefully across the slick surface of the pressure-treated boards. This area is muddy and low. At a culvert where the ponds drain, you may see schools of good-sized smallmouth bass.

Views to the west reveal Stissing's fire tower. The trail rises above the pond now and remains dry. In the dense cattails, we saw several large, rust-colored king rails, a critically imperiled species in its northernmost habitat limits, now substantially farther north than the range mapped out by Roger Tory Peterson in 1980.

As you reach the trail's northern terminus, a stand of Norway spruce grows beside an open cornfield, at the edge of a new housing development. As the desirability of scenic home sites in this area increases, you'll appreciate the efforts of FOSL and The Nature Conservancy that have led to the preservation of this remarkable place. Hunting, trapping, fishing, camping, bicycling, motorized vehicles, and fires are prohibited in the preserve, which is why it is still pristine. However, cross-country skiing and canoeing are allowed.

Bear left as you reach the road and cross the outlet of Stissing Pond. The trail entrance appears to the left as you complete the loop.

TRIP 18
NORRIE POINT

RATING: Easy
DISTANCE: 5.0 miles
ELEVATION GAIN: 200 feet
ESTIMATED TIME: 3 hours
MAPS: USGS Hyde Park; Staatsburg State Historic Site (Mills-Norrie State Park) Trail Map

A shoreline hike along the Hudson River, and a fine example of a Hudson River mansion and estate. A great family outing.

DIRECTIONS

Take Exit 19 of the NYS Thruway (I-87) at Kingston; bear right out of the toll pavilion and set your odometer to zero. Cross over the Thruway and bear right on to NY 209, headed north toward the Kingston-Rhinecliff Bridge. At 5.5 miles, you cross the bridge (toll), and as you enter Dutchess County, NY 209 becomes NY 199. At 7.9 miles turn right (south) at River Road (CR 103). Bear right at the fork you reach after 8.6 miles. Following open vistas of the Catskills on your right, at 11.2 miles turn left onto Rhinecliff Road. At 12.4 miles, you're in the center of Rhinebeck. Set to zero here. Turn right onto NY 9G (south), and at 4.3 miles, turn right onto Staatsburg Road. At 5.3 miles, turn right into the Staatsburg State Historic Site. (This is also Taconic Parks Region Headquarters.)

TRAIL DESCRIPTION

What distinguishes this hike from others in the Hudson Valley is its proximity to the river. For more than 2.5 miles you walk next to the water, enjoying far-reaching views up and downriver. When you've finished the hike, you can take a look at the Mills Mansion (fee), or just sit on the open sweep of lawn above the Hudson to ponder the opulent lives of one of the Gilded Age's wealthiest couples—Ruth Livingston and Ogden Mills.

Drive through the grounds. The mansion appears on your left. Take the first right into a shady parking area adjacent to the beautiful old brick carriage houses that serve as the grounds maintenance buildings. This is the designated parking area for hikers and sledders (the latter is very popular on the long, sloping hillside in front of the house). Take Gardener's House Lane from the southwest corner of the lot, and head for the river between rows of elegant sugar maples.

As you walk down the road toward the river, you pass a stone boathouse on the right that you can explore. Continue past the gardener's house, the large, elegant brick homestead on the left, and you're at water level, looking north toward the Esopus Meadows Lighthouse. Just as the road begins to rise, watch carefully to your right, and follow the white trail markers into the woods along the river's edge. You will rise to Dinsmore Point, as the trail turns south over the craggy hemlock-shaded path and provides several open vantage points. The trail is rooty and rocky, so watch your footing. In icy conditions, be careful—there are several spots where the ledges drop vertically into the river. Continue, passing an abandoned pump house and keep your eyes on the white markers, as they become sparse in spots. You'll notice a few old fire pits dating from the park's origins in the 1920s. Shortly, you will arrive at a grassy spot

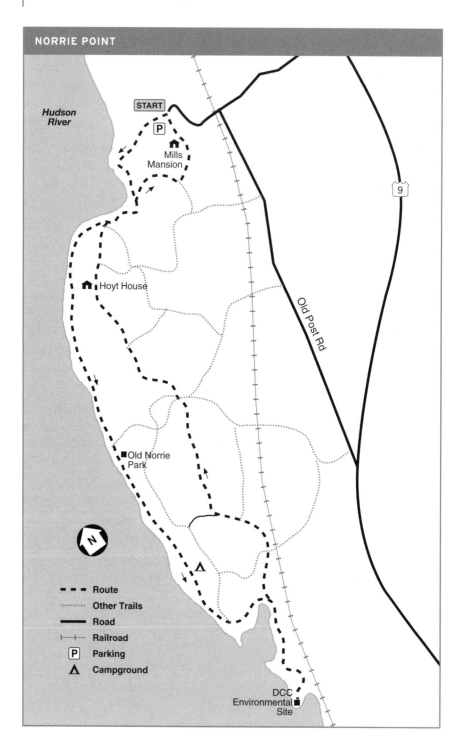

NORRIE POINT

Hudson River

START

Mills Mansion

Hoyt House

Old Norrie Park

Old Post Rd

9

DCC Environmental Site

- - - Route
.... Other Trails
——— Road
I—+— Railroad
P Parking
△ Campground

Looking from Norrie Point toward Esopus Meadows Lighthouse and the Catskills.

with several picnic tables, enclosed by old stone foundation ramparts.

Follow to the right on a paved road along the river next to a large gazebo with a fireplace in it. This area is accessible by car, and during the season, many people drive down for a look at the river. The white trail continues on the south side of this cul-de-sac, making its way into secluded woods again. At a point where the riverbank becomes steeper, the trail veers uphill and east, goes through a hardwood forest of large, mature oaks, and climbs gently above the river to the cabin camping area. Keep the cabins to your left and continue with the river on the right. Markers become scarce here—but only momentarily. At the rear of the last cabin, the white trail turns right, dropping downhill toward the park road. Cross a small wooden bridge and turn right at the road, leaving the Indian Kill to your left. Continue across the stone bridge (the short, dull remains of the white trail venture left here, into the woods) and straight along the road (yellow markers appear), very shortly passing the marina, and continue to the Norrie Point environmental research station that you see straight ahead. This aquarium, museum, and field station belonging to Dutchess County Community College is open to the public (hours are posted). Treat yourself to a rest amid the far-reaching southerly views across the river from the dock on the south side of the building and watch for the harbor seals—they have been seen sunning themselves off the northern tip of Esopus Island.

Return to the stone bridge and go north on the road beyond the white trail, to an intersection. The train tracks run along here and you can wave at the passengers. Go left at the blue/yellow trail junction, and in 50 feet, go right on red markers, following the multi-use trail (also marked as a horse trail). Ascend gently through a young sugar maple woods and cross the park road, continuing on the red trail through secluded woods. At the next road, which leads to the river gazebo you passed earlier, turn left and very soon thereafter, go right (north) on the blue-marked carriage path. The blue trail will take you past the Hoyt House, its reclaimed gardens, barn, and carriage house. This parcel on Dinsmore Point was given to the Mills' daughter, Geraldine, and her husband, Lydig Hoyt. The large cedars and runaway ornamental Norway spruce trees hint at what the place must have been like in the mid-1800s. To get a better idea, continue to the park road (Gardener's House Road) where you were earlier, turn right, and leaving the gardener's house to your right, follow the green trail along the south side of the mansion grounds to the garden complex. To the north, a footpath crosses the lawn to the mansion, its gift shop, and offices.

Ogden Mills' father, Darius Mills, found wealth in the California gold rush, and became one of the richest men in the business by the age of 30. He invested heavily in railroads with his son, a realtor, businessman, banker, and among many other things, the vice president of the Metropolitan Opera House. Ruth Livingston was the daughter of Maturin Livingston, a great granddaughter of Robert R. Livingston. At one time, the Livingstons owned one million acres in the Hudson Valley. She inherited the Mills Mansion, formerly known as Livingston Manor.

TRIP 19
TIVOLI BAYS

RATING: Moderate

DISTANCE: 5.0 miles

ELEVATION GAIN: 400 feet

ESTIMATED TIME: 3.5 hours

MAPS: USGS Saugerties; Hudson River National Estuarine Research Reserve, Tivoli Bays

A more secluded hike along the Hudson's marshy eastern shore, through the largest of the Hudson River National Estuarine Research Reserves.

DIRECTIONS

From NY 199 and NY 9G in the town of Rhinebeck, go north 5.2 miles to Kidd Lane. Turn left and go 0.7 mile to the Tivoli Bays trailhead parking area on the left.

TRAIL DESCRIPTION

The trails of Tivoli Bays will introduce you to the rich estuary habitat of the Hudson River, as you hike its forests and enjoy far-reaching views of the Catskills from its shores. The Bays are part of the Hudson River National Estuarine Research Reserve (HRNERR), designated by the Coastal Zone Management Act as a field laboratory for research and education. There are four such diverse wetland communities on the Hudson River: Stockport Flats, Iona Island, Piermont Marsh, and Tivoli Bays—at 1,700 acres, the largest of the Hudson's reserves with the most extensive foot-trail network. If your visit coincides with low tide, you can also access Cruger Island when the trail is not submerged.

With the addition of new trails to the north and south, it is now possible to hike from the village of Tivoli (not described here), south to Blithewood Road at Bard College, for a total return distance of about 10 miles. The hike described here will introduce you to the most established and scenic trails, and point out additional mileage and areas of interest. These trails can be muddy along the river, and they are hilly, calling for boots with good traction.

Begin at the trailhead parking area on Kidd Lane, off of NY 9G at the information kiosk. Marking is usually adequate, although signage is inconsistent

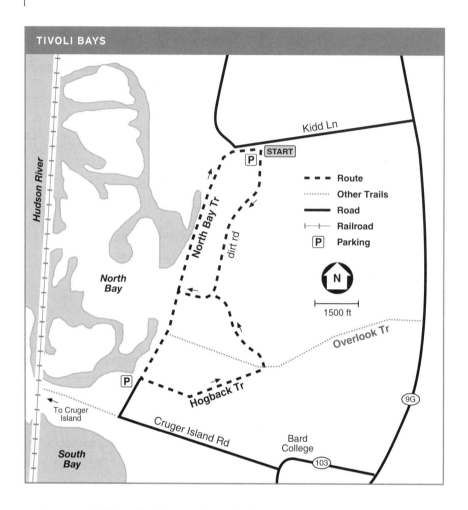

TIVOLI BAYS

Kidd Ln

START

P

- - - Route
.... Other Trails
—— Road
⊢—+—⊣ Railroad
P Parking

N

1500 ft

North Bay Tr

dirt rd

North
Bay

Hudson River

Overlook Tr

P

To Cruger
Island

Hogback Tr

9G

Cruger Island Rd

Bard
College

South
Bay

103

at this time. Follow the dirt road south, through a reclaimed field of juniper thickets, into dense hardwoods. Pass a yellow-marked trail (not on the map) on the right that leads back to Kidd Lane. Within a few minutes of leaving a barn ruin to your left, bear right at the next Y, where red pines appear to the right, and walk through a white pine woods. Just beyond this Y is a wheelchair-access parking area on the right (auto access to this point is seasonal). Cyclists and cross-country skiers also use this trail complex, but only the dirt road is usable for wheelchairs.

The dirt road winds north and descends to the canoe launch parking area at North Bay, and the North Bay Trail (blue markers), where you get your first views of the Hudson (although this is the designated canoe launch, the best place to launch is from the Cruger Island Road parking area). The trail fol-lows down the steps to the river's edge where you peer out over the marsh at

Magdalen Island and the Catskills from a well-built dock and launch. Sign in at the trail register and turn left (south) along the edge of the marsh, toward the Cruger Island parking lot.

The trails can be muddy and rooty through here. You'll see where a wood-duck house has been protected from predators by the use of metal flashing on the tree. You walk next to the marsh and then climb away from it into hemlock woods, crossing a wooden bridge spanning a creek. This up and down shoreline and forest pattern continues until you rise to a scenic lookout at a trail junction. Just above the hamlet of Glasco on the west shore of the river you see from left to right, Ashokan High Point, Slide Mountain (276 degrees), Overlook Mountain, and numerous Catskill peaks and foothills. At this junction, the red-marked Overlook Trail departs to the east for the NY 9G trailhead. You can use it to shortcut the hike if you wish, by following it to the Manor Road junction and bearing left (north). Your route continues south, on the blue-marked Overlook Trail. Continue south, crossing another bridge to arrive at a T where the Overlook and Hogback trails meet. Go right into the Cruger Island parking lot, take a moment to observe the river from an observation point on the lot's northwest corner, and follow the dirt road to its junction with Cruger Island Road. If the tide allows, go right and walk through the swamp, east to the island. At low tide this area is wet and muddy. Be careful; high-speed trains come north and south here on the Metro-North tracks, and you must cross them to reach the island. Explore the Cruger Island Trail, a loop that may take you an hour or so. There are several quiet, scenic spots and rock outcroppings on the river's edge.

Return to the Cruger Island Road parking area and go east on Hogback Trail (yellow markers), climbing easily up a white pine knoll. Turn north, passing a row of big oaks on the right, at the edge of an open field where you look at Bard College's performing arts center, and a large Tudor-style mansion next to it. Cross a gully into an open field where a line of white pines stands to the north. The red-marked Overlook Trail appears midway across the field. Turn left on it, within 300 feet arriving at a junction. (The North Bay Trail is to the west now; you've almost come in a complete circle.) Bear north at the junction, following the dirt road, which descends easily, to cross a tiny concrete bridge, and ascend thereafter, easily, to the junction with the access road, which you'll recognize. Retrace your earlier steps to the boat launch and North Bay Trail, descend the stairs to the junction, and go right (north) on the North Bay Trail. This pretty trail follows the marsh edge to Stony Creek, past a little waterfall through the hemlocks, and arrives at Kidd Lane, west of the parking area. Turn right (east) and walk the road 0.3 mile back to the trailhead parking area.

TRIP 20
POETS' WALK ROMANTIC LANDSCAPE PARK

RATING: Easy

DISTANCE: 2.0 miles

ELEVATION GAIN: 200 feet

ESTIMATED TIME: 1.5 hours

MAPS: USGS Kingston East; Scenic Hudson, Poets' Walk Romantic Landscape Park Map (available on-site and online)

A scenic river walk among open fields and stone walls with rustic gazebos and unforgettable views of the Catskills. Great family outing.

DIRECTIONS

Take Exit 19 of the NYS Thruway (I-87) at Kingston; bear right out of the toll pavilion and set your odometer to zero. Cross over the Thruway and bear right on to NY 209, headed north toward the Kingston-Rhinecliff Bridge. At 5.5 miles, you cross the bridge (toll), and as you enter Dutchess County, NY 209 becomes NY 199. From center span of the bridge you will see the Rondout Lighthouse a few miles to the south, on a small island off the western shore. To the north, along the east shore are the marshes of Tivoli Bays. Closer to the bridge and just beneath you as you approach the east shore are the fields of the old Astor and Delano estates, the location of Poets' Walk. Take the first left off the bridge onto River Road, which is also known as CR 103 (you're 7.8 miles from the Thruway now), and at 8.5 miles, turn left into the Poets' Walk parking area.

TRAIL DESCRIPTION

This scenic park, located within a few minutes' drive of Tivoli, Red Hook, and Rhinebeck villages, offers one of the prettiest, easiest walks in the valley. It is regarded by many as the crown jewel of Scenic Hudson's open space preservation efforts. At just over 2 miles round-trip, the walk can be done in an easy hour's time by almost anybody. Plan to stay longer if you can, to ponder what Scenic Hudson rightly calls the "breathtaking, unparalleled vistas" of the Hudson Valley and the Catskill Mountains. The park has proven to be very popular with locals who often visit the grounds and its rustic pavilions to cavort, picnic, walk, write, paint, and do nothing.

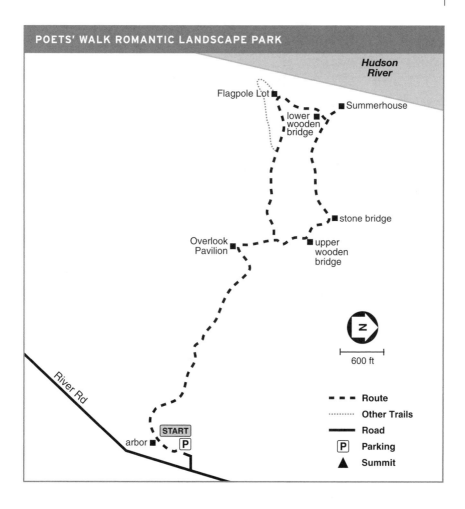

Orient yourself at the information kiosk at the trailhead and get on the path, heading west into open fields that are cloistered by mature hardwood forests. At the next rustic kiosk (the Arbor), there are interpretive notes and a box containing maps. Help yourself to a trail map and a copy of Scenic Hudson's *Adventure Guide to Parks, Preserves, and Trails.* Don't worry if the trail maps are all gone; the trail is self-guiding and well posted (you can print out your own map from Scenic Hudson's website ahead of time). Continue along the gravel path.

The sunny fields of the park offer a warm western exposure. There are benches along the path as it winds in and out of the hardwoods over gentle terrain. The theme of the park—that of the Romantic "sublime," a notion which captured the imagination of the valley's early poets and writers— commemorates Washington Irving (1783–1859) and his friend/mentee, the

The Poets' Walk trails offer sweeping views of the Catskill Escarpment.

Knickerbocker writer Fitz-Green Halleck (1790–1867). The period takes its name from Irving's fictitious character, Diedrich Knickerbocker, the sobriquet under which he penned *A History of New York* and *Rip Van Winkle.* Also a satirist and lesser-known poet, Halleck, a banker by trade, served as John Jacob Astor's personal secretary, an errand that brought him to these grounds. It is unlikely that Irving frequented these same grounds.

At approximately 0.65 mile, you arrive at the Overlook Pavilion, an elegant rustic gazebo and the focal point of the park. Here you can sit back and enjoy views of the Catskills' eastern escarpment, the long wall of ridges and peaks that form the northeast headlands, reaching from Overlook Mountain (325 degrees), at the edge of the Indian Head Wilderness Area, and north past Kaaterskill High Peak and Round Top to the North Mountain Wild Forest. You see the Catskill High Peaks as well, from Peekamoose and Table in the south all the way through the Burroughs Range, including Slide (284 degrees), Wittenberg, and Cornell. Countless other peaks and low hills invite your curiosity and stir your romantic imagination.

Continue along, arriving at a signed trail junction. Go left (west, toward the river) and descend gently to the Flagpole Lot, where there are three rustic benches overlooking the river. After a brief respite, proceed to the right and downhill, descending a flight of steps into the woods. Cross a tiny creek and ascend easily through a wooded glen, arriving at a T. Turn left to see the Summerhouse, a large cedar gazebo facing west. We can imagine Frederic Church having mixed feelings to learn that the cedar used in the structures at Poets' Walk came from Olana, his picturesque estate. The trees are actually junipers, or eastern red cedar. The Summerhouse is the most secluded space along the trail. Retrace your steps to the T and ascend easily into the east along the northern edge of the grounds, crossing a pretty stone bridge and another wooden one before arriving back at the trail junction below the pavilion. In the woods before the junction, you may see an odd-looking, crumbling newspaper "sculpture" of sorts, a seemingly deliberate but unsightly attempt to blend recycled waste into an otherwise pristine landscape. The hive-like mass is disintegrating, as it was apparently meant to do, shedding paper across the forest floor.

Be aware that dogs are allowed in the park and must be leashed and cleaned up after. However, many of their owners do not observe the rules. For this reason you will find it useful to carry a stick, so dogs will be less likely to approach you, and you'll be prepared to ward them off if they do. In deference to their owners, however, it does seem as if most of the unleashed animals are generally well behaved.

At this point you are back at the Overlook Pavilion. From here the trail retraces its steps to the parking area.

TRIP 21
OLANA

RATING: Easy
DISTANCE: 3.5 miles
ELEVATION GAIN: 250 feet
ESTIMATED TIME: 3 hours
MAPS: USGS Hudson South; Olana State Historic Site Trail Map

A stroll-like hike amid the grounds of Frederic Church's Persian-style castle home and through the picturesque landscapes of pond, gardens, and woods created by this second-generation member of the Hudson River school of landscape painting.

DIRECTIONS

From Exit 21 of the NYS Thruway (I-87) in Catskill, turn left onto NY 23B and set to zero. At 0.5 mile, turn left (east) after going under the NY 23 overpass, onto NY 23 itself, heading toward the Rip Van Winkle Bridge. At 2.2 miles, at the intersection of NY 23 and CR 385, go straight. (At this intersection, look diagonally across NY 385 to the right, or southeast, and you can see Thomas Cole's yellow house, Cedar Grove, also open to the public. Built in 1815, Cole resided there until his death at 47 years of age.) As you cross the bridge, you can see Olana up on the hill ahead of you. At 3.8 miles, bear right (south) onto NY 9G. In just under a mile, turn left onto the Olana entrance road, and travel uphill to the ticket booth. Fees are collected during the season only—the rest of the year you can enter for free during the week. It's 1.0 mile from the entrance to the upper parking area next to Olana.

TRAIL DESCRIPTION

Frederic Church was the best-known living artist in the world between 1850 and 1860. Primed by his predecessor and mentor Thomas Cole (and first-generation Hudson River school painters such as Asher Durand), the public received the unveiling of Church's debut full-length landscape, *Niagara* (1857) with celebratory awe. Exhibited "in the flesh," such creations were the visual blockbusters of the times—images that nineteenth-century viewers went to

see just as today we go to see a movie premier. At its unveiling, *Niagara* was the only painting on display in New York's Corcoran Gallery. It sold for $12,500 in 1859, and the artist's ensuing affluence enabled him to conceive, design, and build Olana on the rolling lands and dense forests that became his personal vision of the "living landscape." Today, the grounds of his Moorish-style castle are surrounded by a series of carriage paths and trails that were created by Church himself, in the picturesque style of landscape design.

Olana, presented in the picturesque style.

Olana's carriage paths provide only a few miles of trail suitable for walking and cross-country skiing—but what miles! Although the ornate house itself (one of very few intact artists' residences and workplaces in the country) attracts over 25,000 people a year, the trails seem to get little use. Because they are fairly flat, they make for easy winter walks and ski tours. It can be muddy in springtime, when views of the river and the Catskill Mountains are at their best, though hardly as spectacular as in Church's day, when he "cut" the forest to use scenery as a canvas to set against his own favorite points around Olana.

From the parking lot, descend the large brick stairway. There's a visitor center on your right, and the trail loops begin to your left (north). Cross the entry road and go through a cedar gate to a T. There are trail markers on a tree at the T, but this is the last you'll see of them. Reference the map and you won't have a problem. This is a wide, flat, cinder path, ideal for families with children.

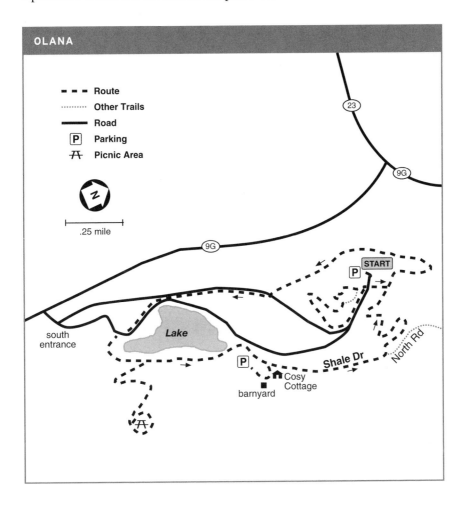

Turn left onto Ridge Road. This road was Church's pride and joy—the (1878) route from which he showcased the Hudson Valley for his family and friends, and the vantage from which he painted Autumn View from Olana. At one time, the area before you was open fields, but the views are limited today. The path bends north and then south, traveling to the west of the house through evergreen forests with the Hudson on your right. Interpretive signs (with maps and helpful "You are here" stars) exist along the entire carriageway system. On your right is an obstructed overlook with a sign illustrating an 1870 oil sketch, hardly representative of his earlier, more realistic Expansionist Phase (the artist's right arm had become almost useless from rheumatism at this point, so he contented himself to use "nature as my palette").

Continue, passing beneath the house through a sugar maple/oak woods, ignoring an unmarked trail that descends to the right (north). Arriving at a gate on the approach road, turn right and descend, with views of the lake on your left, beyond which, in the southeast foreground is Blue Hill and extensive farmlands. Leave the ticket booth to your right and follow the road to the end of the lake; take the Park and Lake carriageway, which is not identified in the field, but that you can't miss. Bear left here and ascend slightly to a vantage point of the "castle" with an interpretive sign (a trail going off to the south here leads off the property). Proceed north along the lake, and within a few minutes arrive at a Y, with (unmarked) Crown Hill Road (1885) on the right. This spur path climbs very gently to a picnic table overlooking a cut view of the house and buildings. But the "historic" view doesn't seem worth the trees that were sacrificed—there is no shortage of house views on this property, and the cut area looks ragged and unnatural. Return to the Y. Proceed right to the lower lot and the barn complex, where a little picnic area leads to the quaint Cosy Cottage (Church's original 1860–72 dwelling during the years of Olana's construction).

Leaving the cottage to your right, climb Shale Drive, which has become grassy, and look to the east at the extensive farmlands and woods of the Claverack, Taghkanic, and Gallatin townships, with the Taconic hills in the tri-state area visible on a good day. This is perhaps the most interesting view from Olana, and receives the least praise. The path enters the woods and arrives at a Y with the intersection of North Road, which leads, as you might expect, north—and off the property. It provides a bit more of a walk, but the hemlock trees Church praised so lavishly in his day are no more; storms in the 1970s and 1980s destroyed the remnant climax forest and the resulting understory is second-growth hardwood, yet with some fine specimens of oak.

From the Y, climb easily back to the first T and the upper parking lot.

TRIP 22
ROOSEVELT WOODS

RATING: Moderate

DISTANCE: 5.0 miles

ELEVATION GAIN: 200 feet

ESTIMATED TIME: 2.5 hours

MAPS: USGS Hyde Park; National Park Service, Hyde Park Trail

A shore and forest walk on easy carriage roads to points along the Hudson River, from the museum, library, and home of Franklin D. Roosevelt.

DIRECTIONS

The Franklin Delano Roosevelt National Historic Site is located on the west side of NY 9 in Hyde Park. Drive into the main entrance on FDR Drive, heading straight back to the visitor parking area past National Park Service (NPS) headquarters. You can enter the grounds and visitor center free of charge; however, there's a fee for the museum, library, and house tours.

TRAIL DESCRIPTION

The beautiful trails of Roosevelt Woods, lying within the heavily wooded estate of the Franklin D. Roosevelt Home, Library, and Museum complex, are patrolled and maintained by the National Park Service. On this hike you are introduced to each loop in the woods (the Cove, Forest, and Meadow trails), with a short side trip to Crum Elbow Point on the Hudson River's banks.

These trails are unlike many of the foot trails you may be familiar with in the valley; they are wide, well marked, and immaculately maintained "carriageways." Today, they are footpaths only (bicycles are not allowed). Because the elevation change is minimal, and the trails are generally flat and wide, this is a walker's paradise, leading you through parklike woods in a peaceful, wild setting with views of the Hudson. Because they are so gently contoured, they are ideal trails for children and seniors. Dogs must be leashed at all times. The FDR National Historic Site, including Springwood (Roosevelt's birthplace), is joined by a trail to Val-Kill, the home of Anna (Eleanor) Roosevelt; but that trail is 5.0 miles round-trip over poorly managed, ATV-impacted trails (Scenic Hudson Land Trust).

The Roosevelt Woods trail system is a part of the Hyde Park Trail (HPT), a cooperative effort of several organizations, including the NPS, the Town of Hyde Park, Scenic Hudson, Winnakee Land Trust, and several private landowners. With the exception of the trail to Val Kill, it is a model trail system under continued development with the help of the Hudson River Greenway.

Before heading into the woods, take a look at the visitor center and request a trail map. Curiously, the map ("Hyde Park Trail") provided by the NPS is far from ideal for navigation on the trails, but it does provide a helpful overview to the area. Trails are accurately designated and well-marked, however, so there's very little chance of getting lost or even disoriented. Because the Hyde Park Trail is a long, linear park trail (in progress), you'll be walking only a short section of it here.

Begin your hike on the paved walkway to the south of the visitor center that runs next to the museum, a long, fortress-like, hand-laid stone building. A

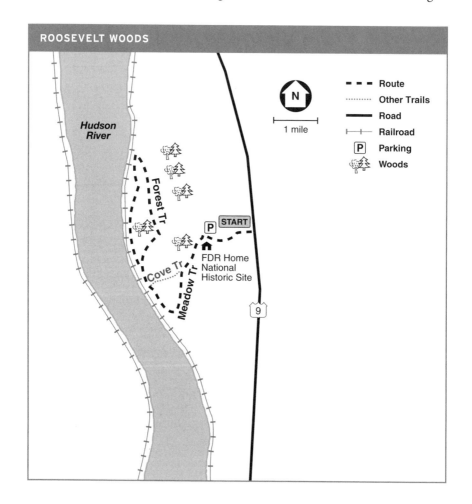

small sign near a cluster of Norway-spruce trees indicates the Hyde Park Trail to your right. From here you are led a short distance to the trailhead, where there's a signboard and map, with information. Follow the paved path down-hill, and it soon turns to dirt at the point where the Meadow Trail goes south and the Hyde Park, Cove, and Forest trails go straight ahead.

Immediately you will note the fine, mature forests of red oak, hemlock, pop-lar, hickory, and sycamore, most of them planted and managed by Roosevelt and his father, who imported many varieties from Europe with the interest of beautifying the grounds of Springwood. Roosevelt continued his boyhood interest in forestry, making it a matter of national interest when he later formed the Civilian Conservation Corps (CCC). Many of the regional plantations we enjoy today—and the trails that run through them (such as those of the Catskills), were CCC projects. You pass a pond and seasonal waterfall to your right, descending through a shady glen.

Bear right at the first trail junction, where the Cove Trail goes left (south). Now you're on the Forest Trail. The HPT goes north, beyond the NPS bound-ary, to the Vanderbilt Mansion (signed at 2.4 miles from this junction), but that is a trip for another day. Unfortunately, the HPT follows paved roads for some distance once it leaves these woods, and you may not find it very ap-

Springwood, Franklin Delano Roosevelt's birthplace.

pealing. Continue, passing the return loop of the Forest Trail on your right (you'll emerge from that trail later). Within 15 minutes or so, you will arrive at a junction where the Forest Trail departs to the right. Bear left here, remaining on the HPT. This is the NPS boundary. Bear left, and within a few hundred yards, bear left again. This will take you across the Metro-North tracks on a trestle bridge, directly to the river's edge at Crum Elbow Point. There's a large, bright navigation day-marker here to help shipping navigate up the channel. You'll have close-up views of tankers and tug barges, most of them carrying oil to the Port of Albany. This is a fine spot to sit on the grassy point and wile away the day, and aside from the estate grounds themselves, is the best place to have a picnic.

Retrace your steps to the junction of the HPT and Forest Trails. Follow left onto the latter as you curve around into the north and east along the park boundary. Following a knoll of red pine on the north side of the trail, bear right once again onto the Forest Trail, walk amidst stately hemlock and very tall white pines, and join the HPT, bearing left now. Walk back to the Cove Trail junction, and follow the Cove (and Meadow) Trail to the right (south). The Meadow Trail continues south, while the Cove Trail goes west (right). This very short (0.2 mile) spur trail takes you along the fringes of a pretty, tidal cattail marsh, and dead ends at the railroad tracks. The large building you see on a hill to the south is the Culinary Institute of America. More interesting yet are the bright yellow blooms of marsh marigold you see everywhere in early spring, their flowers submerged by the incoming tide.

Now you retrace your steps to the Meadow Trail, bear right, cross the stream on a wooden bridge, and enter a hemlock wood. The trail turns east soon, and then north along the edge of a broad meadow where Springwood comes into view. You are soon back at the first junction, where you turn right to the trail-head and estate grounds. Take a few moments to look at Springwood and the magnificent, soft hues of the Hudson's hills, and walk through the rose garden and the Roosevelt gravesite. Treat yourself to a look at the sculpture of two figures, cut from the thick concrete of the Berlin Wall and fashioned into art by Winston Churchill's great granddaughter, Edweena Sandees. Follow your way back through the grounds to the parking area to complete the walk.

4

THE SOUTHERN TACONICS

THE TACONICS GET THEIR NAME FROM the ancient continental collision known as the Taconic Orogeny, or mountain-building process. Originally formed near the location of today's Costa Rica, about 470 million years ago the Taconic Island Chain moved northward to collide with Proto North America. This event marked the beginning of a mountain-building episode stretching from the Canadian Maritime provinces to North Carolina, and lasting another 35 million years. (The Taconic Orogeny was distinct from the east- and north-advancing Acadian Orogeny that created the Northern Appalachian Mountains.) At the time, the Iaptus Ocean covered most of North America. Achieving an elevation of around 4 miles, the Taconics were eroded during the Mesozoic and Cenozoic eras, and in the Quaternary Period, the mile-high glaciers of the Great Ice Age finished the final, billion-year process by sculpting the Taconic landscape we see today. Their northern and southern ranges define the Taconics from Williamstown, Massachusetts, to the borders of New York and Connecticut. The Nature Conservancy has named the South Taconic Range lying in New York, Connecticut, and Massachusetts, one of the Earth's "Last Great Places" because it is among the largest and healthiest contiguous forests in the Lower New England Ecoregion (Maine to Virginia). It is also considered one of the most diverse forests in Southern New England, supporting many rare natural communities such as the scrub oak and pitch

The northwestern viewshed from the Southern Taconic Trail highlights the Catskills.

pine woods found on cliff and talus slopes, and the rare species that inhabit them, including Gerhardt's underwing moth and the purple clematis. Both ranges are heavily forested with northern hardwood species and dense hemlock woods in wet ravines.

Protection of the Taconics began around 1920, with the acquisition of lands that eventually became the Taconic State Park on the New York side of the range, the Mount Washington State Forest and Bash Bish Falls State Park in Massachusetts, and the Mount Riga State Park in Connecticut.

THE SOUTHERN TACONICS

This 36,000-acre mountain range is bounded in the north by Hillsdale, New York, and South Egremont, Massachusetts, and in the south by Millerton, New York, and Lakeville, Connecticut. The plateau's highest peak is Mount Everett (2,602 feet). The average elevation of the ridge is 2,000 feet above the surrounding valley, or 2,700 feet above sea level. Two major trails cross the Southern Taconic Plateau. The Appalachian Trail (AT) enters the ridge in the south, at Salisbury, Connecticut, and follows its eastern edge along the Housatonic watershed, crossing Bear Mountain, Mount Race, and Mount Everett before leaving the range in Egremont. On the west side of the range is the South Taconic Trail (STT), a 15-mile scenic ridge trail with its southern trailhead in the town of Northeast, New York. The STT traverses South Brace Mountain, Brace Mountain (passing west of Mount Frissell and the highest point in Connecticut), Alander Mountain, and Bash Bish Falls before descending to the Taconic State Park and continuing north to Mount Fray and Hillsdale. Several trails join the ridge from the east and west sides, providing a number of access options. The STT was built by volunteers in the early 1970s, and is maintained by the NY–NJTC.

For more information contact:

Renssealaer-Taconic Land Conservancy
www.rtlc.org

Berkshire Natural Resources Council
(South Taconic Range and Greylock Maps)
20 Bank Row
Pittsfield, MA 01201
413-499-0596
www.bnrc.net

State of New York
Office of Parks, Recreation and Historic Preservation
Taconic Region
P.O. Box 308
Staatsburg, NY 12580
845-889-4100
www.nysparks.state.ny.us

Appalachian Mountain Club, Connecticut Chapter
www.ct-amc.org

TRIP 23
BRACE MOUNTAIN

RATING: Moderate

DISTANCE: 3.8 miles

ELEVATION GAIN: 2,300 feet

ESTIMATED TIME: 4 hours

MAPS: USGS Copake; Berkshire Natural Resources Council, South Taconic Range; NY-NJTC South Taconic Trails

A short, very steep climb followed by a ridge walk across the scenic southern Taconic Plateau, featuring valley and mountain views.

DIRECTIONS

From Millerton, NY, follow NY 22 for 5.4 miles to Whitehouse Crossing Road and turn right. At 6.1 miles, turn left on CR 63. Just under 0.2 mile, turn right onto Deer Run Road, and left onto Quarry Hill Road. Go an additional 0.5 mile and look for the small (obscure) trailhead parking area on the left. A sign identifies the Taconic State Park Brace Mountain Area.

TRAIL DESCRIPTION

Brace Mountain (2,311 feet), together with its sister peak, South Brace (2,304 feet), are the southernmost trailed peaks in the Taconic State Park. This is the tri-state highlands area of New York, Massachusetts, and Connecticut (nearby Mount Frissell, at 3,453 feet, is Connecticut's highest point), the watershed divide of the Hudson and Housatonic rivers. Climb Brace on a very clear day, when the exceptional views include points from Mount Greylock and northwest through the Helderbergs and Catskills, south along the Shawangunks, and as far away as the Hudson Highlands.

Like most of the steep western approaches to the Taconic Plateau, the South Taconic Trail is no exception, and because of its rocks and ledges, this trail is not recommended under icy conditions. But the climb, while steep, is short, and you'll reach ridge elevation at 1,800 feet from the trailhead elevation of 1,000 feet in about one hour.

Begin hiking along an open field, following the white-blazed trail. These blazes (and ridge cairns) may be all you ever see of any trail identification—signage, typically sparse in the Southern Taconics, is scarce here. The climb is gentle until, at 1,200 feet in elevation, a shallow gorge appears to the right side

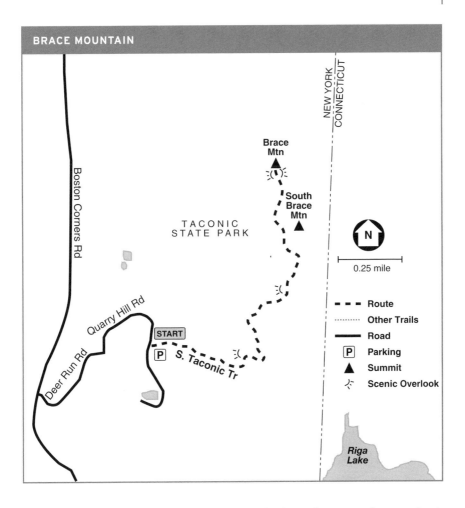

BRACE MOUNTAIN

NEW YORK
CONNECTICUT

Brace
Mtn

South
Brace
Mtn

TACONIC
STATE PARK

N

0.25 mile

Boston Corners Rd

Quarry Hill Rd

START

P   S. Taconic Tr

Deer Run Rd

Riga
Lake

- - - Route

.... Other Trails

——— Road

P   Parking

▲   Summit

⅄   Scenic Overlook

of the trail. Now the trail follows uphill steeply through a magnificent red oak woods, following the scoured and exposed boulders of this once much larger stream course. As the trail steepens, a high-angled cascade of about 60 feet is encountered. Now the trail veers north away from the falls and requires an all-fours approach for the next 10 minutes, as you vault your way upward through ledges with increasing views west and southwest. The trail relaxes at 1,700 feet, and arrives at a flat spot on the ridge, where you turn left. This was the old junction with the red-blazed trail to the high ledges of New Point that you can see just to the south, but the blazes have disappeared and the trail has vanished. You can still follow the vague footpath to the right a little way to take a look at a fairy glen, where a tiny falls creates a clear pool beneath a small, thick hemlock stand. Hunters have left fire rings and evidence of makeshift bivouacs here.

The South Taconic Trail heads north now, and is well marked with white blazes. You face some additional climbing, but it is spread out as the trail walks level for a while along the western ridge, then climbs through oak woods and scattered laurels. Soon you will cross a small, grassy slab with sweeping views south over Riga Lake and South Pond. Climb a bit farther, and you arrive on South Brace, its summit identified by a cairn. Here, your views to the west develop into a wider panorama of the Hudson Valley, while you begin to see more in the east as well, including Mount Frissell, Round Mountain (2,298 feet), Gridley Mountain, and Bear Mountain. On the other side of that ridge, the Appalachian Trail (AT) corridor runs up over Lion's Head and Bear Mountain, through Sage's Ravine to cross Mount Everett. From here you can see the burnished open balds of Brace. As the trail makes its way north again around the scenic, windy western side of South Brace, it dips down into a sheltered saddle and climbs gradually up the south slopes of Brace. The summit is identified with a more impressive rock pile than South Brace's. This broad, open, grassy summit looks directly at Mount Frissell, and across nearby Alander Mountain to the north, in Massachusetts. Hidden behind Mount Frissell is Mount Everett, but lying in the northeast like an inverted molar is the unmistakable Mount Greylock (Massachusetts' highest peak at 3,491 feet), pale gray in the haze, with Mount Prospect forming the left part of the tooth. The viewshed is spectacular and complex, and in order to fully identify surrounding mountain ranges and river valleys, you will need USGS metric topographical maps in the 1:100,000 scale. The westerly Catskill skyline is the most comprehensive, including most of the prominent peaks from the Blackhead Range to the southern Sundown Wild Forest area. A dizzying complex of mountains and unnamed peaks dissolve across Berkshire County, in the direction of Great Barrington and Lee, and away to the north northeast. The north northwestern flatlands rise imperceptibly to the low Helderbergs, and to the east across Litchfield County you can see the Housatonic State Forest and the bumpy hills of Canaan. No matter what point of the compass you sit and face, you will enjoy extensive open space.

At one time, this hike could have been fashioned into a loop trail, using the blue-blazed trail to Riga Lake and an informal trail back to the South Taconic Trail. However, private lands to the west prevent this. Several of the maps still in use for this area are no longer accurate, so be careful. For example, note that the blue-blazed trail from South Beacon to Lake Riga has been erased, covered with tree paint and posted by the Mount Riga Corporation. Return the way you came.

Charcoal makers who supplied the iron furnaces and manufacturing needs of the Revolutionary War effort actually denuded the countryside around Mount Riga. The Riga blast furnace, the last such furnace standing in Connecticut, stands at the southeasterly corner of South Pond, north of Mount Riga. It supplied raw product for the iron works in nearby Lakeville, Connecticut, that were owned in partnership by Ethan Allen. When large steel makers began to use bituminous coal for smelting ore, the charcoal industry disappeared and the Southern Taconics began their slow process of reforestation.

To get a good "feel" for the spectacular Southern Taconic Range, take a drive north along Mount Riga Road from Salisbury, Connecticut, to Mount Washington Road and the Mount Washington State Forest area, where you can camp for free (but you have to hike in). (The headquarters has relocated, but the area is maintained by the state. You can get maps here, at the kiosk north of the maintenance building.) Keep in mind that the Connecticut chapter of the Appalachian Mountain Club maintains a rustic camp (Northwest Camp) on its own property just west of the AT on the Massachusetts-Connecticut line, making an ideal, alternate staging point for climbing Brace from the east.

TRIP 24
ALANDER MOUNTAIN

RATING: Moderate
DISTANCE: 8.0 miles
ELEVATION GAIN: 1,600 feet
ESTIMATED TIME: 6 hours
MAPS: USGS Copake; Berkshire Natural Resources Council, South Taconic Range; NY-NJTC South Taconic Trails

A gradual climb to the central Taconic Ridge, with views east over the Hudson Valley and Catskills, with free camping.

DIRECTIONS
From the hamlet of Copake Falls, east off NY 22 (13 miles north of Millerton and 20.5 miles south of Exit B3 off I-90), set your odometer to zero. Take NY 344 east 0.3 mile to Taconic State Park and continue uphill past Bash Bish Falls, into Massachusetts. At 3.2 miles, bear right onto West Street. Turn right at Cross Road at 4.3 miles and follow to its end on East Street at 5.3 miles. Bear

right and go 0.2 mile to Mount Washington State Forest headquarters (no longer staffed). Turn right into the entrance and park next to the maintenance building at the trailhead.

TRAIL DESCRIPTION

Alander Mountain forms the watershed divide between the Hudson and Housatonic rivers, along the high scenic borderlands of Massachusetts and New York. Although at 2,250 feet it may not seem a formidable peak, its position in the Taconic Range allows for generous views westward, giving it the look and feel of a much bigger mountain. Be aware, too, that the open balds and rocky, unprotected ridge trails are open to rapid changes in the weather, and this increased exposure should be considered as carefully here as in any upper-elevation setting. Be prepared with water, food, warm clothes, and raingear.

The Taconic Ridge is very popular with backpackers, among them hiking groups from the Appalachian Mountain Club (AMC), many of whom begin at the Mount Washington State Forest trailhead. There are several reasons for approaching Alander Mountain (or any point on the ridge) from the east, in Massachusetts. First, you get to choose from several different trailheads, all of them beginning at considerably higher elevations than the single western trailhead in New York State off Under Mountain Road (750 feet). In contrast, the Alander Mountain trailhead, in Massachusetts' Mount Washington State Forest, begins from the middle of the Taconic Ridge at 1,700 feet, so right away, you've saved considerable climbing. The time you would have spent ascending is time you can spend on the ridge. Consider the other advantages: Camping is permitted (walk-in), free of charge in Mount Washington State Forest. You can plan a side trip after your overnight to the Sage's Ravine primitive camp on the Appalachian Trail, or take a quick walk up to Guilder Pond in the Mount Everett State Reservation. And you can drive the fascinating, lonely backroads of the Mount Riga area—as wild as it gets in the tri-state area of New York, Massachusetts, and Connecticut. But the best part is that with some prior planning and preparation you can stage from the AMC's (Connecticut chapter) rustic Northwest Camp off East Street, 2.3 miles south of the trailhead. Seldom will you see a cabin as appealing as this one. (There is also a cabin near Alander's summit that's open all year and available to hikers on a first-come-first-served basis. It has sleeping platforms, which comfortably hold six hikers—and floor space for more, and a wood stove.)

Begin at the state forest headquarters. The trail departs just north of the maintenance buildings. There's a kiosk with handout maps that are not reliable for way-finding or navigation. Head west into open bluet fields, threading

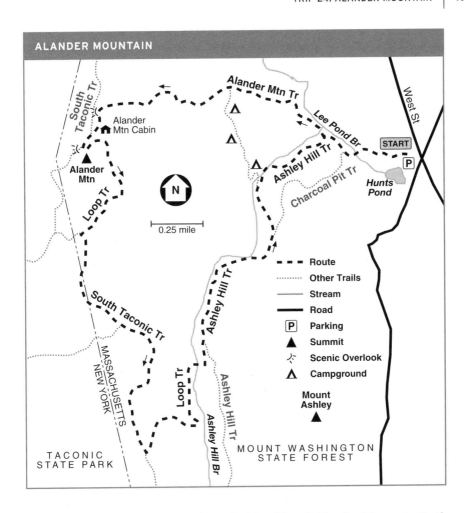

ALANDER MOUNTAIN

your way in and out of the woods on the blue-blazed Alander Mountain Trail. The trail is well defined and frequently traveled. Marking is good. Pass the Charcoal Pit Trail and then the Ashley Hill Trail on your left as you walk in proximity to enchanting Ashley Hill Brook. Cross the brook at an idyllic spot on a hand-hewn stringer bridge, and climb easily into a patch of hemlock trees where a sign indicates the primitive camping area at 0.5 mile. The trail assumes the character of a garden path as it passes a blue-blazed connector trail leading to the primitive camping area. Continue straight ahead, remaining on the Alander Mountain Trail. Spring-blooming wildflowers appear in profusion—common blue violets, downy yellow violets, and, notably, the (critically imperiled, Audubon blue-listed milkwort) fringed polygala, or gaywings. Its little orchidlike purple blooms look like a tiny airplane, complete with propeller.

Climbing to a point next to a small brook, you may notice a tin strip on a tree, perforated with the statement Last water in dry period. The trail turns hard right (keep your eye on the blue markers) and climbs more steadily now. At the appearance of the cabin—remaining from the days when Alander had a fire tower—you arrive in a shallow saddle cleaving Alander's ridge. Imagine having this place to yourself some night, sitting by the wood stove when the wind is shrieking across the summit, bringing new snow for the next day's descent on cross-country skis or snowshoes!

Continue on blue markers to the four-way intersection with the South Taconic Trail (STT), blazed in white, which goes west. Don't take it, but bear left on blue Alander Loop Trail and cross the true summit and the subsequent, open ridge rock of Alander. Views to the west are far reaching, including the Catskills from north to south, Stissing Mountain, the Hudson Valley lowlands, and points southwest. Variations of this view continue as you make your way south in a setting like the Scottish Highlands.

Dropping down off the ridge into a col, the trail makes a sharp right turn, descending briefly west before turning south again below the ridge, to join the white-blazed STT. Bear left on the STT at a place identified by a weathered sign that says *Gentz's Corner* and climb easily and steadily thereafter on an old grassy tote road that led to a bygone farmstead. The atmosphere is airy and remote; the forest floor is covered in ferns. The trail takes you around the west side of a hill and gradually up to ridge elevation again (avoid the unmarked trail to the left), where fine views appear from a solitary rock. As you descend this ridge, watch carefully to your left; take the blue trail that departs northeast over a small rise, and then descends. As you hike through the upper elevations of the Ashley Hill Brook headwaters, join the Ashley Hill Trail as the terrain levels out. After 20 minutes or so, leave the Charcoal Pit Trail to your right (without the trail sign you'd miss it), and continue on the Ashley Hill Trail, where you turn right (east). You may be surprised to see a latrine here. Its purpose is to serve the primitive campsites below, along the creek. If you look down the hill across from the outhouse, you'll see a fire ring on the creek's edge. What a pretty campsite! Follow the level Ashley Hill Trail along the lip of a magnificent, steep hemlock ravine. This will bring you to the junction of the Alander Mountain Trail, which you'll recognize. Bear right and follow the trail back to the parking area.

TRIP 25
BASH BISH MOUNTAIN

RATING: Moderate

DISTANCE: 3.0 miles

ELEVATION GAIN: 1,200 feet

ESTIMATED TIME: 3 hours

MAPS: USGS Copake; Berkshire Natural Resources Council, South Taconic Range; NY-NJTC South Taconic Trails

Rugged, rocky, and steep with a stream crossing and a spur trail to Bash Bish Falls.

DIRECTIONS

From the hamlet of Copake Falls, east off NY 22 (13 miles north of Millerton and 20.5 miles south of Exit B3 off I-90), set your odometer to zero. Take NY 344 east 0.3 mile to Taconic State Park and continue a short distance past the park entrance to the Bash Bish Area parking lot on the right. Cross the creek on the cabin access road.

TRAIL DESCRIPTION

One of the most picturesque and popular wilderness destinations of the nineteenth century, Bash Bish Falls, its gorge, and the sky-clear Bash Bish Brook remain very popular today. Although only a small percentage of the falls' visitors hike the loop using the South Taconic Trail (STT) and the Blue Trail, this hike is the best way to get a complete feel for this unusually rugged and special place.

This hike is a loop that begins and ends at the Bash Bish Area parking lot on Bash Bish Mountain Road (NY 344). Before heading out, read the historical information at the kiosk in the parking area, where there is a comprehensive map. Adjacent to the parking area and just out of sight on the other side of Bash Bish Brook, the Taconic State Park Commission maintains a number of rustic cabins. From the parking area, follow the cabin access road, cross the bridge, and walk along the south side of Bash Bish Brook among several large Norway-spruce trees until you see the first cabin. Watch carefully to the right, where the white-blazed South Taconic Trail appears next to the cabin. Signs indicate Bash Bish Mountain at 2.0 miles. Immediately, the trail ascends, following a small brook through a hemlock forest. The trail switches back a few times as it climbs the steep northwest shoulder of the mountain through northern hardwood forests.

Just under a mile into the hike, at 1,500 feet in elevation, look for a faint, blue-blazed spur to the left (northwest) of the STT. This is easy to miss and you'll be given few clues. (At the head of the spur, the trail flattens out only slightly before turning east and climbing again.) You've ascended nearly 900 feet at this point, and will welcome a break. Follow the spur downhill slightly to a small rocky lookout, where you look straight down into a bowl of pastoral land between Washburn Mountain (1,642 feet) and the ridge you're standing on. You see nearly the entire Catskill range, from Windham High Peak in the northwest, along the Escarpment, north to south, and beyond Overlook Mountain into the Burroughs Range (Slide, Wittenberg, and Cornell), and farther south. If you continue a little farther on the blue-blazed spur, you'll

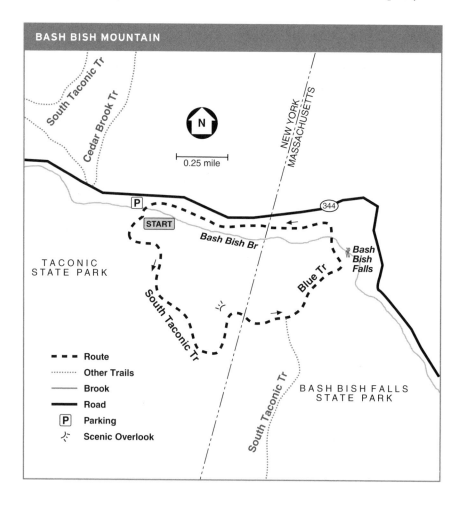

discover a pitch pine outcropping where a limited exposure to the north allows a taunting peek at the north wall of Bash Bish Gorge. This spur provides the hike's best views—don't miss it. You're right at the New York–Massachusetts border here. Backtrack to the STT and continue into Massachusetts.

At 1,600 feet, the forest type changes suddenly into a pleasing montage of hemlocks, mountain laurel, and thick blueberry heaths. Hardwoods appear to the right, conifers to the left. The trail flattens, and suddenly, you're at a (once again) vague junction where the STT leaves south to Alander and Brace mountains. An old Taconic Trail sign is nailed to a tree to the left of the trail here. The sign *Alternate Route to Bash Bish* is intended for those coming north on the STT, who could go either left or right here, depending on the season. The sign also advises *Must ford stream—use only when water is low*. This is a judgment call on your part. You will ford above the falls, where the brook is relatively tame and shallow, but it is wide, and when the water table is very high or flooding, you may indeed get wet. However, even in a late, wet May, I crossed with dry boots. (You can always take your boots off.)

Continue straight ahead on the well-marked Blue Trail, descending gradually, then steeply into the ravine. The trail turns east as it approaches the safety perimeter. The cable acts as a convenient handrail. An engraved rock on the trail itself (you may step over it without noticing) was carefully inscribed by one John Williams, '46. Judging by the style and script, this stone was carved in 1846, around the time that John Frederick Kensett (1816–1872), a leading figure among the second-generation Hudson River school painters, was making preliminary field sketches for a series of five paintings of the falls, most notably his first *Bash Bish Falls* (1851). Other versions followed, leading to his 1855 masterwork by the same name. Be very careful as you descend; hemlocks cling tenaciously to the slope. You'll be using them—and sometimes all fours—to steady yourself. The vertical drops into the cataract beyond the fence are a nerve-wracking 200 feet high. Due to the many fatalities here (many of them connected with alcohol and associated acts of derring-do), observers, under threat of fines, are not permitted beyond the fence. This descent ends at the brook above Bash Bish Falls.

From the small gravel apron at the edge of the brook, the trail continues on the other side, bearing right along the bank. The falls are not in view. Walk upstream to find a good crossing point. (This is where that hiking staff comes in handy.) Once you arrive safely on the brook's northeast banks, look around for the blue blazes and follow the trail up to the parking area of Bash Bish State Park in the Mount Washington State Forest of Massachusetts. The cluster of rock to the left is not worth exploring and offers only obstructed views. Your route continues downhill on the Blue Trail, well identified on the west side of the parking area. Descend past the trailhead kiosk, and walk on a storybook section of trail through a hemlock ravine. As you hear the sounds of falling water, the trail jogs hard left and joins the dirt service road that comes up from the parking area where you began. Bear left to look at the falls, and then descend the stone steps to their base. Here a rock protrudes from the lower falls, split by centuries of falling water, the cascade ending in a viridian pool of remarkable clarity. Bash Bish is the highest falls in the state of Massachusetts, falling in multiple tiers to a final drop of 80 feet. Many casual visitors content themselves with painting, writing, photographing, and meditating here; however, few have really seen "the whole picture," as you have.

Return to your starting point, 0.75 mile back along the Blue Trail (service road) heading west, keeping the brook to your left until you reach the parking area again. Bash Bish Brook continues without you, to join the Roeliff-Jansen Kill and onward, to dissolution with the Hudson River.

TRIP 26
HARVEY MOUNTAIN

RATING: Moderate

DISTANCE: 3.0 miles

ELEVATION GAIN: 480 feet

ESTIMATED TIME: 2.5 hours

MAPS: USGS State Line; Harvey Mountain State Forest

Little-known trail with views of the southern Taconics from a blueberry knoll and free camping.

DIRECTIONS

From NY 22 in Austerlitz, NY, 5.5 miles south of Exit B3 of I-90, turn left (east) onto East Hill Road, where you'll see the post office. Go 2.5 miles to the Harvey Mountain trailhead parking area on the left.

TRAIL DESCRIPTION

Few scenic vantage points in the southern Taconics' tapering northern hills offer such unusual views of the Taconic Plateau as Harvey Mountain (2,065 feet). From the east and west as it is viewed from the valley, the range looks like a

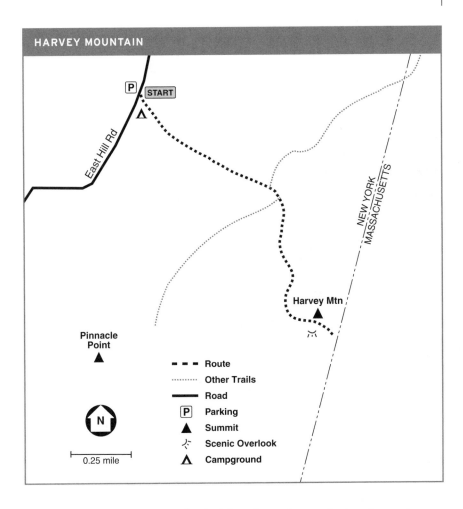

long, low ridge with minimal relief, but from the north the plateau is seen longitudinally, and the fact that the Taconics are a "real" mountain range—the result of tectonic collision and uplift, not just a dissected plateau—becomes strikingly apparent.

Harvey Mountain State Forest (HMSF) is a recent (1996) addition to the state forest system. In addition to the Harvey Mountain Trail itself and its connector trails to the Beebe Mountain fire tower and Barrett Pond, HMSF offers a dozen primitive, no-fee, drive-up campsites. Camping permits are required for more than three consecutive nights, or for groups of ten or more. Come prepared—there are no water sources, fire pits, or pit privies, and on-site management is limited to occasional ranger patrols, mostly on weekends. Hunting is permitted here as in most state forests; dress accordingly.

Die-hard hikers may take umbrage with the fact that there is a road to

Fern glades on Harvey Mountain.

the summit of Harvey Mountain. However, both the summit road—a washed-out four-wheel drive route—and the HMSF's dead-end campsite access road see very little use from the sightseeing public. Parking is provided in the well-identified lot on East Hill Road. The Harvey Mountain trailhead is located diagonally across East Hill Road from the parking area, on the northeast side of the Harvey Mountain camping area access road opposite Campsite 1. Follow blue markers.

The trail begins with a sharp ascent, and then levels out through hardwoods over a smooth, wide dirt surface. Within 0.3 mile, the trail register appears at the junction of the red-blazed trail to Barrett Pond and the fire tower in Beebe Hill State Forest. Bear right, following the blue markers into a vigorous, young sugar-maple forest on this flat and pretty section of trail. Within 15 minutes of the trailhead, the trail departs left at a Y (where a rough road continues straight ahead), and soon becomes a narrow path, descends slightly adjacent to a steep ravine where Harvey Mountain can be spotted ahead, and crosses Big Moon Brook. Now the trail rises consistently but never very steeply, as it sidehills up the western slopes of the mountain. (A spur trail to the Chance of Thunder Lean-to is being built in this vicinity at this writing.) Soon after ascending through a white pine stand the trail rises to an open blueberry heath. Though not the highest point of the mountain, this spot is, for all practical purposes, its summit. At this writing there is a rickety picnic table with a loosely attached plaque that says, *Harvey Mountain, 2,065 feet.* The views to the south are the most interesting, showing the long, thin Taconic Ridge with its dramatic eastern slopes pitching steeply down from Mount Fray into Egremont, Massachusetts, followed by the cluster of peaks around Mount Everett. The highest point of the eastern ridge defines the route of the Appalachian Trail as it makes its way from northern Connecticut, through the Southern Taconics, and drops sharply off the eastern shoulder of Jug End, heading for the Greylock Range. You can see the Beebe Hill fire tower at 310 degrees. Continue up the hill to the east of the summit, where a herd trail leads across a field and into the woods. Look left along a stone wall for the New York–Massachusetts state-line marker. The state forest ends here. Return the way you came.

The town of Austerlitz's historian, Sally Light, has identified several home-stead foundations in the state forest dating from 1755, when an iron industry flourished here. In 1882, on a lot believed by duped investors to contain gold ore, a prospector named Oliver Beckwith murdered and cannibalized his part-ner, Simeon Vandercook. Beckwith fled to Canada and the ensuing manhunt took several years. Beckwith was brought to justice in 1882; he was the last person hanged in Columbia County. (This has given rise to many rumors about Beckwith's ghost haunting the forest).

Just outside HMSF, on East Hill Road along the upper fringes of the Stee-pletop Estate, is the Millay Poetry Trail, a short walk posted with selections of Edna St. Vincent Millay's nature poetry from 1917 to 1935. (Millay won a Pultizer for her collection *The Harp Weaver and Other Poems* and was noted for her sonnets.) This short trail (about 0.4 mile) leads through quiet woods to her grave and that of her mother Cora Millay, and her husband, Eugen Jan Boissevain. The trailhead is 0.2 mile west of the Harvey Mountain trailhead parking area. There's a sign and parking area. The nearby Millay Colony for the Arts, established by the poet's sister Norma, is an active artist-in-residence colony. Aside from special events, it is not open to the public.

TRIP 27
SUNSET ROCK

RATING: Moderate
DISTANCE: 3.5 miles
ELEVATION GAIN: 740 feet
ESTIMATED TIME: 3 hours
MAPS: USGS Copake; USGS Hillsdale; Berkshire Natural Resources Council, South Taconic Range; NY-NJTC South Taconic Trails

A walk along a creek and upland ridge environment, amid pinxter blossoms, mountain laurel, evergreen plantations with an optional spur to Bash Bish Falls.

DIRECTIONS

From the hamlet of Copake Falls, east off NY 22 (13 miles north of Millerton and 20.5 miles south of Exit B3 off I-90), set your odometer to zero. Take NY 344 east 0.3 mile to Taconic State Park and continue a short distance to the Bash Bish Area parking lot. The trail begins on the north side of NY 344.

TRAIL DESCRIPTION

Combine this hike with a visit to Bash Bish Falls, and you'll begin to get an idea of what the Taconics are all about. Sunset Rock is a small, isolated lookout lying along the New York–Massachusetts border, offering a western exposure to the Catskills from Columbia and Dutchess counties. It can be hiked in a half day, but, like most scenic destinations in the Taconics, there's about 900 feet of elevation gain. However, because the gain is gradual, this hike feels considerably easier than the more involved (and longer) outings to Alander, Bash Bish, and Brace mountains.

You can begin most conveniently from the Bash Bish Area parking lot on NY 344, a.k.a. Bash Bish Mountain Road. (If you're staying at the campsite, several trailheads leave from the tenting area; the southernmost trailhead next to Loop A will bring you to the start of this hike.) From the parking area, take the time to walk the 0.75 mile to Bash Bish Falls. If you save this short detour for the end of the hike, you can soak your feet in the brook.

Directly across Bash Bish Falls Road from the parking area, you'll see the Cedar Brook Trail right next to the bridge. Follow the blue blazes uphill through a dense hemlock stand along the creek. This was an early picnic area where you'll see a few old fireplaces. Amid the emerald, moss-fringed pools of Cedar Brook and the white clustered flower bunches of blooming viburnum, make your way uphill. The trail crosses the shallow brook several times before it turns east, then north, to ascend a dry (seasonal) hemlock gully. Watch for a sign at the junction that states *Alternate route to South Taconic Trail*. This section of trail is steep. You will arrive out of breath at the top of the slope, where the Cedar Brook Trail joins the South Taconic Trail (STT, white blazes) and the red-blazed, Sunset Rock Trail. Go right (northeast). You're grateful for a bit of level ground here, but the trail soon ascends. You'll see vestiges of an early settlement—probably a farm homestead—stone walls and shallow foundation pits. The trail is roadlike, though washed out and rocky. As you rise through the hardwoods, the trail turns west and you sense the top of the ridge ahead. Somewhere around 1,700 feet, there is a sudden, marked forest type change as you rise above the rich slope soils onto the harder, poor soil of the ridge. Suddenly, pitch pines, stunted oaks, and mountain laurel appear.

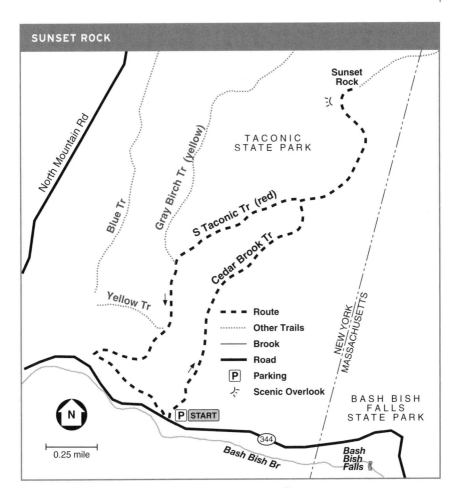

Look carefully along the trail at this point for the elusive and stunning pink lady's slipper (spring blossom, pink moccasin flower), one of the largest native orchids. And look at all the blueberries! In a few moments you will reach a flat opening at the ridge's near summit. Look carefully to the left of the STT for the unmarked spur to Sunset Rock. This trail is well established and leads, in a few hundred feet or so, to the small rock lookout, where brush has been pruned to allow for a wider view. The broad, rolling farmlands of the valley stretch away to the east, north, and south. Standing to the west and appearing oceanic in volume are the Catskills. The long Escarpment is seen from Windham High Peak to Overlook. The Devil's Path, that line of east-to-west-running peaks from Plattekill to Hunter, defines the Indian Head Wilderness Area. And to the southwest, you can see the interior high peaks around Slide and Wittenberg, collectively known as the Burroughs Range for its resident naturalist,

John Burroughs. This is a quiet place. Vultures soar past and mockingbirds thrash in the underbrush. To the north, the STT reaches Sunset Rock Road in 0.3 mile; it is possible to return to Bash Bish on a roundabout course using the road and the blue or yellow trails back through the campsite, but this is a longer option. Immediately to the north (off route) along the STT is one of the most dense mountain laurel "slicks" I have ever seen in the Hudson Valley.

Return to the STT junction with the Cedar Brook Trail. This fast backtrack will bring you along the Sunset Rock Trail as it assumes the character of a woods road. In late May, the remarkably sweet scent of pinxter flowers fills the woods. This member of the heath family (pink azalea) has showy pink flowers that often appear before its leaves are fully grown.

As you're descending gradually through the oak woods, the inviting-looking Gray Birch Trail comes in from the right (northwest). Pass it and continue straight ahead following the red markers and white blazes. At a point along the trail you will be able to look up to the southeast at the steep walls of Bash Bish Gorge, at the lookout on the ridge's northwest shoulder (see Trip 25) and into the high pastures between Alander and Washburn mountains. There is a substantial population of scarlet tanagers in these forests—they prefer oak woods.

Stay left on the STT where the yellow trail goes right. This will bring you through a forest of tall white pines. Jack-in-the-pulpit (Indian turnip) appears along the trail here. At a point where the red trail departs to the right for the campsite, go diagonally into a red spruce stand, following white markers. This is a very pretty section of trail. Where the spruce stand enters hardwoods, the late-afternoon sun turns the forest to an incandescent hot lime. The trail reaches a dirt road (the connecter from the campsite to the falls area). Go left, and within minutes you will arrive at Bash Bish Falls Road (NY 344), right across the street from the parking area where you left your car.

If you're feeling up to the falls walk, have a look at the map kiosk, and follow the trail to the east along the banks of Bash Bish Brook. A relaxed round-trip, including time to admire the falls, will require about one hour.

5

THE NORTHERN TACONICS

THE PART OF THE TACONIC RIDGE that lies along the eastern border of New York and northwestern Massachusetts is commonly known as the Berkshire Hills. To the north are the Green Mountains of Vermont; to the east is the Greylock massif. In the west, the ridge is locally referred to as the Taconic Range, although geologically, it is known as the Greylock Range; i.e. the Berkshire Hills have the same origins. These hills drain eastward into the Hoosic and Hudson rivers. Of interest to long-distance hikers is the Taconic Crest Trail (TCT), a 35-mile scenic ridge trail beginning in Pittsfield, Massachusetts, and linking several state forest areas, sanctuaries, and conservation lands (including White Rocks and the Snow Hole), the multiple peaks of Misery Mountain, Berlin Pass, and the scenic summits of Berlin and Petersburg mountains, before ending in Petersburg, New York.

The Taconic Hiking Club initiated the TCT in 1932. It is maintained and/or managed by several groups, including the Taconic Trails Council, the Taconic Hiking Club, the Appalachian Mountain Club, the Williamstown Rural Lands Foundation, and the National Park Service.

Of major interest to most hikers visiting the area is Mount Greylock State Reservation (established 1898; Massachusetts' first state park), at the confluence of the Green and Hoosic river valleys. (Note: In New York, the spelling is *Hoosic*; in Massachusetts, the common spelling is *Hoosac*. As such, in New

York, it is the Hoosic Valley, while in Massachusetts it is the Hoosac Valley. However, the spelling of Hoosic River does not deviate from state to state, nor does the spelling of Hoosac Ridge or Hoosac Range. For convention, we have used *Hoosic* here for instances when both spellings are acceptable.)

Greylock (3,491 feet) is the highest point in the state of Massachusetts, and is surrounded by several peaks in the 3,000-foot range. Its name came into use in the 1930s and is believed to refer to an Indian chief named Grey Lock, or from the summit's cloud-shrouded appearance. About 12 miles of the Appalachian Trail passes through the reservation, crossing Greylock's summit, and there are 70 miles of additional trails within the reservation. Fantastic, 360-degree views greet the hiker on Greylock, who will also want to climb the War Memorial Tower and visit Bascom Lodge, where meals and lodging can be enjoyed at reasonable prices. Between 1933 and 1939, the Civilian Conservation Corps worked on Mount Greylock, at the site of today's campground on Sperry Road. In recognition of their contribution, the area above 3,100 feet on Greylock was designated a National Historic District by the U.S. Department of the Interior.

A good way to begin your explorations of this fascinating area is with a visit to the reservation's new visitor area (see website for directions) in Lanesborough, or with a driving tour to Greylock's summit (mid-May to mid-October).

Hikers should obtain the excellent *North Berkshire Outdoor Guide*, the authoritative text on the area, produced by the Williams College Outing Club. Included with the book is the pocket map North Berkshire Trails, which identifies the trails around Williamstown, the Greylock Reservation, and the Northern Taconic Range.

For more information contact:

Taconic Hiking Club
Katherine Wolfe, Interclub Liaison
29 Campagna Dr.
Albany, NY 12205

The THC is a small club of about 150 hikers. Every other May, they conduct a supported thru-hike of the Taconic Crest Trail. THC publishes a guidebook and seven-map series for the TCT.

Williamstown Rural Lands Foundation
413-458-2494
www.wrlf.org

Williams Outing Club
39 Chapin Hall Dr.
Williamstown, MA 01267

Mount Greylock State Reservation Visitors Center
30 Rockwell Rd.
Lanesborough, MA 10237
413-499-4262/4263; www.mass.gov/dcr/

Department of Conservation and Recreation (DCR)
251 Causeway St.
Boston, MA 02114
617-626-1250; www.mass.gov/dcr/; email: Mass.Parks@state.ma.us

THE CIVILIAN CONSERVATION CORPS (CCC)

The Emergency Conservation Work Act (1933) brought great numbers of un-employed men and the environment together. Organized by the Departments of Agriculture and Interior, and managed by regular and reserve officers in the Coast Guard, Navy, and Marines, this peace-time army of 500,000 men set about improving federal and state lands and parks. Enlistees were housed in tent camps and paid $25 a month. In 1937, the Civilian Conser-vation Corps (CCC, affectionately known as Roosevelt's "tree army") was introduced, and education and training elements were added. Eventually, every state had a CCC camp—as well as Hawaii, Alaska, Puerto Rico, and the Virgin Islands. In addition to the CCC's primary duties of planting trees and fighting fires, the Corps built 3,470 fire towers and 97,000 miles of truck and fire roads. They also acted as an emergency service organization, helping in flood and disaster control in the Ohio and Mississippi valleys, and in drainage and irrigation of croplands in the Midwest. During the Labor Day hurricane of 1935 in the Florida Keys, after a rescue train derailed on its way to rescue them, nearly 300 CCC veterans were reported as missing or unidentified dead. The CCC came to an end after the attacks on Pearl Harbor focused the president's attention and the bulk of available moneys on the war effort. Although the CCC officially ended by a narrow congressional vote in 1942, its spirit lives on in the state trails and plantation forests you'll experience on many of these hikes.

TRIP 28
MOUNT GREYLOCK

RATING: Strenuous

DISTANCE: 8.2 miles

ELEVATION GAIN: 2,300 feet

ESTIMATED TIME: 7 hours

MAPS: USGS North Adams L; AMC Mount Greylock Reservation; Williams Outing Club, North Berkshire Trails; Department of Conservation and Recreation, Mount Greylock State Reservation and Greylock Glen

A long hike showcasing the Greylock massif, Bascom Lodge, and the memorial tower, following a section of the Appalachian Trail and descending through a sugar-maple forest.

DIRECTIONS

From Williamstown at the corner of MA 2 and CR 43 (Water Street/Green River Road), go south on CR 43, leaving the Green River linear park to your left. At 2.5 miles turn left into Mount Hope Park. Go 1.4 miles to a fork and turn left onto Hopper Road. Go 0.7 mile to the Haley Farm trailhead. (You can also come in from South Williamstown on US 7, turning right (north) onto CR 43, and going 2.5 miles to Hope Park).

TRAIL DESCRIPTION

There are many ways to approach Mount Greylock, but the Hopper Trail is the traditional route of serious hikers, with the possible exception of the Appalachian Trail (AT). According to the Williams Outing Club's *North Berkshire Outdoor Guide*, the trail was created in May 1830 by a group of more than 100 people, most of them Williams College students and faculty members. The Greylock trails are still heavily used by college students and Williamstown residents, who have served as stewards to them for over 100 years.

To the early farmers and romantics of the Hoosic Valley, the steep, narrow gash cleaving Greylock's southwest face resembled a grain hopper. Your route takes you along the Hopper's western defile as you turn gradually northeast to summit Greylock. At 3,491 feet, Mount Greylock is the highest point in Massachusetts. Beginning at 3,000 feet or so, its summit zone is forested with the post-glacial remnants of sub-alpine vegetation. Colder temperatures and

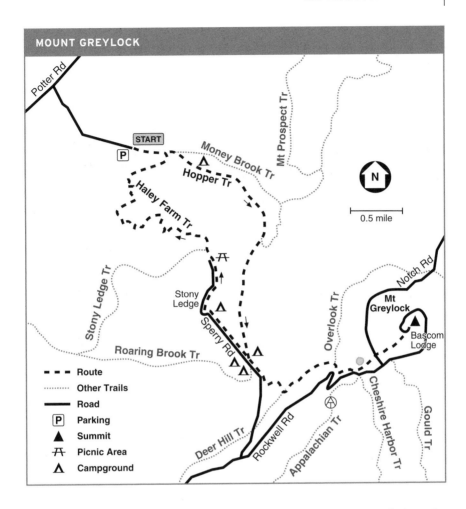

MOUNT GREYLOCK

Potter Rd

START

P

Money Brook Tr

Mt Prospect Tr

Hopper Tr

Haley Farm Tr

N

0.5 mile

Stony Ledge Tr

Stony Ledge

Sperry Rd

Roaring Brook Tr

Overlook Tr

Notch Rd

Mt Greylock

Bascom Lodge

Cheshire Harbor Tr

Gould Tr

Deer Hill Tr

Rockwell Rd

Appalachian Tr

- - - Route
.... Other Trails
——— Road
P Parking
▲ Summit
⊼ Picnic Area
Λ Campground

increased precipitation create favorable conditions for red spruce, balsam fir, paper birch, and mountain ash—the upper-elevation companions that hikers tend to equate with wilderness. And, while Mount Greylock's serenity is minimally imposed upon by the scenic auto byway to its summit, hikers can find isolation very near at hand, just a short way off the summit on any one of the mountain's many trails.

Prepare for a long day's outing with significant climbing. From the parking area at Haley's Farm trailhead, follow the blue-blazed Hopper Trail along an old road lined with sugar maples, through fields of alfalfa. Pass the Haley Farm Trail (your return route) on the right, and the Hopper Brook Loop Trail (a.k.a. Money Brook Trail) on your left. Your route, the Hopper Trail, goes right, off the woods road. (If you were to continue straight ahead another 300 feet you'd reach the dispersed group camping area.)

Mount Greylock as seen from the Hoosic Valley.

The Hopper Trail ascends through hardwoods, sidehilling above Money Brook, growing steeper as it turns southeast, and you have sparse and intriguing glimpses of Greylock up to the left (east). Within an hour's hiking, you'll be happy to find that the trail relents, finally becoming level in a forest where red spruce appears in isolated stands. Now the trail bears left as it reaches a road, where you will walk for about 10 minutes through the heavily wooded Sperry Road camping area. (Many people park or camp in the campground for a substantially easier ascent of Greylock. Still others backpack to this point, make camp, and day-hike to the summit. Reservations for camping are advised.)

Hike a few hundred feet past the campsite check-in cabin where the Hopper Trail goes left (northeast) back into the woods. The steepest ascent lies behind you now, but there's more vertical rise ahead. Rising to a T with the Deer Hill Trail, the Hopper Trail bears left on level ground. Follow it, bearing right at a Y, where the Overlook Trail departs to the left (north). As you ascend easily, you'll draw near to Rockwell Road (the summit road) on your right. At a Y, bear left at the Cheshire Harbor/AT connection, joining in with the Hopper Trail from the right. Walk carefully over a long string of half-log-and-plank puncheons through a wet alpine zone of balsam fir, witch hobble, and paper birch, skirting the natural-looking, manufactured pond and disused pump house that originally provided Bascom Lodge with water (the Lodge uses a well now). Just ahead the trail crosses Rockwell Road, and climbs again. Signs for Bascom Lodge appear. One last rocky ascent remains. Soon you pass the communications tower and service garages and cross the access road, where you'll come upon a large, circular, steel relief map of the Greylock Range, just below the summit. Carry on until you reach the expansive overlooks at the base of the memorial tower, where the viewshed is inscribed in stone. To the right is Bascom Lodge, where you can relax, find rest rooms and buy refreshments, AT souvenirs, books, and sundries. Built by the CCC in the 1930s, this rustic stone and wood lodge accommodates 34 guests in both bunk- and private rooms. Have a look at the AT thru-hikers' journal, and enjoy a picnic on the enclosed porch with its remarkable 100-mile views and mountain house atmosphere. (The only drinking water on the mountain is located outside, in the back of the Lodge.)

After climbing the tower for the 360-degree view, you can watch hang gliders and sport kites taking off and landing in the valley, far below you. Also of interest is the Thunderbolt Shelter (built in1934), located adjacent to the parking lot. This rustic emergency hikers' shelter was originally the ski lodge of the Mount Greylock Ski Club, the organization that hosted the first U.S. Eastern Amateur Ski Association downhill championship races.

Retrace your steps to Sperry Road and the campground, back to the point where the Hopper Trail joined the campsite road next to Site R7. Leave the Hopper Trail to your right now, and remain on the campsite road as it makes its way northwest to Stony Ledge. From the scenic overlook and picnic area at Stony Ledge (where you'll be treated to a spectacular close-up of Mount Greylock, Mount Prospect, and the Hopper) follow the Stony Ledge Trail to the north (it appears on your left as you look toward Greylock). Pass the Stony Ledge Shelter, soon appearing to your right, and watch carefully on the right for the Haley Farm Trail, your route of descent. The Haley Farm Trail is not intensively used. It winds and switches its way back down the mountain through dense hardwoods, meandering west to gentler contours. Within 35 minutes of hiking from Stony Ledge, it cuts back into the north and east, following a graded old farm road through a beautiful and extensive sugar maple forest. Soon you cross the fields of Haley's Farm and turn left on the Hopper Trail, arriving in short order at the trailhead parking area.

TRIP 29
HOPKINS MEMORIAL FOREST

RATING: Moderate
DISTANCE: 4.3 miles
ELEVATION GAIN: 450 feet
ESTIMATED TIME: 2 hours
MAPS: USGS Berlin R; Williams College Center for Environmental Studies, Hopkins Memorial Forest; Williams Outing Club, North Berkshire Trails

A quiet, easy hike through an old settlement area now managed as a research forest and a cross-country ski trail.

DIRECTIONS

From the rotary intersection of US 7 and MA 2 at the site of Field Park in Williamstown, follow US 7 north (past the information booth) 0.3 mile to Bulkley Street (go slowly—it comes up quickly). Turn left and go 1.2 miles to Northwest Hill Road. Bear right, then left into the Hopkins Memorial Forest. Park on the left in the designated lot and walk up to the trailhead.

TRAIL DESCRIPTION

The 2,500-acre Hopkins Memorial Forest lies in the extreme northwest corner of Massachusetts. Essentially a research forest belonging to Williams College's Center for Environmental Studies (CES), its trails are well marked and open to the public.

Local folks like to point out that the beautiful woods and fields of Hopkins Memorial Forest inspired William Cullen Bryant's best-known poem, "Thanatopsis," written in 1811 when the budding writer and Berkshire native was a student at Williams College. At the time, subsistence farms covered most of the area. These farms began to disappear with the construction of the Erie Canal and the inexorable industrialization of New England. Bryant and many of the Knickerbocker writers (Thomas Cole, Washington Irving, and James Fenimore Cooper among them) were repelled by such changes, and found solace in nature. Bryant's somber tone is reminiscent of the English Graveyard school of poetry.

Consisting of two loops that form a figure eight, this hike offers two options for hikers, snowshoers, and cross-country skiers. The first, or Lower Loop, is

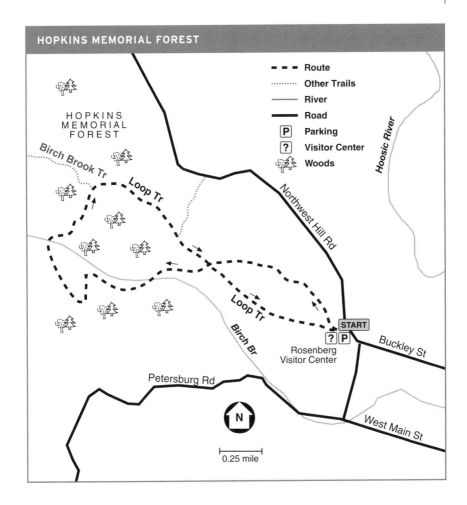

HOPKINS MEMORIAL FOREST

- - - Route
········· Other Trails
———— River
———— Road
P Parking
? Visitor Center
  Woods

HOPKINS
MEMORIAL
FOREST

Birch Brook Tr

Loop Tr

Loop Tr

Birch Br

START

? P
Rosenberg
Visitor Center

Buckley St

Petersburg Rd

West Main St

Hoosic River

Northwest Hill Rd

N

0.25 mile

an easy 1.5-miler; the Upper Loop is steeper and longer, at 2.8 miles. The trail follows an old settlement road over rolling terrain, through the dense forests and reclaimed fields of the Northern Taconics' eastern slopes.

Begin your outing from Rosenberg Center, the college's research base, housed in the 1906 carriage house and stables of the original Buxton Farm. Here you will find maps and information, as well as a public rest room. Walk between Buxton Garden and the Moon Barn (the Moons were the original subsistence farmers who lived along the North Branch of Birch Brook), following the dirt road to the northwest. (If you're on skis, go left of Moon Barn onto the Lower Loop to climb the steepest ascent first.) Pass the Outing Club cabin on your right, and the sugarhouse on your left. Soon you will see an open field to your left, where a weather station appears. As you re-enter the woods, see if you can spot the forest canopy platform and walkway 75 feet above you.

The Moon family's original barn, Hopkins Memorial Forest.

Interpretive signs describe many of the CES' research projects.

As you ascend, a red pine plantation appears to your left. The trail flattens out at the intersection of the figure eight, where a ski-trail map is located. Continue diagonally across the intersection, onto the Upper Loop. The wide, dirt road descends slightly, crosses a plank bridge over the north branch of Birch Brook, and follows the south branch, passing a tiny hemlock glen. As the trail turns away from the forest's blazed southern boundary, it ascends into a sparse red spruce wood, then into beech and oak woods. At the top of the loop, the trail becomes narrower and bumpier; skiers will want to have a good base and some new snow to negotiate this section safely.

The apex of the trail is at its crossing of the Birch Brook's middle branch. Thereafter the trail descends, crossing a bridge on the north branch where the Birch Brook Trail appears on the left. (The Birch Brook Trail climbs the eastern ridge to join the Taconic Crest Trail north of White Rocks and Jim Smith Hill. See Trip 31.) Soon you will walk through an open, airy wood along a flat section of the trail where you can see the Taconic Ridge up to your right. Avoid the Carriage Road Trail that appears to your left, continuing straight ahead to the intersection of the loops. Go straight through the intersection now (skiers should turn left here). This is a flat and sometimes wet section of trail that passes first through a monospecific glade of hay-scented fern (see the interpretive sign describing the ongoing research). Farther on, you will pass a Norway-spruce stand, and many large specimens of field-grown oak. Soon, the relocated, reconstructed Moon Barn comes into view again amid the old reclaimed fields and stone walls of Buxton Farm, at one time considered the "agricultural showplace" of Williamstown.

Fortunately, although he remained and is remembered as a poet, William Cullen Bryant did not sustain his early fondness for graveyard verse. He did become a humorist, critic, and popular essayist, taking on the editorial leadership and part ownership of the *New York Evening Post*. He is recognized in scholarly terms for his translations of *The Iliad* and *The Odyssey* in 1870–1871.

While in Williamstown (population 9,000), take the time to visit its many points of historical interest. Founded in 1750 as West Hoosuck, its first settlers were soldiers who served at the northern front of the French and Indian wars. Their leader, Colonel Ephraim Williams, provided the means by which Williams College was established in 1791 (provided that the town be renamed Williamstown). The small house in Field Park (a remnant of the original town green) is a handmade reproduction of a 1753 "regulation" house (in order to gain title to a lot, a settler's house had to measure 15 by 18 feet), built in 1953 for the Williamstown Bicentennial.

TRIP 30
PINE COBBLE

RATING: Moderate
DISTANCE: 3.2 miles
ELEVATION GAIN: 1,000 feet
ESTIMATED TIME: 2.5 hours
MAPS: USGS North Adams L; Williams Outing Club, North Berkshire Trails; AMC, Mount Greylock Reservation

Williamstown's most popular short hike to a quartzite limestone summit overlooking the Hoosic Valley and the Greylock Range.

DIRECTIONS
From Williamstown at the corner of Cole Avenue and MA 2 (at the only light in town), turn north on Cole Avenue. Cross the Hoosic River at 0.7 mile. Turn right on North Hoosac Road (note the variance in the spelling of "Hoosic" is accepted) and go another 0.4 mile to Pine Cobble Road. Turn left and park on the left at 0.1 mile in the designated trailhead parking area.

TRAIL DESCRIPTION
The short, scenic hike to Pine Cobble (1,893 feet) is Williamstown's most popular short outing. Lying north of the Hoosic River on the southernmost slopes of the Green Mountains less than 2.0 miles from the Vermont border, it

represents the northeastern-most hike in this book. What makes Pine Cobble such an interesting landmark is its position between the Greylock massif, the Green Mountains, the Hoosac Range, and the eastern slopes of the rambling Northern Taconics, where the Green River valley and the fertile farm flats of the Hoosic floodplain sprawl out before you.

Although relatively short, this hike has a few steep sections and a substantial vertical rise, so be prepared for a moderately strenuous outing. (Another, longer, less popular approach is along the Appalachian Trail (AT) from Blackinton. See the *North Berkshire Outdoor Guide* for details.)

From the trailhead parking area, locate the blue-blazed trail and signboard across the road and climb adjacent to it for a short distance. The trail soon heads east and away from Hoosac Road, climbing past the unexpected sight of the Pine Cobble development area, where you'll see a handsome residence or

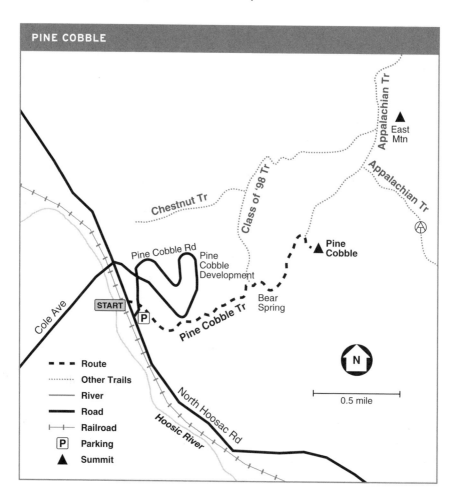

two. Pay attention to the blazes, as there are several unmarked side trails and skid roads. After this initial pitch, the trail departs for the deep woods and relaxes for a while, climbing gently. Soon the trail levels and passes another blue-blazed trail on the left, identified as the "Class of '98 Trail." Bear right, avoiding it (it loops around to the north, connects with the Chestnut Trail, and ascends East Mountain to a point south of Eph's Lookout on the AT). This marks the halfway point at 0.8 mile. Now the trail ascends, and within a few minutes brings you into the Pine Cobble Summit Natural Area, owned and stewarded by the Williamstown Rural Lands Foundation (WRLF).

The trail climbs steeply now, joining an unidentified old tote road, thereafter climbing to a marked T with a trail sign. To the left the trail joins the AT, to the right it leads 0.1 mile to Pine Cobble summit. Bear right, and note that the trail splits, the right fork leading to the ledges above Williamstown and the left to those facing North Adams. Both forks have the character of herd trails at this point, and faint trails appear here and there on the "summit," a collection of isolated south-facing outcroppings with extensive east-to-west views.

The most pronounced of the two trails—the left fork—will lead you to an easterly lookout, where a series of open rock ledges face the long ridge of the Hoosac Range stretching north and south above North Adams. The predominantly hardwood summit area yields a few pitch pines and white pines, and a sparse blueberry heath. The summit rock is a curious-looking quartzite limestone, resembling unpolished marble. Most prominent of the peaks on the Hoosac Ridge is Spruce Hill, and north of it, West Summit, both lying across the Hoosic River's north branch; more arresting by far is the view looking across Blackinton where the AT comes down from Greylock to cross the Hoosic Valley. Then you gaze up the long ridgeline south of Braytonville to the summit of Mount Williams, companion to

Williamstown and the Hoosic Valley from Pine Cobble.

Mount Greylock, rising unmistakably in the south in company with westerly Mount Prospect. Move to the southwest now. With a little searching, locate a faint trail that leads to the views over Williamstown. A good-looking village, Williamstown looks even better from above, with its college halls, spires, playing fields, farms, and woodlands; beyond, the eastern slopes of the Northern Taconics flatten into the valley where prominent Mount Brodie juts into the floodplain. Easily identified across the Hoosic's west branch are Petersburgh and Berlin passes splitting the long Taconic Ridge, where the Taconic Crest Trail roughly defines the border between New York and Massachusetts. White Rock (Trip 31), Mount Raimer, Berlin Mountain, Bald Mountain, and Misery Mountain extend the ridge to the south. The centerpiece of this rural dominion is the Greylock massif itself, lying squarely across the southern viewshed, a wrinkled jumble of hills created, remarkably enough, by the smashing of the South American continent into North America. Imagine that you are looking at the floor of a 1,000-foot-deep glacial lake (Lake Bascom), easily recreated in your mind if you were to pour water to the tops of the surrounding ridges.

The "pocket" wilderness represented by the unexpectedly wild landscape of the Hoosic River valley is in the heart of a natural wonderland that lies at the gateway of yet another. To the north, the Green Mountains present a route into the Northeast Kingdom, cordially defined by the 265-mile Long Trail that begins just north of Pine Cobble on the Vermont-Massachusetts border. You may be tempted to extend your hike by continuing to its trailhead north of Eph's Lookout (named for Ephraim Williams, founder of Williams College), or by visiting the closer summit of East Mountain, where you can set foot on the AT—just to say you did.

Return the way you came.

TRIP 31
WHITE ROCK

RATING: Moderate

DISTANCE: 5.5 miles

ELEVATION GAIN: 300 feet

ESTIMATED TIME: 3.5 hours

MAPS: USGS North Pownal; USGS Berlin R; Williams College Outing Club, Northern Berkshire Trails; Williams College, Center for Environmental Studies, Hopkins Memorial Forest

An easy, east-facing, scenic ridge hike along the Taconic Crest to the Snow Hole, a deep, icebound crevice.

DIRECTIONS

This section of the Taconic Crest Trail (TCT) begins at the Petersburg Pass Scenic Area on NY 2, at the height of land equidistant between Williamstown, Massachusetts, and Petersburg, New York. Find the trail on the north side of NY 2.

TRAIL DESCRIPTION

This fairly relaxed hike will take you along the skyline trail that roughly defines the border between New York, Vermont, Massachusetts, and Connecticut—the TCT. On the TCT you will walk briefly through Vermont, and come within a few feet of the Massachusetts border. But, because most of the TCT in this section travels through the forested crest of the ridge or just below it on the Taconics' western slopes, your views will be only west-facing.

Some confusion surrounds the placename and location of the area defined as White Rocks. White Rocks is a topographical feature identified on maps close to the Petersburg Pass trailhead of the TCT, whereas a scenic lookout on this hike, White Rock, lies farther to the north. Because of the appearance of white quartz in this area, the first mile or so of this trail is locally referred to as White Rocks, while the landmark, White Rock, is at 2,400 feet in elevation, just under 2 miles north of the trailhead. Your turn-around point is the unmistakable Snow Hole, a deep fissure at 2.75 miles from the start.

From the trailhead parking area, head north and climb a short distance, passing the prettiest trail kiosk you've ever seen as you enter Hopkins Memorial Forest. What a difference this privately managed forest makes from

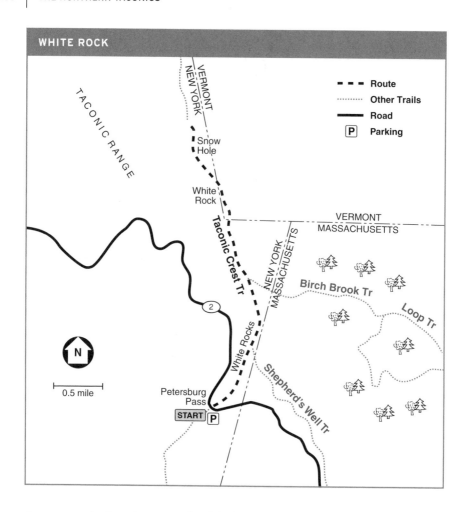

WHITE ROCK

the contrastingly, mismanaged public lands of south-lying Berlin Mountain. There's a map posted here, along with a box of trail maps.

The TCT is marked with white diamonds against a blue background. Marking is often scarce but the trail is well defined. To the left (west) above this initial steep rise, a short herd trail leads to an overlook. Continue as the trail flattens out, passing a spring on the right. At the 0.5-mile point, you will pass the Shepherd's Well Trail on your right (signed). The trail remains mostly level now, making its way through thick mats of hay-scented fern and an overstory of hardwoods, where a few apple trees appear, escapees from the early subsistence farms that covered the eastern slopes in the town of Williamstown. (The upper elevation western slopes are too steep to farm.)

At 1.1 miles, the Birch Brook Trail (also signed) appears on the right, and descends to the Upper Loop Trail in Hopkins Memorial Forest (Trip 29).

The Taconic Crest Trail provides interesting views to the west.

Climb the TCT, up a long, easy ascent to a point where the trail divides in a patch of ferns, where you may notice an unmarked logging trail leading to the right, to private lands. Continue left on the TCT, where the forest cover diminishes to the west, revealing views to the southwest of Berlin Mountain (2,828 feet) and west. Just ahead another 5 minutes, there's another viewpoint with a fire ring or two, and finally, after walking through Vermont for a while, a third (and best) lookout at White Rock. An old sign here is barely recognizable and not long for this world. Views to the west across the Hudson Valley are far reaching, including the northern Catskills and the Helderbergs. You're about an hour and a half into the hike at this point.

Continuing, the TCT begins to descend. In 10 minutes or so, look for red trail markers to the right. Avoid this trail; it is the southerly end of the nameless loop trail around the Snow Hole, now faint and unmaintained. Instead continue on the TCT to a point where the better-marked northerly part of the red trail appears on the right. There is an informal hand-painted sign indicating the Snow Hole. Follow the red trail to the right, a few hundred feet to the

Snow Hole, an unlikely looking, deep fissure that emits cool air. This crack is said to hold snow through the summer, or well into it, and has proven a curiosity over time. Old etchings scrawled by early visitors are inscribed among newer, poorer ones. The Hole is sometimes "spelunked" by caving enthusiasts who warn against doing so without proper guidance and equipment. It seems odd to think that such an isolated spot in the woods would ever have been discovered at all, until you realize that this was all open pastureland—70 percent or more of it cleared for graze by the 1700s.

Hikers will appreciate the nature of the self-limiting terrain and careful management that has acted to limit abuse by all-terrain vehicles (ATVs) in Hopkins Memorial Forest. Just across the pass to the south in New York State, Berlin Mountain (originally a candidate for this book) has been badly impacted and consciously abused by unchecked ATV use, including pick-up trucks. The level of trail damage—and the failure of state forest management to enforce protection of these public lands—is the worst I've ever seen in any state forest.

Turn around here, retracing your footsteps to your point of origin in Petersburg Pass, passing, along the way, lumps of white rock contrasting against the green ferns.

THE TACONIC HIKING CLUB

The oldest and most active hiking club in the Taconics (1932), with the exception of the Williams Outing Club of Williams College (1873), the Taconic Hiking Club (THC) is the guardian spirit of the Taconic Crest Trail. The THC leads outings each weekend throughout the year in a variety of activities (hiking, canoeing, biking, cross-country skiing, and snowshoeing) in the Adirondacks, Catskills, and Berkshires.

The club initiated the Taconic Crest Trail in 1948. The THC offers an end-to-end hike and patch, and leads a supported thru-hike of the trail every other year. They also offer a winter patch. A newsletter is provided with an annual membership fee of $10. THC conducts socials and events with other regional hiking groups, and within its own membership of 150 hikers.

The club publishes the *Taconic Crest Trail Guide and Map Set*, available in some nearby retailers, and by mail (see introduction).

6

THE CATSKILLS

The Catskills, in the high mountain parts, are a plateau, a land of folk tales and very interesting old people in the back areas on doubtful looking roads.

—A.T. Shorey, DEC employee, circa 1950

THE CATSKILLS ARE THE LARGEST GEOLOGICAL PROVINCE described in this guide. They occupy 1,102 square miles (705,500 acres; 287,514 of these publicly owned), and next to the Adirondacks (6 million acres), are the highest and most rugged mountains in the state. Slide Mountain (4,205 feet) in the central high peaks area is the highest peak, and there are over 100 peaks in the Catskills above 3,000 feet in elevation. In spite of their rugged appearance and character, the Catskills are not mountains in strict geological terms, that is, the result of tectonic collision. Instead they are a dissected plateau, formed by the erosive action of rivers and streams when vast sheets of thick glacial ice melted and retreated along a north-south axis. The rivers that were defined at that point remain today. The Schoharie Creek drains the plateau to the north, a tributary of the Hudson River via the Mohawk. To the east, the Rondout, Esopus, and Kaaterskill creeks join the Hudson. To the south and west, the Delaware and Neversink rivers form the major drainages.

The rocks found in the Catskill plateau are relatively soft, consisting mainly of the sands and gravels deposited in the rivers and shallow seas of the Devonian Period, about 350 million years ago. These sands and gravels became the sandstones and conglomerates that have been uplifted and tilted. However, they have not been significantly folded, faulted, or changed by igneous and metamorphic activity. Thus they differ from many other mountain ranges such as the Appalachians or the Adirondacks.

The Catskills may have been a peneplain (almost a plain) at sea level before they were uplifted to their present elevation. The deep dissection (erosion) occurred when streams were rejuvenated during uplift. The resistant rocks remained, while the softer strata washed away. In some regions joint patterns in the rock controlled erosion to produce the deep cloves (clefts) and wildly scenic hollows that steeped the Catskills in mystery and romance, and contributed to the art and literary imagination of early America.

The uplift of the Devonian sediments took place in several stages, and the Miocene and later stages were influenced by several episodes of Pleistocene glaciation. Today the higher peaks are located where the uplift was greatest and where their conglomerate sandstones were able to resist erosion by the advance of the continental ice sheets and later by glacial meltwaters.

What is perhaps most interesting about the underlying geology of the Catskills is the soil and hence the vegetation that flourishes there. The region represents the southernmost occurrence of boreal coniferous forests on glaciated uplands in North America. In contrast with this summit forest of spruce fir and paper birch is the valley forest type, known as the Carolinian Zone Forest, which consists of oaks, hickories, occasional black birch, tulip trees, and, until recently, chestnut. According to Catskills ecologist Michael Kudish, "The proximity of the Carolinian and Canadian zones, especially in the eastern Catskills, together with the effects of man over two centuries, produces a rich, diverse flora, and creates a vegetation so complex that it nearly defies explanation."

While they are unique florally and geologically, the Catskills have yet another distinguishing characteristic: their youth. All the surrounding ranges are considerably older. To the east lie the 450-million-year-old Taconics, formed during a continental collision that displaced older sediments in a period called the Taconic Orogeny.

South of the Catskills are the Shawangunks, and although they are close to the Taconics in age, their evolution is more related to the Catskills. Extensive sands and quartz-rich gravels were deposited in a shallow sea during the Silurian Period, about 450 million years ago. Much later the resulting sandstones and conglomerates were uplifted and differentially eroded.

After the Contact Period and its destructive consequences for the indigenous people of the valley, these same people sold for pittances large blocks of lands that were then "granted" to small groups of patentees. The largest of these was the Hardenburgh Patent, a grant by Queen Anne of England of over 2 million acres of Catskill wilderness to Johannes Hardenburgh and six other men in 1708. The lands were leased to tenant farmers who struggled to make a living in the rocky and inhospitable mountain areas. For the next hundred years or so, the Catskills remained agricultural. Very little westward expansion was undertaken during the period before the Revolution—people were afraid to invest money without knowing the future political landscape, and there were still Indian worries. But with the 1781 capitulation of the British, and the remainder of General Washington's troops still in New Windsor, the Catskills began to grow. Farm products grown in the Catskills were shipped to New York City on sloops. Dairy products and fruit followed wheat. In 1825, the Erie Canal opened, creating a widening market and turning a good deal of commerce away from Canada. Gristmills turned to steam power by the middle of the eighteenth century, and by 1840, over 100 steamships plied the Hudson, offering twenty-hour, $5 round-trips from Albany to New York. With the introduction of the tanning industry, roads were built. By the late 1700s, a road led from Schoharie to Prattsville, coming in from the west. The Escarpment was still an obstacle to early road builders who worked by hand. Eventually, these roads reached the Hudson River at Malden, near Saugerties, and the full exploitation of the Eastern Catskills by the tanlords and quarrymen was underway. With the completion of roads into Dutcher Notch in the north and Stony Clove to the southwest, the Catskills were exposed to the full force of the extractive resource industries of tanning and later, bluestone quarrying. Still, by the mid-eighteenth century, permanent settlement of the original Hardenburgh Patent was limited. Rent was too high and farmers were just scraping by. Ultimately finding the rents crippling, the farmers organized and resisted making the payments; they banded together in disguise, calling themselves the "calico Indians," and began the so-called Anti-Rent Wars (1839–1845). Ultimately, members of the anti-rent movement were elected to office and the great Hardenburgh Patent was dissolved.

Alongside the tanbark industry, and later, commercial bluestone quarrying, the great era of hotel tourism began on the high Catskill ledges. Hotel owners were uneasy about the destruction these industries wrought upon their saleable assets—namely the scenic beauty and, less and less it seemed, the peace and serenity of the wilderness. The Catskill Mountain House set the standard for leisure tourism as early as 1823 when it opened on the Escarpment in Haines Falls, the same year that James Fenimore Cooper, then 34 years old, published the fourth of his popular romantic Leatherstocking Tales, *The Pioneers*. This was relatively early in terms of new American literature. Thoreau was 6 years old. His mentor, William Ellery Channing, was in his 40s (Channing's ideas helped to formulate Transcendentalism, which in turn contributed forcefully to the preservation movement). William Cullen Bryant was 29 years old, Washington Irving, nearing 40. Thomas Cole, the British-born founder of America's fist recognized school of painting (and a poet in his own right) was a lad of 21. The English Romantic poets, Coleridge and Wordsworth, were middle-aged. Even William Blake was alive (died 1827). Cooper's fictional hero, Natty Bumppo, was himself on the threshold of old age, lamenting what the Catskill hoteliers seemed already to realize: The wilderness he so loved—and for which he waxed so eloquently—was fast disappearing. No doubt, Cooper knew all about the Hardenburgh Patent and wrote his tales of a vanishing wilderness with just such things in mind. The mountain houses enjoyed exclusivity until the Gilded Age of the steamship, railroad, and horse and buggy gave way to the automobile. Some of the more successful mountain and valley boarding houses hung on into the middle 1900s.

The biggest dividend the patent would yield was not for its patentees—even less for its farmers, but for the unintended preservation of open space, a fact that led directly to the creation of the Catskill Forest Preserve. In 1885, by an act of Congress, the forest preserve was created in the Adirondacks and the Catskills, leading to the famous "forever wild" clause in the state's constitution: "All lands now owned or which may hereafter be acquired by the State of New York . . . shall be forever kept as wild forest lands." Many people feared that the kind of deforestation that characterized the leather tanning industry and later the chair, glass, and charcoal production industries that used second-growth hardwoods following hemlock deforestation, would denude the Catskills' slopes and threaten the region's water quality.

The state responded with a progressive acquisition policy and annexed additional lands to the preserve. By 1887, there was a log observatory on Balsam Lake Mountain. In 1892, the state financed the first trail up Slide Mountain. The Catskill Park was created in 1904, and the first fire tower appeared in 1905, replacing the original log structure on Balsam Lake Mountain. Between 1926 and 1931, four public campsites were created. President Roosevelt formed the Civilian Conservation Corps (CCC) in 1933, which led to a vast reforestation and trail building era. In the ensuing years, the park grew. State commissions were formed to strengthen acquisition and management policies, and to develop land-use classifications. Master plans were designed, historic preservation and open-space projects were developed, and heritage initiatives were funded and continue to be.

Today, in the four forest-preserve counties of Delaware, Greene, Sullivan, and Ulster, there are 143,000 acres of wilderness, 130,000 acres of wild forest, and 5,200 acres of intensive-use lands. There are 7 campgrounds, 303 miles of hiking trails, 76 miles of snowmobile trails, 30 miles of horse trails, 33 lean-tos, and 187 primitive campsites. Based on recent trail register sign-ins, a half million people use the forest preserve annually.

LONG-DISTANCE TRAILS IN THE CATSKILLS

There are three trunk trails contained within the forest preserve itself (the Escarpment, the Devil's Path, and the Delaware Ridge trails, each roughly 25 miles long). Two longer regional trunk trails, the Long Path and the Finger Lakes Trail, pass through it. (See the Long Path sidebar on page 248.)

The Finger Lakes Trail (FLT) is incomplete at this time, with the exception of the main trunk section in the Catskills. Planned to connect the Allegheny Mountains with the Catskills using the most remote sections of New York State's Southern Tier, the trail will provide hikers with the opportunity to hike nearly the entire length of New York State. Now complete in the Catskills, the FLT uses existing DEC-marked trails, with the FLT logo at trailheads and trail junctions. At this time the trail passes through the Delaware Wild Forest, the Balsam Lake Mountain Wild Forest, the Big Indian Wilderness, and the Slide Mountain Wilderness.

NYS DEC DIVISION OF LANDS AND FORESTS

For further information contact:

Central Office, NYS DEC
625 Broadway
Albany, NY 12233
518-402-9405
www.dec.state.ny.us

The DEC manages the New York State Forest Preserve lands of the Catskills and detached parcels of state land outside the Catskills. The DEC is responsible for search and rescue, planning for management, supervision of campsites, and issuing of camping permits. (Unless expressly prohibited, campers may stay for up to three nights in one location on state land without a permit and may apply for a permit for longer stays. Permits are required for groups of ten or more.) The DEC also publishes an official regional trail map and guide (*The Catskill Park*). However, because each state region is run independently, it is easiest to obtain local information from one of the regional offices listed below.

NYS DEC Region 3 (Ulster and Sullivan counties)
21 S. Putts Corners Rd.
New Paltz, NY 12561
845-256-3000

NYS DEC Region 4 Sub Office (Delaware and Greene counties)
65561 State Highway 10
Stamford, NY 12167
607-652-7365

NYS DEC Region 4 Headquarters
1150 N. Westcott Rd.
Schenectady, NY 12306
518-357-2066

JOHN BURROUGHS

John Burroughs (1837–1921)–naturalist, poet, and essayist–is generally regarded as the guardian spirit of the Catskills, the John Muir of the East. From his boyhood on a farm in Roxbury, New York, to his later years at Riverby in West Park on the Hudson, he rose to international prominence as a spokesman for American wilderness. Most of his writing was done at his handmade cabin, Slabsides, built in 1895, now a National Historic Landmark. Visitors to the cabin included Theodore Roosevelt, John Muir, Thomas Edison, and Henry Ford.

In his lifetime, Burroughs had become the most popular author in the field of nature writing. He bridged the gap between the early Romantic artists and writers, alerting his readers to the more concrete, physical wonders of nature. He wrote *Wake-Robin* (1873) while a bank examiner and clerk in the treasury department, and followed with another 24 books, among them the first biographical volume on Walt Whitman (*Notes on Walt Whitman*).

There are 2.0 miles of hiking trails on the Burroughs Sanctuary, which is open year-round, and free of charge. Slabsides is open for tours on the third Saturday in May and the first Saturday in October. The sanctuary is located 10 miles south of Kingston, 0.5 mile off US 9W on Floyd Ackert Road in West Park, New York.

TRIP 32
SLIDE MOUNTAIN

RATING: Strenuous
DISTANCE: 7.0 miles
ELEVATION GAIN: 1,700 feet
ESTIMATED TIME: 5.5 hours
MAPS: USGS Phoenicia; USGS Shandaken; AMC Catskill Mountains; NY-NJTC Southern Catskills

A day-long hike up the Catskills highest peak in the Slide Mountain Wilderness area. Very scenic.

DIRECTIONS
From Exit 19 of the NYS Thruway (I-87) in Kingston, take NY 28 west 31 miles to CR 47 (Slide Mountain Road) in Big Indian. Set your odometer to zero. Turn left (south) on CR 47, passing the Giant Ledge trailhead at 7.3 miles, and Winnisook Lake at 8.4 miles. At 9.0 miles park at the Slide Mountain trailhead parking lot on the left side of Slide Mountain Road.

TRAIL DESCRIPTION
John Burroughs would never have suspected that the mountain, which had so successfully defied his climbing efforts in the early 1880s, would become the Catskills' most popular peak. In Burroughs's time, Slide (4,180 feet) was, as he suggested, "probably the most inaccessible; certainly the hardest to get a view of, it is hedged about so completely by other peaks, the greatest mountain of them all and apparently the least willing to be seen; only at a distance of 30 or 40 miles is it seen to stand up above all other peaks." Yet within a few years of Burroughs's 1885 ascent, Jim Dutcher, a bark peeler living at the foot of the mountain, introduced the mountain to hikers. Some of Dutcher's trail (constructed in 1886, with many stone steps) remains to this day, but it leads onto the private lands of the Winnisook Club.

There are several popular approaches to Slide, but the easiest (and fastest) route is from the northwesterly Slide Mountain trailhead parking area, using a combination of the Phoenicia–East Branch Trail (PE, yellow markers), the Wittenberg-Cornell-Slide Trail (WS, red markers), and the Curtis-Ormsbee Trail (CO, blue markers). For the final ascent you again join the WS Trail.

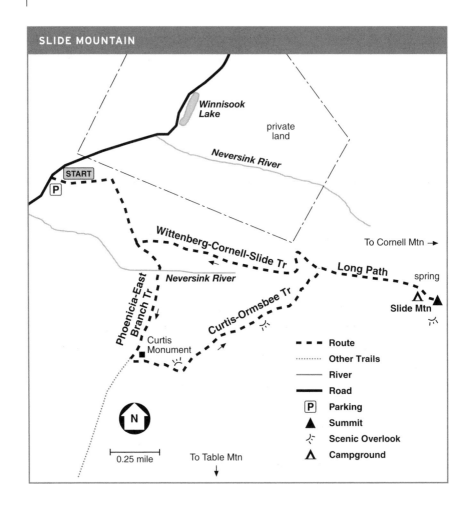

SLIDE MOUNTAIN

Winnisook Lake

private land

Neversink River

START

P

To Cornell Mtn →

Wittenberg-Cornell-Slide Tr

Long Path

spring

Neversink River

Slide Mtn

Phoenicia-East Branch Tr

Curtis-Ormsbee Tr

Curtis Monument

- - - Route
.... Other Trails
——— River
—— Road
P Parking
▲ Summit
Scenic Overlook
△ Campground

N

0.25 mile

To Table Mtn ↓

Orient yourself at the map kiosk, and locate the yellow-marked PE Trail. Once afoot you immediately cross the upper reaches of the Neversink's West Branch (often dry here, but can present a problem at very high water), which flows into the Delaware River. Originating on Slide's northwest watershed is the Esopus, running down through Big Indian Hollow into Phoenicia and the Ashokan Reservoir water supply, its "wastewater" continuing to the Hudson.

Ascend through a stand of maples over rocks and roots, up a flight of stone steps, and within 15 minutes bear right at the T, following a level jeep trail (a.k.a. the Truck Trail, the Bridle Path, the Firetower Trail). After 5 minutes on this section, you pass a spring on the left side. Soon you arrive at a junction with the red-marked WS Trail that goes off to the left. (The WS Trail follows the old truck trail up Slide Mountain. It is the shortest way up, but it's rocky

Slide Mountain, king of the Catskills, from the western shoulder of Cornell Mountain.

and without views. Instead, this road will be used for the descent.) Continue straight ahead on the yellow-marked PE Trail. Cross a wooden bridge over an unnamed tributary of the Neversink's West Branch. From here, the trail climbs slightly. In another 15 minutes you'll reach the Curtis-Ormsbee Trail (this is the Long Path). Bear left, following blue markers.

Note the vandalized stone monument near the junction. William "Father Bill" Curtis and Allen Ormsbee, for whom the trail was named, both died of hypothermia caused by a sudden snowstorm on Mount Washington, New Hampshire, in the summer of 1900. They were on their way up the mountain to attend a meeting of the Appalachian Mountain Club. This trail was laid out to commemorate them. (It's good to bear in mind that these men were among the most experienced hikers of their time, and still, they were caught unprepared.)

The trail ascends. Soon you will arrive at a small ledge with westerly views, including Doubletop, Graham, Wildcat, and various peaks in the Big Indian Wilderness Area. In another 15 minutes, after a steep but short climb, you encounter a beautiful viewpoint to the north. The trail now levels off, soon passing the 3,500-foot sign, and within 5 minutes, a short, marked spur trail to the right leads 200 feet to an outstanding overlook at 3,550 feet. Below and ahead of you is the valley of the East Branch of the Neversink River. Table Mountain, distinguished by its long, flat summit, is directly ahead, and Lone Mountain is to its left. You also see Rocky and Balsam Cap. With binoculars, you can see High Point Monument on the Kittatinny Ridge in New Jersey. You'll probably want to rest here for a few minutes and savor the spectacular view.

After leaving the viewpoint, the trail remains relatively level for a while and then resumes its ascent of Slide's southwestern slopes in thick spruce-fir forest. Within 40 minutes of the previous lookout, following a fairly steep climb, you arrive at the junction of the WS Trail.

Bear right (east). This section of trail is relatively flat, and you have only about another 200 feet of elevation gain and an additional 20 minutes of hiking before you reach Slide's summit. Extensive views appear from a northeast-facing outcropping on the left of the trail. Continue ahead to the summit, passing the site of the former fire tower to arrive at a flat rock with good views to the east. (In Burroughs' time, the encroaching spruce-fir forest had been cut down.) Ahead of you and just to the left are Cornell and Wittenberg mountains, and the Ashokan Reservoir is visible beyond. Directly below the ledge, affixed to the rock face is a plaque commemorating John Burroughs, which reads in part: "Here the works of man dwindle in the heart of the southern Catskills."

Slide's views include nearly 70 named Catskill peaks as well as a wide view of the Hudson Valley, Green Mountains, Berkshires, Taconics, Hudson Highlands, and Shawangunks. This is the same view that Commissioner Cox, climbing Slide in 1886 (to recognize the Catskills as members of the New York State Forest Preserve), pronounced to be "every bit as fine as anything to be seen in the Adirondacks." Slide was not recognized as the Catskills' highest peak until Arnold Guyot, a Princeton professor of geology, published his map of 1879. Previously, Kaaterskill High Peak and later Hunter Mountain competed for the title in the days when a carpenter's level was the critical tool used for measuring mountains.

Highly recommended is a short descent (off route) to a year-round spring, ahead on the WS Trail, 200 feet lower in elevation and about a twenty-minute hike beyond Slide's summit along the trail (as if continuing to Cornell Mountain). The trail switches back across Slide's eastern face before descending two flights of log stairs, after which the spring appears at the end of an unmarked spur on the left.

To return to your car, retrace your steps on the red-marked WS Trail, leaving the CO Trail to your left and continuing on the red markers. Writers and historians have commented on the presence of white quartz here, giving the trail the appearance of a "garden path." Where this stratum of rock continues into Pennsylvania, it is overlain with anthracite coal. Geologists believe that if the Catskills were 500 feet higher, they would have contained coal.

Descend for 40 minutes or so over the rocky footpath. Soon after passing a designated campsite on the left, you arrive at the junction with the yellow-marked PE Trail, which you'll recognize. Turn right and follow the yellow markers to the next T (the trail continues to Winnisook lands and is usually barricaded with sticks), where you bear left and descend to the parking lot.

BICKNELL'S THRUSH

A regular visitor to Slide Mountain in the later years of the nineteenth century, John Burroughs noted, "Slide Mountain enjoys a distinction which no other mountain in the state—so far as I know, does—it has a thrush peculiar to itself." Burroughs would later learn of the work of amateur ornithologist Eugene Bicknell, who collected a species of thrush on Slide in 1881. Bicknell shot for collection what he thought was a gray-cheeked thrush, but on further examination, and to the ornithological community's surprise, it seems Bicknell had discovered a new species. The taxonomic status of the thrush remained in question for a long time, however, until recent DNA examinations confirmed that the Bicknell's and gray-cheeked thrush shared no common ancestor in the last million years. Not until 1995 did the American Ornithological Union's Committee on Classification and Nomenclature grant full species status to Bicknell's thrush.

The thrush is in general a very shy and reclusive species. Bicknell's thrush, said to be the shiest of them all, is found only in the high boreal "fog forests" like Slide Mountain's. It is seldom seen in the open, and is small—the size of a sparrow, olive-brown, gray and white underneath, and yellow at the base of the lower bill. It can be distinguished by its song, a higher, throatier sound than the gray-cheeked thrush, a thing both Bicknell and Burroughs noted as peculiar to the species.

Burroughs reserved his finest prose to describe it: "It is . . . a musical whisper of great sweetness and power. It seemed as if the bird was blowing in a delicate, slender golden tube, so fine and yet so flutelike and resonant the song appeared . . . a strain as fine as if blown on a fairy flute . . . it was of the purest harmony. It was but the soft hum of the balsams, interpreted and embodied in a bird's voice."

TRIP 33
WITTENBERG AND CORNELL MOUNTAINS

RATING: Strenuous
DISTANCE: 9.4 miles
ELEVATION GAIN: 2,480 feet
ESTIMATED TIME: 7 hours
MAPS: USGS Phoenicia; USGS Shandaken; AMC Catskill Mountains;
NY-NJTC Southern Catskills

A steep climb from the rustic Woodland Valley to an area that is a favorite of many Catskill hikers.

DIRECTIONS
From NY 28 and NY 214 in Phoenicia, drive 0.6 mile west on NY 28 to Woodland Valley Road. Follow Woodland Valley Road to its terminus at the Woodland Valley Campsite (4.8 miles). The trailhead parking area is located opposite the campsite, 0.1 mile east of the campground entrance.

TRAIL DESCRIPTION
Wittenberg Mountain (a.k.a. The Wittenberg, 3,780 feet) is a favorite among hikers who regard its scenery as among the Catskills' finest. A key figure in the skyline peaks of the Burroughs Range (Slide, Wittenberg, and Cornell), Wittenberg's popularity, based on hiker registrations, lags only slightly behind that of Slide, the Catskill's highest peak, and nearby Giant Ledge, the shortest scenic hike in the Slide/Panther Wilderness Area. An interesting side trip with open views to the northeast (or for camping) is reached from the Terrace Mountain Trail (TM), a short hike from its junction with the Wittenberg-Cornell-Slide Trail (WS).

Park in the hikers' parking area on the north side of Woodland Valley Road, and pay the (seasonal) parking fee at the campsite office 0.2 mile farther along the road. ($4 at this writing.) Note that the WS Trail does not leave directly from this parking lot, but from the south side of Woodland Valley Road. From the parking area and map kiosk, walk across the road and bear left, keeping the campsite to your right. Within 300 feet, you'll find the red-marked WS Trail on the right. Follow the red markers into the campsite area, bearing left along the edge of Site 46, and cross Woodland Valley Creek on the wooden bridge. The trail ascends at once, soon passing the trail register and climbing thereafter

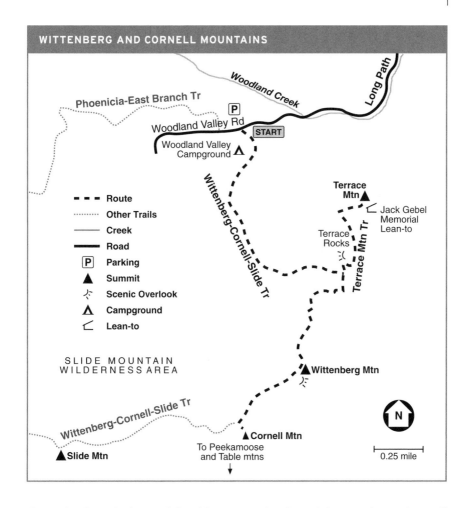

WITTENBERG AND CORNELL MOUNTAINS

Woodland Creek

Long Path

Phoenicia-East Branch Tr

P

Woodland Valley Rd

START

Woodland Valley Campground ▲

Terrace Mtn ▲

Jack Gebel Memorial Lean-to

Terrace Mtn Tr

Wittenberg-Cornell-Slide Tr

Terrace Rocks

- - - Route
.... Other Trails
——— Creek
▬▬▬ Road
P Parking
▲ Summit
𝅘 Scenic Overlook
Λ Campground
∠ Lean-to

SLIDE MOUNTAIN
WILDERNESS AREA

▲ Wittenberg Mtn

N

Wittenberg-Cornell-Slide Tr

▲ Slide Mtn

▲ Cornell Mtn

To Peekamoose and Table mtns

0.25 mile

through a heavily forested, boulder-strewn hardwood forest. The trail is well marked here, but because of its many boulders, it is not always self-guiding. Keep an eye on the red foot-trail discs.

After 20 minutes of hiking, you'll note the dramatic change in forest type to a nearly pure hemlock stand on a flat ledge at 1,950 feet, with spare, seasonal views to the east. Late-coming backpackers will find many suitable places to camp in the hardwood flats to the right (west) of the trail as they continue past the hemlock stand. After this welcome break, the ascent resumes and a seasonal brook is crossed before the trail switches back hard to the left at an obscure arrow (south southeast). The ascent continues, not as steeply now, through attractive hemlock ledges and soon relaxes, becoming nearly level as the trail turns east southeast along Wittenberg's northern flanks at 2,700 feet. Often lively but nameless seasonal brooks increase in volume as you travel east. Beyond the last of these you'll enter the transition zone from mixed northern hardwoods to stunted paper birch and spruce-fir, and suddenly the trail junction appears in the low saddle between Wittenberg and Terrace. At this point, you are one and a half hours or more into the hike. Wittenberg is 1.3 miles to the right (south and 1,100 feet higher), and the Terrace Lean-to is 0.9 mile to the left (north, 200 feet lower) on the yellow-marked Terrace Mountain Trail (TE).

Since the removal of the very well-loved, old suspension bridge in Woodland Valley (which many hikers still remember crossing on the old trailhead to Slide Mountain), Terrace Mountain has seen few visitors. However, a 10-minute detour on the TE Trail from the WS/TE junction will prove an interesting diversion, bringing you to a fine place to rest and eat while enjoying the excellent views from the high side of Terrace Rocks. Twenty minutes beyond the Rocks is the Jack Gebel Memorial Lean-to, erected by the Adirondack Mountain Club in 1998. On the grassy flats of Terrace's treed-in "terrace" there is room for a dozen or more tents. Backpackers who plan to visit Wittenberg (but not Slide) will find the terrace a closer and more practical choice for camping than the designated sites in the col between Cornell and Slide (see Trip 32).

The ascent to Wittenberg from the WS/TE Trail junction is characterized by attractive (albeit steep), terraced ascents, sedimentary rock ledges, and penetrating vertical crevices. The forest cover will have changed notably into spruce and fir at 3,000 feet. Within 45 minutes to one hour of fairly strenuous hiking from the junction, you will arrive at the summit, an east-facing, exposed ledge. Although not panoramic, Wittenberg's view encompasses a 180-degree hemisphere of mountain and valley extending north over the Devil's Path Range and the Escarpment, east over the Hudson and Taconics, and south over an expanse of hills and valleys, where the Gunks taper off into endless flatlands. To the southwest the hiker is enticed by intimate observations of the nearby peaks of Peekamoose and Table, along with the trailless Lone, Rocky, Balsam Cap, and Friday, each of the latter being popular bushwhacking summits above 3,500 feet. In the eastern lowlands, hikers will see the Ashokan Reservoir (part of New York City's water supply), the impoundment created by the damming of the Esopus Creek. Wittenberg's summit impressed John Burroughs, who reached it after a "long and desperate" attempt at Slide: "The view from The Wittenberg is in many respects more striking, as you are perched immediately above a broader and more distant sweep of country . . . and the earth falls away at your feet and curves through an immense stretch of forest until it joins the plain of Shokan, and thence sweeps away to the Hudson and beyond."

Climbing a ledge on the ascent to Cornell Mountain.

After experiencing Wittenberg, you may feel up to the short hike to Cornell (add 30 minutes each way) via the "Bruin's Causeway," an interesting, boreal section of the WS Trail. As you gain Cornell's summit (requiring the ascent of one low but nearly vertical ledge that can be hazardous in icy conditions) a short, unmarked spur trail to the left will take you to the summit. This is Cloud Cliff, the site of an illegal, impacted campsite with limited views. Only Cornell's nearby westerly shoulder provides a good view to the west, including the slide on Slide's north side that occurred around 1820. To see this memorable view, proceed west 0.1 mile on the trail as if hiking to Slide.

This trail and its dedication to John Burroughs dates back to 1880, when the naturalist haunted the range, relating anecdotes of the porcupines in volume six of his complete nature writings, *Riverby*. And if you've dropped your pack off on Cornell's summit to find the westerly view of Slide, don't be surprised to discover the omnivorous quill pig sorting through its contents.

Return the way you came.

TRIP 34
GIANT LEDGE

RATING: Moderate

DISTANCE: 3.0 miles

ELEVATION GAIN: 1,000 feet

ESTIMATED TIME: 2.5 hours

MAPS: USGS Phoenicia; AMC Catskill Mountains; NY-NJTC
Southern Catskills

**A short and rewarding hike to the scenic cliffs of a glacial cirque in
the epicenter of an ancient meteorite impact zone.**

DIRECTIONS

At the intersection of NY 28 and CR 47 (Slide Mountain Road) in Big Indian,
set your odometer to zero, turn left and drive south on CR 47, to the Giant
Ledge trailhead at 7.3 miles.

TRAIL DESCRIPTION

This fairly short, rewarding hike will take you to the vertical lip of a glacial
cirque in the heart of the Catskill High Peaks area. The Giant Ledge–Panther
Mountain–Fox Hollow Trail (GP) to Giant Ledge has become extremely popular with day-hikers and backpackers, so expect company, especially on weekends. Aside from its tremendous appeal as a scenic destination hike, Giant
Ledge is an ideal overnight trip for those new to backpacking or wishing to
"shake down" for longer outings.

Giant Ledge (3,200 feet), so-named for its vertical cliffs, forms the lower,
southerly ridge of Panther Mountain (3,720 feet). On the east it is flanked
by the extensive wilds of Woodland Valley and the Slide Mountain Wilderness Area, and to the west, by the Big Indian Wilderness Area. It is here that
the Esopus Creek (an important source of New York City's drinking water)
gains momentum, nurtured within Panther's long ridge and the west-lying Big
Indian Valley with its Bavarian-style homesteads and rustic mountain hotels.

The trail to Giant Ledge begins across the road from the parking lot where
it is well identified. Enter the woods and follow the yellow markers of the
Phoenicia–East Branch Trail. Within 300 feet of the road you'll see the trail
register and information kiosk. The initial section of trail climbs steeply at
times, over a rough and rocky footway, crosses a streambed (seasonal) on a

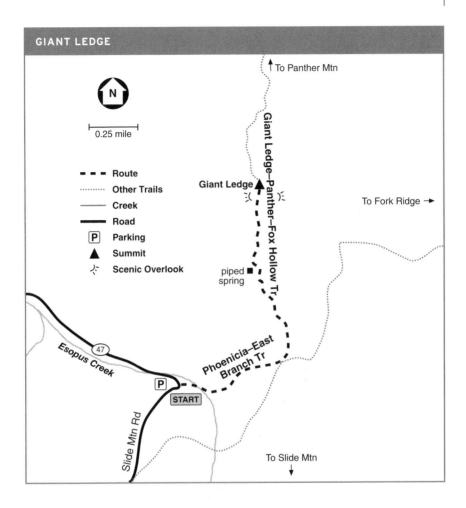

GIANT LEDGE

To Panther Mtn

0.25 mile

Route
Other Trails
Creek
Road
P   Parking
▲   Summit
⚘   Scenic Overlook

Giant Ledge ▲

Giant Ledge–Panther–Fox Hollow Tr.

To Fork Ridge →

piped ■
spring

Esopus Creek
47

Phoenicia–East Branch Tr.

P

START

Slide Mtn Rd

To Slide Mtn

wooden bridge, and again ascends through a hardwood forest. The rest of the hike is easier, except for the last short pitch to the ledges.

Within 20 minutes or so of rigorous ascent, the trail flattens out at 2,700 feet in the col between Slide and Panther mountains. Avoid the faint, unmarked trail to your right at this point, that heads southwest across the lands of the Winnisook Club (this is a legal and significant shortcut to the Slide Mountain trailhead for hikers doing the "loop" from Woodland Valley across the Burroughs Range). Bear left here, and within a stone's throw you will be at the trail junction where the PE Trail heads for Woodland Valley, passing the blue-marked GP Trail to Giant Ledge. Bear left again (north) on the GP Trail, following blue markers now. The trail is flat for a while, and hops across a series of stones where the footway is often muddy. These conditions vanish as the trail rises again, ascending a long set of stone steps to arrive at a Y. At this

Barry Knight, an Overlook Mountain fire tower steward, spots the Overlook Tower from Giant Ledge.

point a spur trail marked Spring goes left (west) 600 feet to a piped spring. (Pass the first small pool of water appearing next to a boulder and continue to the pipe. This is the only reliable water source on the GP between here and Fox Hollow.) Bear right over level ground for a while and then ascend steeply as the trail rises to ridge elevation, where the first of several herd trails leads to a ledge on your right (east). Explore more lookouts to the north along the trail, each of them very exposed and dangerous, most of them poised on fractured sandstone ledges above high, vertical drops. The views are spectacular.

From these easterly points, you look toward Fork Ridge and into Woodland Valley, with Terrace, Cornell, and Wittenberg to your right (southwest). To the northeast you can identify the lower peaks of Garfield and Sheridan, with Romer to the east and Tremper beyond it, including various peaks of the Devil's Path Range from northeast to east. You can see (usually you'll need binoculars) three of the Catskills' five fire towers from here: Overlook (easy to spot), Hunter (around the middle of the long ridge top to your left, northeast), and Mount Tremper (the cab can be seen sticking up between you and the col of Twin Mountain). From a point roughly in the middle of Giant Ledge, a trail leads to the west into the designated camping area, marked with yellow discs. Continue through the campsites—there are two crude fire rings—where you will discover a west-facing rock with a view revealing Hemlock, Spruce, Fir, Big Indian, Eagle, Haynes, Balsam, and Belleayre mountains in the Big Indian Wilderness Area. The appeal of Giant Ledge is that it's a short, fairly easy, and massively scenic hike. You're likely to find many friendly people wandering around or camping here on a nice weekend. But to have the place to yourself, plan to come on an off-season weekday.

Giant Ledge is predominantly forested with maple, beech, cherry, and birch, but at its north end there is a virgin spruce grove, extending to the ledge's base. A few remaining drought-killed red spruce can still be seen below the eastern cliffs. More recently, forest tent caterpillars and gypsy moths have defoliated much of the mid-elevation forest here, the long-term results of which remain to be seen.

Many hikers elect to continue to Panther's summit for a longer day's outing. Panther is another 1.75 miles beyond Giant Ledge and an additional 750 feet in cumulative elevation. If you'd like to extend your hike from Giant Ledge to Panther's summit, you have another 40 minutes of hiking (each way), dropping slightly downhill at first and then climbing vigorously through large boulders and thick hardwood forest. On the ascent you will have several views of Slide, Wittenberg, and Cornell as you cross open rock terraces, most of them similar if not inferior to Giant Ledge's. Panther's "summit," is a very small scenic outcropping beneath the true, viewless, fir-clad summit. The trail (completed in 1936) continues to the north and descends to the Fox Hollow trailhead. Most thru-hikers on the GP Trail spot a car at both ends. (Consult the AMC's *Catskill Mountain Guide* for details.)

From Giant Ledge, return the way you came.

TRIP 35
PEEKAMOOSE AND TABLE MOUNTAINS

RATING: Strenuous

DISTANCE: 10 miles

ELEVATION GAIN: 2,200 feet

ESTIMATED TIME: 5 hours

MAPS: USGS Peekamoose Mountain; AMC Catskill Mountains; NY-NJTC Southern Catskills

A remote wilderness hike to a pair of quiet boreal summits with southwesterly views.

DIRECTIONS

From NY 28 in Big Indian, go south on CR 47 through Oliverea, Winnisook, and Frost Valley, and turn left in Claryville onto CR 19 (Denning Road) to the trailhead parking area, a distance of some 30 miles from Big Indian. Alternately, from NY 28 in Boiceville, turn south on NY 28A 3 miles to West Shokan,

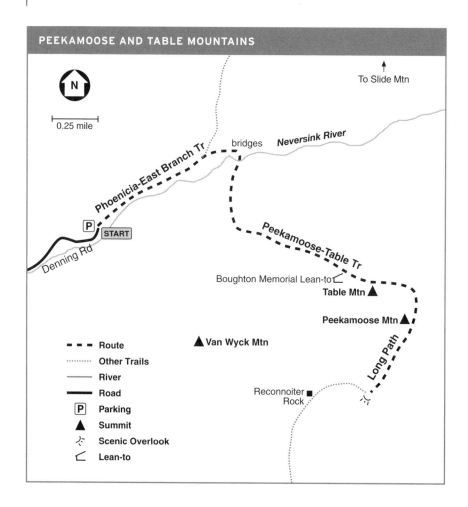

PEEKAMOOSE AND TABLE MOUNTAINS

N

0.25 mile

To Slide Mtn

Phoenicia-East Branch Tr

bridges Neversink River

P START

Denning Rd

Peekamoose-Table Tr

Boughton Memorial Lean-to

Table Mtn ▲

Peekamoose Mtn ▲

▲ Van Wyck Mtn

Long Path

Reconnoiter Rock ■

- - - Route
.... Other Trails
——— River
━━━ Road
P Parking
▲ Summit
⅄ Scenic Overlook
⊏ Lean-to

and turn right onto CR 42 (Peekamoose Road), passing the Peekamoose-Table trailhead 10 miles from West Shokan. Bear right into Grahamsville, Unionville, and Curry on NY 55, turning right at Curry to Claryville, and again right into Denning and to the trailhead, also a total of 30 miles. From NY 17 (the shortest approach to this area from the south) take NY 55 east from Liberty, turning north on CR 19 at Curry. Bear right (staying on CR 19) at Claryville, and follow Denning Road to the trailhead.

TRAIL DESCRIPTION

What will impress you most about Peekamoose and its environs are its storybook forests and the remarkable clarity of the Rondout Creek and Neversink River. The Rondout is conceived on the south- and east-facing slopes of Rocky, Lone, and Peekamoose mountains and is joined by the malachite waters of

Peekamoose and Table mountains as seen from the boreal Bruin's Causeway.

Peekamoose Lake as it swells through Bull Run and joins its east branch at Sundown. John Burroughs loved this flashy, pellucid brook, vowing, "If I were a trout I should ascend every stream till I found the Rondout." If you're coming from the west, you follow the Neversink's east branch from Claryville. It, too, is famous trout water.

The most popular approach to Peekamoose Mountain (3,843 feet) is from the southern trailhead in Sundown Wild Forest along the Peekamoose Road, and involves a 2,643-foot elevation gain within 3.5 miles. The recommended (and more interesting) Denning Trail, or Phoenicia–East Branch (PE) Trail, with its crossing at Deer Shanty Brook is the gentler and more scenic option, and it will save you a few hundred feet of (cumulative) elevation. If you wish only to climb Peekamoose (these days it has a better view than Table's), the trail from Peekamoose Road provides the shortest route. The distances and logistics of spotting a car at each trailhead make this an impractical hike to shuttle.

Park at the end of Denning Road where trail signs to Slide Mountain and the Denning Lean-to are posted. The setting is a high farming-valley plain with frequent plots of old-growth forest. You may see deer feeding close to the road here, where old apple trees provide them with seasonal treats.

Follow the PE Trail through a hemlock woods on an old woods road, crossing a small plank bridge and a small seasonal brook. Within 25 minutes you will reach a trail junction, where you turn right on the blue-marked Peekamoose-Table Trail. Go downhill into a wet area (seasonal), keeping an eye on the markers (blue) and continuing downhill to cross two log stringer bridges, one of which spans a dry bed at various times of year. This is the confluence of Deer Shanty Brook and the Neversink. The bridges are kept simple because these two creeks rise considerably during runoff, and they must be replaced frequently. Be careful crossing the stringers. The lean-to that existed mid-stream here has been removed as a non-conforming structure, due to its proximity to the creeks and the difficulty of siting a privy so close to a water source, but there are a few legal, designated campsites in the area. Most of the heavily impacted, old (illegal) sites along the banks of both Deer Shanty Brook and the Neversink have been closed for recovery.

Continue uphill through a lush forest of fern, oxalis, club moss, and huge birch. Within a half hour the trail will level somewhat, skirting a ridge exposing Woodhull and Van Wyck mountains to the southwest. The trail varies in pitch, generally gaining elevation as you go through thin stands of hardwood, climbing through broken rock ledges. Within 45 minutes of leaving the confluence, you reach a ledge among the cherry trees with a view of Peekamoose to the south. Several more spur trails lead to the right 20 or 30 feet off the trail, some with worthwhile views. Beware—these are dangerous ledges. Through the trees to the left (north) as you continue, you may see Slide and its neighboring peaks, and, as you gain in elevation, you'll identify Panther, parts of Giant Ledge, Lone, Rocky, Balsam Cap, and Friday. Just below the 3,500-foot mark (and a short way beyond a spur to a piped spring), a spur trail to the right leads to the Boughton Memorial Lean-to.

Within 2 hours of the Denning Lean-to you reach Table's summit (3,847 feet). There is no view here. At one time, a herd trail led to an extraordinary north-facing viewpoint, but this location has been lost over time, obscured by heavy spruce-fir growth. Several herd trails appear in the summit area, heading nowhere in particular and creating an undesirable pattern of sustained overuse.

Continue on the main trail to Peekamoose; you can see it ahead as you descend. Some faraway views are available along this downhill section of trail—extending beyond the Shawangunks and into the Highlands. Even Anthony's Nose and the deep gulch spanned by the Bear Mountain Bridge can be seen with binoculars, or good eyes.

As you drop into the fragrant, balsam saddle between Table and Peekamoose, the trail becomes wet, and within 10 minutes you begin climbing again. You may see a vague Y in the trail as you approach the summit of Peekamoose. Go right to reach the summit, where a large boulder sits in a small clearing surrounded by scrub evergreens. This boulder can be climbed for more views, but they are inferior to those ahead.

Continue south another 0.6 mile, following steeply downhill through a series of ledges and overlooks, following the backbone of a long ridge extending south southwest. Within half an hour of leaving the summit, following frequent blue trail markers, you will cross several open areas with interesting ledges and flats, to reach an outstanding viewpoint at 3,500 feet, exposing the Rondout, Neversink, and Mongaup valleys; Samson Mountain, Bangle Hill, Breath Hill, and Little Rocky; and some interesting ridges and peaks to the west, among them Big Indian, Doubletop, and Balsam Lake Mountain with its fire tower (319 degrees). Any additional descent to see the limited (seasonal) views from Reconnoiter Rock would be counterproductive—the views are better here on the high southern flanks of Peekamoose.

Return the way you came.

TRIP 36
ASHOKAN HIGH POINT

RATING: Moderate
DISTANCE: 7.5 miles
ELEVATION GAIN: 1,980 feet
ESTIMATED TIME: 5.5 hours
MAPS: USGS West Shokan; AMC Catskill Mountains; NY-NJTC Southern Catskills

A gradual climb to a scenic and extensive blueberry heath with intimate views of the high peaks.

DIRECTIONS

Turn south onto NY 28A from NY 28 in Boiceville, west of Kingston. (At this time, automobiles cannot use the Ashokan Reservoir route on Monument Road.) Follow NY 28A for 3.0 miles to West Shokan. Follow Peekamoose Road (NY 42) west. Reset to zero. At 4.0 miles, turn right into the Kanape Brook parking area. Cross the road to the footbridge and the trailhead.

TRAIL DESCRIPTION

The trail to Ashokan High Point (3,080 feet) follows an old but very well-built settlement road along hemlock-fringed Kanape Brook. Bluestone walls and ditches constructed by the Civilian Conservation Corps in the 1930s have protected the trail from erosion, and trail maintenance is carried out by a local Boy Scout troop from the Rip Van Winkle Council.

Follow the trail uphill through a slope forest of beech, birch, and maple, gently climbing up and away from Kanape Brook, to your right. Within 10 minutes you cross one of several stone culverts running under the trail, draining the northwest watershed of the mountain. These are structures you ordinarily won't see on Catskill trails. Several are entirely handmade; the ditch itself is lined and capped with large, flat stones. You will see some very attractive bluestone walls along this part of the trail, as well as some stone bridges

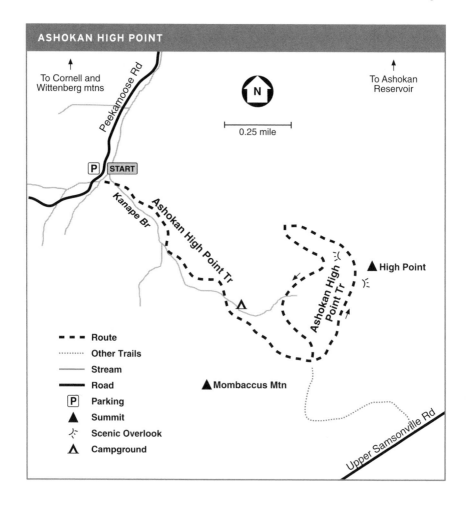

ASHOKAN HIGH POINT

To Cornell and
Wittenberg mtns

Peekamoose Rd

N

0.25 mile

To Ashokan
Reservoir

P START

Kanape Br

Ashokan High Point Tr

Ashokan High Point Tr

High Point

- - - Route
.... Other Trails
——— Stream
——— Road
P Parking
▲ Summit
⋏ Scenic Overlook
Δ Campground

▲ Mombaccus Mtn

Upper Samsonville Rd

spanning seasonal creeks. You cross two such bridges and climb gradually but steadily into an area where mountain laurel appears.

Within 30 minutes or so of beginning the hike, at 1.4 miles and at 1,600 feet in elevation, the trail crosses Kanape Brook at a clearing with a designated campsite. This is a pretty spot—the brook forms a large pool as it flows from the shady Norway-spruce forest upstream. Keep going uphill, never strenuously, for another 20 minutes through a second-growth forest. Curving gradually toward the east, the trail soon reaches higher open forest, becoming level and grassy amid the oak and laurel. Within 5 minutes you arrive at a T in the airy, forested saddle between High Point and Mombaccus Mountain (trailless) at 2.5 miles and 2,060 feet. This is the border of state land. The adjoining property, south to Freeman Avery Road, is private.

Turn left (north) at the trail junction for the 1.0-mile, 1,000-foot ascent to Ashokan's summit. Slightly beyond the trail intersection take note of another red trail marker (this is where you'll come back to the main trail if you choose to complete the loop), but continue straight ahead, climbing gradually over broken rock. Views appear as you climb through this hardwood forest over steeper, terraced terrain. The vague side trails you may notice lead to older, treed-in views. From saddle to summit takes nearly one hour.

At 3.5 miles from the trailhead, Ashokan's summit is a rock ledge with an east-to-southwest aspect, revealing the edge of the Ashokan Reservoir, the Kingston-Rhinecliff Bridge, the Shawangunks from Mohonk to Minnewaska (Sky Top Tower and the Mohonk Mountain House are visible at 165 degrees), down to Sam's Point and deep into the Hudson Highlands. Weathered carvings from 1878 show in the summit stones, along with several anchor bolts from an early observation tower and a few benchmarks. There is a shallow overhang just beneath the summit ledge. The best is yet to come.

From the summit, the trail continues to the north, crossing open balds with exciting, close-up views of Slide, Friday, Balsam Cap, Rocky, Lone, Table, and Peekamoose. Most hikers will stray from the trail here to explore the bald and the broken views of the Ashokan Reservoir to the east through the trees. The popularity of camping (legal) is obvious on the bald, where there are a few large, informal fire rings. Very few places in the Catskills provide such an intimate look at the interior high peaks area. But what may astonish you the most are the low-bush blueberries, ranking easily as the best in the Catskills; patches remain from the era of commercial harvesting that persisted into the early 1900s. The thick heaths cover the entire unshaded summit.

Many hikers take the short bushwhack to Little High Point (2,800 feet), which, along with the Ashokan High Point Trail, was originally described in

50 Hikes in the Hudson Valley (1984) and in every Catskill guidebook since. As a result, herd trails have developed. From Little High Point, you can see almost the entire Ashokan Reservoir, appearing as a long, flat strip of indigo. Spun into the scene are the somber, drab outcrops of rock that pockmark the summits and ranges beyond, and short stilts of wind-battered, nut-brown tree trunks, festooned with the scarlet berry clusters of mountain ash. Looking left (north) from east to west, you observe the Devil's Path Range. To the north are Wittenberg and Cornell. To the east and beyond the reservoir are the Taconics and the Berkshires. Moving westward is the long Shawangunk Ridge and the plain of the Neversink, Rondout, and Mongaup. Suddenly Mombaccus again fills your eye, and you've covered about 270 degrees for what promises to be one of the best overlooks in the Catskill Mountains. Return to Ashokan High Peak summit and descend the way you came.

You can also complete the loop discussed earlier, time allowing. To do so from Ashokan High Point's summit (where the benchmarks are), follow the trail as it skirts the balds on the mountain's northwest side, soon descending through a thick and viewless forest. This is a longer (add about 2 miles) option than returning the way you came; its only advantage is that it's a little easier on the knees. The descent back to the main trail will take an hour plus. The loop is completed near the saddle between Ashokan High Point and Mombaccus, where you turned north for the final ascent. (It is much easier to return the way you came, and safer if your time is running short. It's not a good idea to be caught in low light on the less established, sometimes vague loop connection—it's not as well marked or as self-guiding as the main trail. If you plan to spend the day and do both Little Ashokan Point and the loop, it's a good idea to carry a headlamp and extra provisions.)

TRIP 37
RED HILL

RATING: Moderate
DISTANCE: 2.2 miles
ELEVATION GAIN: 890 feet
ESTIMATED TIME: 2 hours
MAP: USGS Claryville; AMC Catskill Mountains

A short, steep hike to the last fire tower that operated in the Catskills. Great for family outings.

DIRECTIONS

Take NY 55 from NY 209 north of Ellenville, or from NY 17 in Liberty. Take CR 19 6.5 miles to Claryville and turn right onto Red Hill Road. In 3.2 miles, go left onto Dinch Road, 1.5 miles to the trailhead parking area on the left.

TRAIL DESCRIPTION

The bare, bright footlands of the Neversink highlands were cleared long ago, the earth sown with potatoes. Large open fields remain in this exposed country above beautiful Claryville, lying south of the Big Indian and Slide Mountain wilderness areas at the confluence of the Neversink River's east and west branches. Seldom will you see a more alluring blend of upper elevation pastureland abutting deep, dark forests anywhere in the Catskills. Red Hill belongs to the Sundown Wild Forest management unit, a 27,000-acre parcel forming the southeasterly border of the Catskill Park.

On Red Hill, you will stand on the watershed divide between the Delaware and Hudson river basins.

An Allegheny serviceberry bush grows near the Red Hill trailhead, planted by the friends of Red Hill's fire tower observer, Don Wood. See if you can find it as you prepare for this short but steep hike to the tower—the last fire tower to operate in the Catskills. The Red Hill fire tower committee manages the trail, tower, and observer's cabin, and has created an interpretive guide for the trail that you can usually find in the kiosk at the parking area.

The trail begins innocently, working its way across a tributary of the East Branch, and rises through broken ledges amid the hardwoods. It remains level for some time; the footway is soft soil, following through thick mats of wood

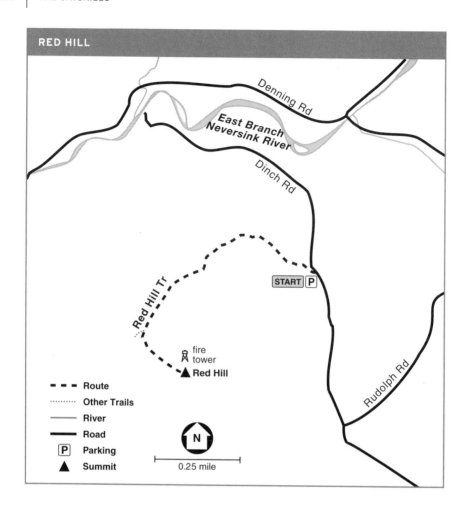

RED HILL

Denning Rd

East Branch
Neversink River

Dinch Rd

Red Hill Tr

START P

fire
tower
▲ Red Hill

Rudolph Rd

- - - Route
·········· Other Trails
——— River
—— Road
P Parking
▲ Summit

N

0.25 mile

fern as it circles the north slopes of Red Hill. In addition to the ferns, you'll see two varieties of club moss, shining pine, and ground cedar amid even-age forests of sugar maple. Twenty minutes into the hike the trail turns south-west and begins to climb, departing from an older, abandoned woods road that continues straight ahead. A sign on the right indicates a spring that can be found 400 feet from the trail; the path is not entirely self-guiding but the spring can be found by following closely to ledges on the left.

The trail climbs steeply now as it curves around the mountain into the south-east, soon leveling in a grassy plot on Red Hill's summit (2,990 feet). There's a picnic table here, adjacent to the observer's cabin and close to the tower, where my friends and I were attacked by ferocious black flies in early July. The tower, built in 1920, is 60 feet high, and the cab is open and staffed on most summer weekends. This tower also served as a communications tower, before the existence of radio repeaters in the southern Catskills. The 360-degree views are the highlight of the hike.

From Ashokan High Point, look north through the Catskill high peaks, close-at-hand and including Peekamoose and Table (5.0 miles away), Slide and Panther; then you'll see the fir summit of Doubletop, then Graham with its abandoned TV station and tower,

Getting up in the world on the Red Hill fire tower.

and Balsam Lake Mountain (note the fire tower). You see from the Big Indian Wilderness Area in the northwest to the Rondout reservoir in the south, and beyond it, the Shawangunk Ridge, including Sky Top and Eagle Cliff. Just below, along Denning Road, is Frost Valley's (YMCA) education camp.

Return the way you came.

TRIP 38
MOUNT TREMPER

RATING: Strenuous

DISTANCE: 5.6 miles

ELEVATION GAIN: 1,960 feet

ESTIMATED TIME: 4 hours

MAPS: USGS Phoenicia; AMC Catskill Mountains; NY-NJTC Northeastern Catskills

An interesting hike past a quarry and two lean-tos to the summit fire tower.

DIRECTIONS

The Phoenicia Trail begins on the east side of the Esopus Creek, 2.3 miles northwest of Mount Tremper Corners and 1.6 miles southeast of Phoenicia, off CR 40 (Old Plank Road or old NY 28).

TRAIL DESCRIPTION

The hike up Mount Tremper (2,740 feet, previously Timothy Berg) is most direct and interesting from the southwest, following the red-marked Phoenicia Trail. This trail, a long-time favorite with Catskill hikers and backpackers, has become even more popular with the re-opening of its (reconditioned) fire tower. Volunteers staff the tower on summer weekends.

The trailhead lies along the northeastern banks of the Esopus Creek, an important trout fishery and New York City water source. Mount Romer (2,240 feet) can be seen to the southwest across the Esopus Creek from the trailhead parking area. Follow the trail across two wooden bridges to a flight of stone steps. The trail levels, heading northwest to join an old truck trail at 0.5 mile. Turn right (northeast), passing the trail register.

Several larger feeder streams intersect the trail. Evidence of logging is visible in the abundance of second-growth hardwood. Yellow blazes running north and southwest mark the forest-preserve boundaries. This piece of trail also sports a few of the Long Path's blue blazes.

As the trail steepens to 15 or 20 degrees, you cross an energetic brook that cuts a deep gully in the mountainside as it bursts from an uneven-aged hemlock stand. The large drainage area of Mount Tremper's southwestern slopes crosses the trail here, causing it to be very wet at times.

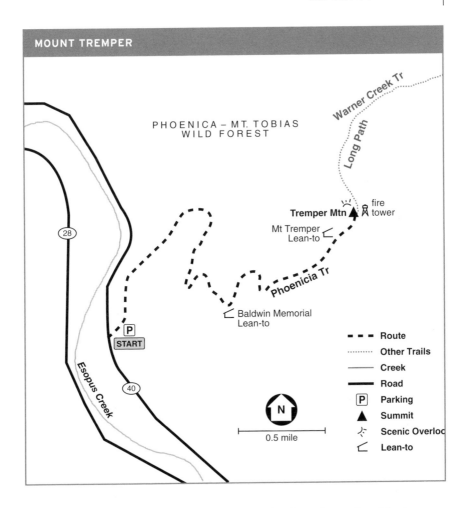

MOUNT TREMPER

PHOENICA – MT. TOBIAS
WILD FOREST

Warner Creek Tr

Long Path

Tremper Mtn ▲ fire tower

Mt Tremper Lean-to

Phoenicia Tr

28

Baldwin Memorial Lean-to

P

START

Esopus Creek

40

N

0.5 mile

- - - Route
.... Other Trails
——— Creek
▬▬▬ Road
P Parking
▲ Summit
Scenic Overlook
Lean-to

You will have reached the first switchback when the trail suddenly turns south and uphill, where large maple and ash dominate an understory of young hemlock. To your left (east) and uphill, a long outcrop that has slid in many places begins an interesting visual transition. Water appears from a spring on your left. Fallen rock can be seen below the trail to your right, now heavily covered with moss and accumulated forest litter.

As you turn through the next switchback, you see a huge pile of quarry tailings on the left; the broken stone that was shoved aside as longer slabs of bluestone were mined. The pile now forms a sort of manufactured ridge covered with thin soil and vegetation. The quarry itself is accessible from a small, overgrown roadbed on the trail's left that ascends gently into the quarry, covering an acre or two. You can follow it to a high, right-angled face, where the slabs were removed. Other than this vertical stone wall, only a small foundation and a few rusted iron remnants bear testimony to the once-thriving industry. During your exploration, beware of the quarry-dwelling rattlesnakes, which habitually bask in the warm sun of early spring. (There is a documented den here.)

Many of the nineteenth-century hotel owners disliked the imposing quarries. By the early 1880s Major Jacob H. Tremper's Tremper House was competing for business with the Catskill Mountain House, so it could ill afford competition with the nearby bluestone quarries that robbed the hills of their peace and quiet.

The trail continues along a flatter section into an oak forest, joined by the laurel cover typical of higher elevations in the Catskills. At about 1,800 feet above sea level, you switchback about 120 degrees on a steepening grade, where paper birch and an occasional white pine appear. You'll have a few glimpses southwest toward the southern high peaks during early spring. Once through the switchback, you can look to the northwest at Sheridan Mountain.

The trail steepens, heading directly uphill, nearly due east. Within a few minutes you'll see the Baldwin Memorial Lean-to on your right. At this point you are 2.0 miles from the trailhead, at 2,000 feet in elevation. Keep a sharp eye out for this shelter if you intend to use it, because it's off-trail, positioned somewhat downhill, and facing south. It is in better condition than the summit lean-to, is more private, and has a water source nearby (uphill 0.1 mile off the trail) but no summer views.

Finally, after one more switchback you climb slightly and walk a long ridge. Just as you expected the summit to appear, you discover that the ridge continues for another 0.5 mile through a canopy of twisted oak, tormented and battered by exposure. After 20 minutes of hiking, you reach a stand of bright-barked beech trees on your left, and soon after that the Mount Tremper Lean-to. This hike ends here, but the trail continues to the north, joining the Warner Creek Trail to Silver Hollow (the Long Path route), and the Willow Trail into Hoyt Hollow and Willow.

The fire tower is just ahead and offers a 360-degree view. Plattekill, Indian Head, both summits of Twin, and Plateau Mountain in the Indian Head Wilderness Area are in view to the northeast. You see Blackhead and Black Dome in the far distance, and (closer) Hunter (looking carefully, you can find Hunter's fire tower with binoculars), Southwest Hunter, West Kill, and the seemingly endless array of peaks in the central Catskills, including Belleayre and Balsam. To the south are Ashokan High Point, bits and pieces of the Ashokan Reservoir, and several high peaks including Wittenberg and Slide. To the right of Slide is Giant Ledge and Panther. To the east you can see Cooper Lake

(Kingston's water supply), as well as Overlook Mountain. You can see Sky Top and Eagle Cliff in the Shawangunks to the south, and the Hudson Highlands beyond.

This tower was built to replace the one on Slide, after the Mount Tremper tract was acquired between 1906 and 1910. The extractive resource and tourist industries followed the usual patterns here. In addition to intensive quarrying, the area gave heavily of its hemlock stands between 1836 and 1879, with one local tanner recording an all-time harvest of 170,000 cords of bark. The Tremper House Hotel was built in 1879 near the existing railroad bed at the base of the mountain. It was the Catskill's first railroad hotel, built in an era when remoteness was more in fashion, and was visited by so many colorful personalities that it threatened even the popularity of Charles Beach's Catskill Mountain House. Oscar Wilde patronized the hotel (it was on his lecture circuit) by assuring the owners that "the top of a mountain is no place for a mountain house it should be put in the valley, there the picturesque and beautiful is ever before you." The hotel was named for its manager, Major Jacob H. Tremper Jr., who renamed the mountain as well. The confluence of the Esopus and the Beaver Kill, on the flat plain of the Ashokan, was a convenient corridor for moving freight and munitions, and became the site of a fort during the Revolutionary War.

Return to the parking area the way you came.

TRIP 39
CODFISH POINT

RATING: Moderate

DISTANCE: 3.5 miles

ELEVATION GAIN: 680 feet

ESTIMATED TIME: 3.0 hours

MAPS: USGS Kaaterskill; AMC Catskill Mountains; NY-NJTC Northeastern Catskills

An historic hike to an old quarry with views overlooking the Hudson River, with a spur to Plattekill Falls.

DIRECTIONS

To reach the trailhead, turn south off NY 23A at the (only) light in Tannersville onto CR 16 (Spring Street). At 1.3 miles this road intersects Bloomer

Road, where you bear left. At 1.8 miles mile you will reach a Y where you bear left onto Platte Clove Mountain Road (still CR 16). At 4.6 miles you pass Dale Lane on the right (trail to Sugarloaf, Twin, Pecoy Notch). Stay on Platte Clove Mountain Road, and at 5.7 miles you see Prediger Road on the right. At 6.5 miles from Tannersville, turn left onto the dirt entrance to the Kaaterskill Wild Forest Area parking lot. (See Huckleberry Point for alternate seasonal directions through Platte Clove.)

TRAIL DESCRIPTION

This little lookout point, deep within the magical realms of the Platte Clove quarries and tanbark haunts, has never been treated as a destination hike, but it deserves to be. Only a few miles round-trip, the hike can be done in two to three hours, allowing enough time to explore and relax, with a view of the

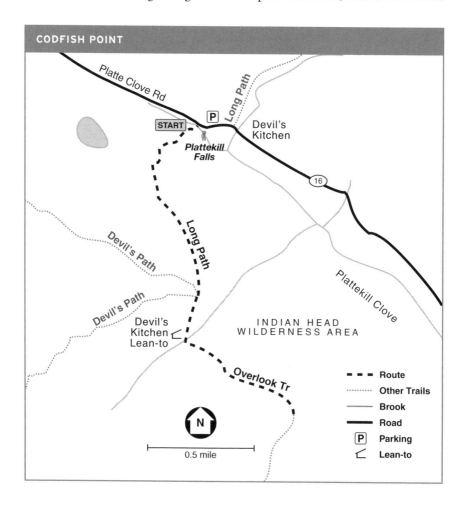

Hudson and its rolling, eastern midlands. Afterwards, you can descend the trail from the Platte Clove Preserve to sit in the cooling mists of Plattekill Falls.

Codfish Point is a spur off the Overlook Trail. The trailhead for Codfish Point represents the northern portion of the historic Old Overlook Turnpike, often used by hikers as an alternative to reach the Devil's Path, which begins 1.0 mile to the west at the top of Prediger Road. From the forest preserve access parking walk to the right (west) along Platte Clove Road, 250 yards to the trailhead on your left (south). This is the Catskill Center for Conservation and Development's (CCCD) Platte Clove Preserve, through which you walk to reach the Overlook Trail. You'll find trail signs at the roadside. To the left of the trailhead you will see the CCCD's little red artist-in-residence cabin. Go down the embankment and cross Plattekill Creek on a timber bridge, following green CCCD diamond trail markers and aqua Long Path blazes, heading south. There are CCCD interpretive signs posted along the trail. Due to intensive erosion of the original turnpike roadbed, the trail has been rerouted and is not yet entirely self-guiding. Watch the markers. You slowly gain elevation through this pretty hemlock woods until leaving the preserve and entering state land (Indian Head Wilderness Area) at around 2,000 feet in elevation.

Soon you arrive at the junction with the Devil's Path (red), which comes in on your right from its trailhead at Prediger Road. Just before it, there's a small but interesting quarry on the left (east) of the trail. Continue straight ahead to another junction only a short distance beyond, where the Devil's Path departs to the southwest toward Indian Head, and the Overlook Trail (blue) begins. Follow blue markers now, and within 10 minutes you will arrive at the Devil's Kitchen Lean-to. Here, the trail crosses a wooden bridge above the Cold Kill (folk typonomized from Coal Kiln). This was the site of an old

Plattekill Falls in the Platte Clove Preserve.

settlement where a coal-fired kiln was used to make charcoal. Extensive quarrying took place here, and wide-spread talus fields appear off-trail to the west.

Now the trail begins to climb up the old eroded roadbed, rising 350 feet in elevation in the next 0.7 mile. After a half hour or so, be aware of the trail changing direction into the south. Just as it does so it levels off, following even terrain along the east shoulder of Plattekill Mountain. As the trail levels out, watch very carefully to your left (east) for the Codfish Point spur trail. It is not adequately marked at this time (although narrow, the trail is well established) and there is normally a rock cairn at the intersection and a flat rock with an etched directional arrow lying in the junction. The trail is very short

BLUESTONE

The bluestone quarrying period in the eastern Catskills lasted from 1840 to 1880, in uneasy partnership with the tanbarking industry. In many cases, quarrymen used the same roads that the tanners had cut years earlier, and many of the same laborers—most of them Irish—worked for both as the seasons overlapped.

Settlers and tenant farmers recognized immediately that the bluish, fine-grained sandstone was easily worked and made an ideal building material. They used it for their homes, barns, smokehouses, shops, roads, hearths, and lintels; some even ventured into the commercial end of quarrying. But soon, the big stone dealers who shipped their flagstones by sloop and later, three-masted schooner and railroad, put the small operators out of business.

Bluestone was prized for its ease of handling and shaping. It was used extensively for sidewalks, as it proved durable, attractive, and attainable in volume. As a result, it provided the first pavement for New York City, and quickly found its way to St. Louis, San Francisco, and even to Havana, Cuba. Whereas the tanning industry ended as the result of the near deforestation of the hills, the quarrying industry came to a sudden stop.

As you hike the trails that were once used by quarrymen and their teams, you will see the old quarries, and note where some of the stones lying mid-trail bear the century-old mark of a wedge or chisel. On closer examination, you will still find flags and perfect lintels lying neatly stacked, waiting for the teamsters that never came—testimony to a way of life that was changed nearly overnight by the invention of cement in Rosendale and High Falls, New York.

and brings you into an old quarry. Continue until you arrive at an east-facing lookout, poised above the valley. Where the talus was thrown in order to clear the quarry of debris, a pioneer stand of white birch has taken hold. You can explore this extensive quarry, seeing the face from which the stone was mined and the areas where the flags were trimmed for shipping. There are a few remaining hut foundations, which during operations were typically covered with hemlock boughs and bark shinglings.

The views are very good, extending east to the Taconic Plateau and lowlands, and south along the Escarpment to the summit of Overlook Mountain. (You'll see the fire tower.) You can see Tivoli Marsh and a good stretch of the Hudson River; points in the Shawangunks such as Guyot Hill and Bonticou Crag; and the guardian promontories of the Central Hudson Highlands—Storm King and Breakneck Ridge, far to the south.

Codfish Point takes its name from an incident during the late quarrying days of 1890 when a blizzard marooned the quarrymen for several days. Having exhausted their food supply, they were left with only salt cod. The workers nailed a cod crate to a tree in mock protest, and as a marker to aid their supply party in locating the snowed-under trail. The crate remained for some time and the name stuck. Salt cod was a Dutch staple survival food, dating back a millennia. In its salted state, it could last years.

Retrace the route back down to the CCCD Preserve. If you have the time, by all means take the blue and green diamond marked trail that leads from the CCCD artist-in-residence cabin driveway down to Plattekill Falls, a high, vertical fall and pool at the head of the Plattekill. (The CCCD has requested that hikers do not disturb the artist-in-residence.) From a point along the trail you can get a good look out across the top of Platte Clove itself, facing east. But be careful—there are no barriers or restraints, and the trail can be very slippery when wet (not recommended in icy conditions). This 50-foot fall is a vertical plume that runs heavily following rain, but because of its high elevation and the fact that it lies near the watershed of the west-flowing Schoharie, it runs down quickly.

Return the way you came.

TRIP 40
OVERLOOK MOUNTAIN

RATING: Strenuous
DISTANCE: 5.0 miles
ELEVATION GAIN: 1,440 feet
ESTIMATED TIME: 3 to 4 hours
MAPS: USGS Woodstock; AMC Catskill Mountains; NY-NJTC Northeastern Catskills

A steep hike to the old hotel ruins and the fire tower and Eagle Cliff from Meads, above the town of Woodstock.

DIRECTIONS

From the Woodstock village green turn north onto Rock City Road. Continue straight through the intersection with Glasco Turnpike at 0.6 mile and climb Meads Mountain Road to the trailhead parking area at 2.6 miles.

TRAIL DESCRIPTION

Overlook Mountain (3,140 feet) is Woodstock's own mecca. The trailhead begins at the height of land on Meads Mountain (the high saddle between Overlook and Mount Guardian), opposite the Tibetan Buddhist monastery of Karma Triyana Dharmachakra and adjacent to the infamous Magic Meadow of Woodstock Rainbow Tribe fame. The Catholic Church of Christ on the Mount is here, too, made famous in the 1960s by the "hippie priest," Father William Francis. It does seem silly to deny that this area is a sort of vortex zone; one that has attracted monks, hikers, and artists for 100 years or more. It was because of the view from Meads that Ralph Whitehead built his art colony in Woodstock; one based upon the utopian ideas of John Ruskin and the poetic vision of Walt Whitman. Whitehead only had to marry Jane Byrd McCall to find a name for his art colony, and Byrdcliffe was born in the shadow of Overlook Mountain.

At the Overlook Summit trailhead, locate the map kiosk and trail register. The trail itself is an easy if not dull climb up a consistent grade on a dirt road—all the way to the fire tower. You begin at 1,700 feet in elevation following red markers, surrounded by dark hemlock woods that open up into hardwoods and mountain laurel as the trail climbs. The forest is strewn with large sedimentary boulders, dragged off the mountaintop by retreating ice some

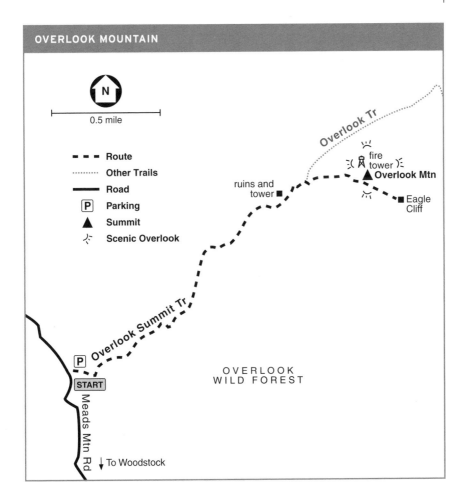

OVERLOOK MOUNTAIN

0.5 mile

- - - Route
.... Other Trails
——— Road
P Parking
▲ Summit
𝟀 Scenic Overlook

Overlook Tr

ruins and
tower ■

fire
tower
▲ Overlook Mtn

■ Eagle
Cliff

Overlook Summit Tr

P

START

OVERLOOK
WILD FOREST

Meads Mtn Rd

↓ To Woodstock

15,000 years ago. The ascent is consistent and at times monotonous, as it follows the TV-tower maintenance road in the presence of electrical wires, having lost the character it certainly had when quarrymen and tanners first built it. But soon, mountains appear everywhere, and Indian Head, a scant 3.0 miles distant, comes out of nowhere in the Devil's Path mountains. Within 45 minutes of hiking, you will come upon the somber ruin of the Overlook Mountain House. The Mountain House opened in 1871, but despite its various distinctions (it was the highest mountain house in the Catskills), it seemed cursed. It burned completely in 1875, was reconstructed in 1878, and burned again in 1924. In 1928, under new ownership, the existing poured-concrete foundation and walls, erected near the old hotel site, were started. Walls, windows, and plumbing were about all that were completed when the stock market crash of 1929 came and the project was abandoned. Trees now grow in the main hall.

The views from the Overlook Mountain fire tower rank among the best in the Catskills.

Artists have pasted biodegradable images and histories to the walls, most of them now faded. Parts of the building have collapsed and the DEC has advised the public not to enter the ruin. Continue on the trail, rising easily, passing the TV and cell tower on your left. At 2.0 miles, pass the blue-marked Overlook Trail on your left. Continue straight, passing several herd trails that lead right (south) to limited views. At 2.5 miles, you will arrive at the summit. There's an observer's cabin, open on summer weekends and serving as a museum to the fire tower, both of them staffed by volunteers. Barry Knight, a local resident and volunteer, has climbed Overlook "hundreds of times in all weather conditions." A tower enthusiast, he located, restored, and rebuilt a dismantled state fire tower on his own property in Hurley. "If it weren't for the efforts of volunteers, these towers would not only be closed to the public," he says, "they'd all be dismantled. What a shame that would be!" You'll agree when you see the view, one that without the tower would not be as spectacular. In 1997, the Overlook Mountain fire tower was recognized by the National Historical Lookout Register for its historical and cultural significance. Barry and his fellow stewards will be happy to show you around the summit and tower.

The summit view is among the Catskills' finest, and includes the Berkshires and Taconics, the Hudson River south to the Highlands, the Shawangunks, the

Ashokan Reservoir, and more Catskill peaks than you can count (remember, the Catskills have 100 peaks over 3,000 feet in elevation). Compasses don't work here because of the steel tower, but a working alidade and the steward will help you identify the major peaks. Six states are seen: New York, Connecticut, Vermont, Massachusetts, New Jersey, and Pennsylvania (and some will argue for New Hampshire). Take the time to visit with the volunteer observer and have a look in the cabin. Follow the trail to the right of the cabin door to a more private view over the immediate valley (beware of the vertical drop). This is Eagle Cliff, so named by the landscape painter Charles Lanman.

Just as inspiring a view is that of Overlook itself from the valley floor, a sight that merited the brushes of Frederic Church and Thomas Cole and prompted the pen of Charles Herbert Moore. The mountain continues to provide inspiration for aspiring artists from the village of Woodstock below. By all means take a drive through Byrdcliffe on your way home, by turning right at the Glasco Turnpike (CR 33) crossroads as you descend from Meads, turning right within 0.5 mile onto Upper Byrdcliffe Road. Byrdcliffe is still a thriving arts colony, with resident artists and writers, and offers many public arts programs conducted in the Byrdcliffe Theater. Attached to the barn is a box of self-guided walking tour maps that will take you through the complex. To complete your outing, visit the Woodstock Artist's Guild (gallery) in town, and grab a slice at Catskill Mountain Pizza on Tinker Street.

Return the way you came.

TRIP 41
INDIAN HEAD MOUNTAIN

RATING: Strenuous

DISTANCE: 6.0 miles

ELEVATION GAIN: 1,573 feet

ESTIMATED TIME: 4.5 hours

MAPS: USGS Kaaterskill; AMC Catskill Mountains; NY-NJTC Northeastern Catskills

An interior forest hike to a boreal summit with exciting views.

DIRECTIONS

To reach the trailhead, turn south off NY 23A at the (only) light in Tannersville onto CR 16 (Spring Street). Set to zero. At 1.3 miles this road intersects Bloomer Road, where you bear left. At 1.8 miles you will reach a Y where you bear left onto Platte Clove Mountain Road. At 4.6 miles you pass Dale Lane on the right (trail to Sugarloaf, Twin, Pecoy Notch). Stay on Platte Clove Mountain Road, and at 5.7 miles you see Prediger Road on the right. Follow it 0.25 mile to the trailhead. Park on the right. (See Huckleberry Point, Trip 46, for alternate seasonal directions through Platte Clove.)

TRAIL DESCRIPTION

Indian Head is a beguiling triad of peaks forming a profile that appears from afar to be a face. It is best seen from the north or east, from the Taconics or from Olana, Frederic Church's Persian castle in Hudson, and from the NYS Thruway and the surrounding valleys. Thomas Cole painted it in 1843 in *River in the Catskills*, the mountain set in vague repose beyond the dark ridges running southeast from Kaaterskill High Peak.

Indian Head is a contender for the position of most rugged and intriguing of the Devil's Path mountains. Its summit ridge is so completely enclosed by thick spruce and fir that you are never certain you are on a mountain at all but feel lost in a sea of endless, aromatic brush. The mountain yields its claustrophobic clutches piecemeal, giving you some extra-rugged views every now and then to lure you onward.

At the trailhead you will see signs identifying the red-marked trail to Indian Head Mountain, Jimmy Dolan Notch Trail, and Echo Lake Trail. This is the Devil's Path trailhead. You will follow the Devil's Path a short distance

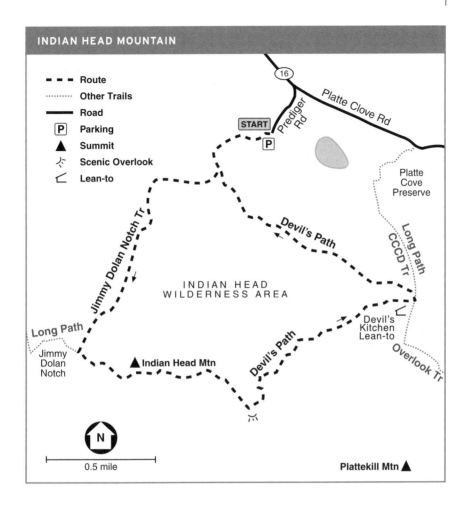

INDIAN HEAD MOUNTAIN

- - - Route
.... Other Trails
—— Road
P Parking
▲ Summit
� Scenic Overlook
⊏ Lean-to

16
Platte Clove Rd
Prediger Rd
START
P

Platte Cove Preserve

Devil's Path

Jimmy Dolan Notch Tr

Long Path
CCCD Tr

INDIAN HEAD
WILDERNESS AREA

Long Path

Jimmy Dolan Notch

▲ Indian Head Mtn

Devil's Path

Devil's Kitchen Lean-to

Overlook Tr

N

0.5 mile

Plattekill Mtn ▲

to the Jimmy Dolan Notch Trail, and join it again as you turn east in Jimmy Dolan Notch to summit Indian Head and complete the loop.

The foottrail leads you into the forest over a stringer bridge across one of several lively creeks that will keep you company until higher elevations are reached. Follow the self-guiding and well-marked (blue and red) old road up-hill, reaching the trail register within 500 feet. Maps are (at this time) posted here. Within 10 minutes you pass a stream on your right, and arrive at a trail junction. Bear right on the blue-marked Jimmy Dolan Trail to Jimmy Dolan Notch and Indian Head.

The Jimmy Dolan Notch Trail rises slightly over a rocky footway with exposed tree roots into a pure beech forest. To your right, in a northerly direction, you can see Kaaterskill High Peak and Roundtop Mountain through the trees in springtime. The trail is not strenuous yet, as you slowly bend to the south, getting a view of Twin's northerly shoulder up to your right.

The trail becomes badly eroded in places where runoff has created a temporary streambed. The various streams you encounter, and the one you can hear in the ravine just west of you, form the easternmost headwaters of the Schoharie Creek beyond a dense and extensive hemlock woods.

As you continue along a steeper section of the trail, you'll have a peek at Indian Head on your left (southeast) and will see more of Twin to the right. Climbing higher, about 45 minutes into your hike (1.5 miles), you can look back (north) at Kaaterskill High Peak, Roundtop, and the Blackhead Range. Within 10 to 15 minutes more you will be happy to arrive in the Notch (3,100 feet) for some rest before the steep summit climb.

In Jimmy Dolan Notch the Long Path intersects with the Devil's Path, showing Indian Head at (a rugged) 0.5 mile, and Platte Clove Mountain Road at 3.9 miles. Jimmy Dolan Notch is in every sense a classic notch, a symmetrical cut through the mountain that is scattered with large boulders and crumbling rock shelves, an ancient river canyon from which the waters have long since run away to a dried-up sea.

The trail climbs and eases alternately as you scramble uphill from the Notch,

heading east. After gaining nearly 400 feet in elevation from the Notch, the trail, thick with hemlock and balsam fir, flattens suddenly. This is the only indication that you have reached the summit, completely surrounded by trees with no view. Within 5 minutes you go downhill slightly to another flat area where climax spruce trees soar above.

Continue along through a pure evergreen forest. Some restricted views of the Sawkill Valley are available to the south if you want to push your way through the trees and explore a little, but the best views lay ahead.

You are now descending to the middle knoll, from the forehead (summit) to the eyebrow of the Indian's

Indian Head Mountain.

head. On the eastern end of the middle knoll, you reach a high overlook that juts out to the east with a vertical, dangerous drop, at 3,200 feet above sea level. A near 180-degree view reveals Ashokan, Shawangunks, Overlook, the Hudson (part of which is obstructed by the east knoll, or nose), and the Highlands, Taconics, and Berkshires. You are roughly midway through the hike, with 3.0 miles behind you.

From here, follow cautiously down a very steep section of trail into a shallow saddle separating the eyebrow and nose. Within 10 minutes you encounter another thick stand of fir that would be difficult, if not impossible, to walk through without a trail. This is a prime example of "cripplebrush." Going uphill and leveling out onto the nose, in 10 minutes or so you reach a spot where views have been maintained by the DEC's cutting. (Many people disagree with maintaining vista cuts in wilderness areas and have questioned its legality.) The result is an outstanding look at the Catskills high peaks area, running from Ashokan High Point over to Slide and beyond. In this collection of peaks are also Peekamoose and Table, Lone, Rocky, Balsam Cap, Samuels, Friday, Wittenberg, Cornell, Giant Ledge, Panther, and many more; you see Overlook's fire tower, the Tibetan Monastery in Meads, the Overlook Mountain House ruin, and as far south as High Point, New Jersey (with binoculars you can see the tower at 219 degrees).

Within a few minutes of leaving this area, you swing toward the north, skirting the nose's easterly rim, which will give you a look at Plattekill's (trailless) western shoulder. With fair views to the east along the trail, you have the opportunity to look deep into Platte Clove, and within 5 minutes you reach Sherman's Lookout (named for General William Tecumseh Sherman, an 1890s visitor to the Catskill Mountain House) which has also been cut over to provide views to the north and a previously unavailable look at the Blackhead Mountains, Kaaterskill High Peak and Roundtop, and the Hudson River. Looking beyond the deep cut of Platte Clove you can see Bash Bish Gorge in the Southern Taconics. This is the last scenic overlook before the plunge into the valley.

After approximately 20 minutes of hiking downhill, with diminishing views to the east, you may find the trail wet as it terraces down, level for a way, then steep again. The footing is red shale and some broken conglomerate. The majestic stands of large virgin hemlock here, some over 30 inches in diameter, reflect the magnificence that was the pre-tanning period, primordial forest.

Within 30 to 40 minutes of leaving the nose, you reach a trail junction. To your right is Devil's Kitchen Lean-to, (this makes for a pretty, 5-minute side trip to the bridge over the Cold Kill) and far beyond it, Echo Lake. Bear left (north), and within 500 feet or so the Devil's Path Trail dodges left (northwest). Watch closely for this turn—it's not too obvious. If you go straight (north) on the Catskill Center for Conservation and Development (CCCD) Trail, you'll wind up a mile east of Prediger Road.

Turning left, or northeast, and back into deep hemlock woods, the trail takes you uphill slightly. In 10 to 15 minutes you cross a creek continuing through a fern glade, crossing another small stream and reaching the trail junction with the Jimmy Dolan Notch Trail. The 1.5-mile section of trail from Devil's Kitchen will take you about 40 minutes. Turn right and you are back at the parking lot in a few minutes.

THE DEVIL'S PATH

Twenty-three miles long, with a cumulative elevation gain approaching 9,000 feet, the Devil's Path is one of two trunk trails in the Eastern Catskills, joining Indian Head Mountain in Platte Clove to West Kill Mountain in the high Spruceton Valley. Crossing six peaks in excess of 3,500 feet (including Southwest Hunter Mountain), this rugged trail, often undertaken as a long weekend backpacking experience, begins on Prediger Road in the town of Hunter. (See Indian Head Mountain, Trip 41, for directions to the Devil's Path Trailhead from the east, and West Kill Mountain, Trip 55, for directions from the west.) The trail can also be done as a series of day hikes from access points in the north. Hikers wishing to add additional miles can begin at the Overlook Mountain trailhead in Meads, adding 2.0 miles and 1,400 feet in elevation (where the Devil's Path ought to begin).

Few trails are so spectacular—and so difficult. Rugged, boreal peaks; deep, weather-ravaged notches; the general scarcity of water; and the steep, rocky terrain characterize the route. Several lean-tos are conveniently located along the way, on or near the main trunk. The Devil's Path retained the reputation given to the eastern portion of the Catskills that inspired fear in early Dutch settlers, on account of its deep, dark cloves (ravines), where the Devil was said to dwell. The DEC created Devil's Tombstone Campsite in Stony Clove Notch, putting a symbolic end to the era of superstition and legendry for which the Catskills are famous. However, today the trail continues beyond Stony Clove, into the west.

TRIP 42
TWIN MOUNTAIN

RATING: Strenuous

DISTANCE: 4.4 miles

ELEVATION GAIN: 1,740 feet

ESTIMATED TIME: 5 hours

MAPS: USGS Kaaterskill; AMC Catskill Mountains; NY-NJTC Northeastern Catskills

A double-peaked mountain with superior views of the Hudson Valley and the Indian Head Wilderness Area.

DIRECTIONS
From Tannersville, turn south at the light (intersection of CR 23C and Railroad Avenue, CR 16) to join Spring Street (CR 16), bearing right onto Elka Park Road at 1.8 miles. Go over the Schoharie Creek, pass the post office, and bear left at 2.8 miles. Go another 1.2 miles to the trailhead and park on the right. The trailhead can also be reached from Platte Clove Road (CR 16) via Dale Lane, by bearing right onto Elka Park Road (a.k.a. Roaring Brook Road) at the intersection of Wase Road and going 0.7 mile to the trailhead.

TRAIL DESCRIPTION
Twin-peaked Twin Mountain is one of the Devil's Path mountains, those craggy and tempestuous summits that you see crowding the western sky as you drive on the NYS Thruway north and south between New Paltz and Catskill. Twin is best hiked from the Pecoy Notch Trail, ascending gradually along the Roaring Kill Trail from Elka Park Road (seasonal, unmaintained in winter but accessible by four-wheel-drive vehicles). Many hikers climb Sugarloaf as well as Twin in a one-day outing. If you choose to do so, factor in an additional 2.0 miles and 800 feet of ascent for a cumulative elevation gain of 2,500 feet. Twin has a far superior view, however. In fact, there's no comparison.

From the Roaring Kill trailhead on Elka Park Road (2,150 feet elevation), take the yellow-marked Roaring Kill Trail 0.25 mile to a junction and follow the Pecoy Notch Trail to the left (southeast). The trail ascends gradually, passing a few quarry pits where you may notice some large, hand-dressed flagstones. Enter a hemlock woods and descend to the left a bit to arrive at

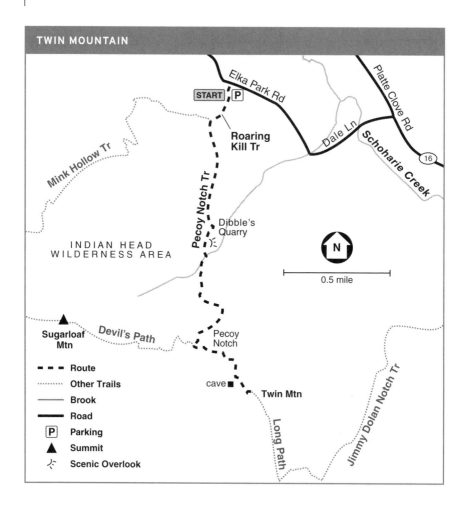

TWIN MOUNTAIN

START

Elka Park Rd

Platte Clove Rd

Roaring
Kill Tr

Dale Ln

Schoharie Creek

16

Mink Hollow Tr

Pecoy Notch Tr

Dibble's
Quarry

N

0.5 mile

INDIAN HEAD
WILDERNESS AREA

Sugarloaf
Mtn

Devil's Path

Pecoy
Notch

- - - Route

.... Other Trails

———— Brook

———— Road

P Parking

▲ Summit

Scenic Overlook

cave ■

Twin Mtn

Long Path

Jimmy Dolan Notch Tr

a large, open quarry face over an extensive talus field providing views to the
north. This (Dibble's Quarry) is probably the best trailside example of a bluestone quarry in the Catskills. Constructed to take advantage of the views over
the Clove toward Huckleberry Point are several druidic bluestone "recliners"
and an odd array of intriguing stone sculptures. You can get a look at Twin
Mountain from here, and to the north and downhill you see the Hutterian
Bruderhof. Kaaterskill High Peak and Roundtop are in the foreground. After
you explore the area, continue along the trail, leaving the quarry and entering
hardwoods, crossing a rustic bridge and ascending.

Soon you will skirt the outlet of a beaver pond on your right. Beaver activity is spotty in this pond that feeds the high, upper Schoharie, but several dams
and lodges have been evident in recent years. The pond, fed by runoff coming
down the northeast slopes of Sugarloaf, attracts wildlife and has a quiet, pri-

Twin Mountain from Cooper Lake.

mordial spirit about it, making a welcome stopover. As you continue, the trail heads uphill, and you begin to get views to the north of the Blackhead Range.

After about an hour's easy hiking, you reach Pecoy Notch, and the Devil's Path Trail. There is no trail out of Pecoy Notch to the south, only a profusion of tumbledown boulders and twisted logs. This is one of the notches, along with its easterly neighbor Jimmy Dolan Notch that can be seen as bright bare scrapes from points as far south as the Shawangunks.

Bear left (east) for Twin, following the Devil's Path (red) and Long Path (aqua, sparse) trails. Twin is 0.5 mile ahead with an additional 540-foot vertical rise to its first (true) summit.

The incline is steep with a westerly aspect, soon exposing Sugarloaf and beyond it Hunter and its fire tower. You pass a large rock overhang that has been heavily used by hikers and is a convenient shelter in the event of rain. The trail is very steep in places, and you will find yourself breathing heavily and resting frequently. Suddenly, through a balsam-thick shoulder of the mountain, you see views opening up to the south, the vertical ledges of stone on your path finally subsiding to a series of flat outcrops that form the northerly summit of Twin.

From this point the view is very good, extending as far south and southwest as the eye can see, but it is blocked to the north and east by mountains in the 3,500-foot class. From this southerly exposure you can survey the southern

Catskills' high peaks just west of the Ashokan Reservoir. You may recognize Ashokan High Point, Samuels Point, Friday, Wittenberg, Cornell, Panther, Giant Ledge, Balsam Cap, Balsam Lake Mountain, and Graham, with many lower surrounding peaks identifiable with the aid of map and compass. You will also have a close look at the foreground mountains, Tremper, Carl, and Olderbark (west to east). During runoff, listen closely and you might hear the noisy waters of the Sawkill or Mink Hollow Brook echoing up from below. Cooper Lake, part of Kingston's water supply, is visible 5.0 miles south southwest of you, with Mount Tobias on its right. There was once a glass factory below in the Saw Kill Valley, and until recent years hikers were able to see the mirrorlike reflections of the waste glass that was cast aside, giving rise to the name, the Glass Plains. The Plains have since been reclaimed by nature.

The southerly summit of Twin is an additional (easy) 0.5-mile hike from here through a saddle of dense coniferous forest, bringing you to another flat rock overlook facing south. Views to the east are of the Hudson River valley and much of the river itself. From here nearly the entire Ashokan Reservoir is visible, as well as the Shawangunks. On a clear day, beyond them, you can see the scattered hills of the Hudson Highlands.

You'll want to visit both of Twin's summits to take in the variety of views that one cannot offer individually. If you have a lunch, plan to enjoy it at the more expansive southerly summit where hikers feel more inclined to loaf. Return the way you came, and while descending the north summit, about halfway down, you can test your lungs against the echoes from Sugarloaf.

TRIP 43
PLATEAU MOUNTAIN FROM STONY CLOVE

RATING: Strenuous

DISTANCE: 6.0 miles

ELEVATION GAIN: 1,840 feet

ESTIMATED TIME: 6 hours

MAP: USGS Hunter; AMC Catskill Mountains; NY-NJTC Catskill Trails 41

A very steep rise out of Stony Clove Notch to a long, level plateau with isolated views.

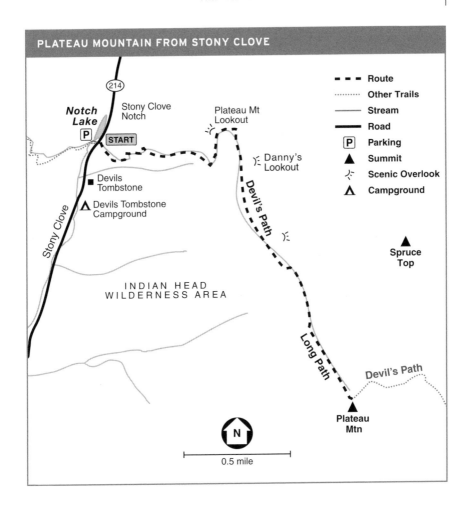

DIRECTIONS

To locate the trailhead, drive south on NY 214 from NY 23A between Hunter and Tannersville, and go 3.0 miles to the south end of Notch Lake. Or from the south at Phoenicia and NY 28, go north 9.0 miles on NY 214. Park at the trailhead parking area (Devil's Tombstone Public Campground day use area) on the west side of NY 214.

TRAIL DESCRIPTION

"If you will believe me that the Stony Clove is a pastoral of lyric beauty with one dramatic climax, instead of the roaring bloody gulch of the fictional folders, I hope that you will also believe that its beauties cannot be more than skimmed by him who trusts only to steam or gasoline for his scenic memories."

So wrote T. Morris Longstreth in his 1918 classic, *The Catskills*, which he promised to be "free of exaggeration." No hiker who ascends the steep paths of Stony Clove will disagree.

Stony Clove Notch is a narrow mountain pass with all the rugged visual appeal Longstreth promises. It is formed by the long ridge of Plateau meeting with that of Hunter and holds at its apex the teardrop of Notch Lake and the Devil's Tombstone State Campground, where the Devil's Path Trail crosses NY 214. This major Catskill landmark can be seen 100 miles away. Take a look at Plateau's western slope and you'll have an idea of the ascent you're about to make. Cross the road to the east where you'll see trail signs and the red markers of the Devil's Path. Plateau Mountain Lookout (a.k.a. Orchid or Orchard Point) is indicated at 1.2 miles, but the mountain's true summit is on the east end of the ridge at 3,840 feet, 2.5 miles from the trailhead. What you will witness from at the lookout will please you more than the boreal, viewless summit. Plateau Mountain Lookout is an outstanding viewpoint at 3,600 feet—one that is grossly underrated in the hierarchy of Catskill vistas.

Climb the steps and ascend over rocky terrain into a tall hardwood forest. Quickly the trail becomes very steep, with makeshift stone steps to aid your ascent. In 10 minutes or more, as you climb over roots and rocks, you encounter isolated rock slides to your left, and views over your shoulder to the southwest of Slide and Wittenberg in the Slide-Panther Wilderness Area, including Cornell, Friday, Peekamoose, Table, Panther, and beyond.

These good views vanish as the trail turns north, with spring beauties and red trillium sprinkled liberally along its edge. If the trillium is in bloom during your visit, you might be surprised at its putrid scent, one that is unbecoming to such a pretty flower. Blooming as it does in very early spring, the trillium's stench attracts pollinating insects in search of decomposing flesh. For this reason it is called a "carrion" flower. All species of trillium are rare, protected, and

Hikers will have to work for the view from Plateau's ridge.

may not be picked. In spring you also will see in bloom the very pretty viburnum, or hobblebush, with its large, heart-shaped leaves, a favorite deer food.

On this flat section of trail at 3,400 feet (the first flat stretch of trail since you set out) you can look back west for occasional views of Hunter Mountain. You cross the 3,500-foot mark and may see a sign indicating this point. In another 10 minutes you traverse some ledges that take you gradually up and onto Plateau Mountain Lookout. This is a nearly 180-degree view, reaching across the range from Colonel's Chair (and the ski trails) to Hunter Mountain's fire tower, Southwest Hunter, West Kill, the high peaks, and the Ashokan Reservoir. You can see Belleayre Mountain, Balsam, Haynes, Eagle, Big Indian (shaped like a molar), and beyond it, Doubletop and Fir. Giant Ledge looks tiny at 246 degrees (with binoculars you can make out the cliffs). Slide Mountain is at 220 degrees. Look down into the col and then at Cornell and Wittenberg. You can plainly see the slide on Slide (snow helps to define it). Wittenberg's steep and sudden drop off is just above Mount Tremper's fire tower (230 degrees). Peekamoose is at 228 degrees. Looking to the left of it you see Ashokan High Point. With binoculars you can see the Lake Maratanza tower farm in Sam's Point Pitch Pine Preserve. Across Stony Clove on the east-facing slope of Hunter Mountain is Becker Hollow, the shortest route to Hunter's summit.

The summit ridge is flat now. Continue following the trail to the east, until you reach an unobstructed overlook (Danny's Lookout) on the north side with a large rock upon which a crude rising sun is carved. Views include the Blackhead Range, North Point, South Mountain, Roundtop, Kaaterskill High Peak, and down into Platte Clove. Hard to your right you will see Spruce Top and then Sugarloaf with its long ridgeline plunging into Mink Hollow to meet Roaring Kill and Schoharie Creek. You can see North Lake at 86 degrees. The distant mountain groups to the northeast are the Taconics, including the Greylock Range.

Continue on the flat ridge over a soft, duff trail—dizzy with trout lilies—for another 5 minutes until you reach an overlook with the same northerly views. Use caution—this one has a dangerous drop. Many blown-down conifers lie upon this exposed ridge, like bleached whale bones against the contrast of verdant life.

Continue through a forest of large spruce and fir, where the trail switches to the ridge's south side. You begin to go uphill slightly in a few minutes, and within another 10 minutes enter a thick understory of balsam reminiscent of Indian Head summit, but not as enclosed. Whipped winds tear along the thin ridge as you peer through trees into Silver Hollow and Stony Clove. The forest remains coniferous on this long walk to the summit; it lends a somehow nostalgic feel, maybe reminding you of favorite walks in places like the Whites or the Maine coast.

In 20 minutes you reach the summit, just beyond a 90-degree left turn where the trail turns south to east. The thick spruce-fir cripplebrush will rub against your shoulders as the trail wanders along the ridge. Follow the trail for another 15 minutes to your final destination—a rock looking east. Jump across a shallow crevasse and survey Sugarloaf, Kaaterskill High Peak, Roundtop, North Point, North Mountain, Overlook, and part of Twin. The view is limited compared to the ones you had already, but it gives you an intimate feeling for the heart of the Devil's Path. And, it's a sight unavailable to "him who trusts only to steam or gasoline for his scenic memories."

Return the way you came, listening for the *"grokk, grokk"* of nesting ravens.

TRIP 44
KAATERSKILL HIGH PEAK

RATING: Strenuous

DISTANCE: 10 miles

ELEVATION GAIN: 1,855 feet

ESTIMATED TIME: 6 hours

MAPS: USGS Kaaterskill; AMC Catskill Mountains; NY-NJTC Catskill Trails 41

A long, remote hike into the isolated Kaaterskill Wild Forest Area, with spectacular views from Hurricane Ledge.

DIRECTIONS

To reach the trailhead, turn south off NY 23A at the (only) light in Tannersville onto CR 16 (Spring Street). Set to zero. At 1.3 miles this road intersects Bloomer Road, where you bear left. At 1.8 miles you will reach a Y where you bear left onto Platte Clove Mountain Road (still CR 16). At 4.6 miles you pass Dale Lane on the right (trail to Sugarloaf, Twin, Pecoy Notch). Stay on Platte Clove Mountain Road, and at 5.7 miles you see Prediger Road on the right. At 6.5 miles from Tannersville, turn left onto the dirt entrance to the Kaaterskill Wild Forest Area parking lot. (See Huckleberry Point, Trip 46, for alternate seasonal directions through Platte Clove.)

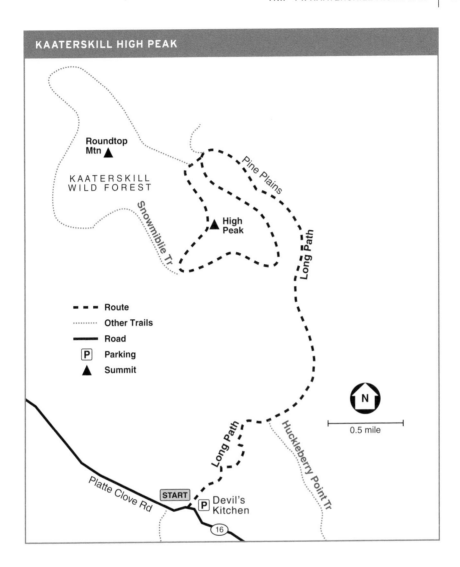

KAATERSKILL HIGH PEAK

Roundtop Mtn ▲

KAATERSKILL WILD FOREST

Pine Plains

Snowmiblie Tr

▲ High Peak

Long Path

- - - Route
.... Other Trails
—— Road
P Parking
▲ Summit

Long Path

Huckleberry Point Tr

N

0.5 mile

Platte Clove Rd

START
P Devil's Kitchen

16

TRAIL DESCRIPTION

High Peak was far more popular 100 years ago during the hotel heydays than it is today. Then, the mountains were defined by hotel magnates who did everything possible to convince visitors that their establishment was indeed positioned in the heart of the Catskills. High Peak (contending with Roundtop) was considered the highest mountain in the range until Arnold Guyot reduced it to a lowly 23rd on the list of Catskill peaks (actually it is 22nd). His authority was considered absolute; his findings challenged local belief to the point that many people claimed they were in scientific error. A veritable empire of tourism had been built on the supposition that High Peak was the very heart and soul of the Catskills, and to question that status was heresy. But science often overrules even the most wishful thinking.

From low in the valley, High Peak does appear to be the highest mountain on the skyline. In *The Catskills*, T. Morris Longstreth describes High Peak and Roundtop from the Hotel Kaaterskill as "sublime breakers just ready to topple over in a universal thunder of white foam." In Cooper's *The Pioneers*, Natty Bumppo says, "Well, there's High-peak and the Round-top which lay back like a father and mother among their children, seeing they are far above all the other hills."

While it is evident from guidebooks and maps of the golden era that Kaaterskill High Peak was a very popular climbing destination, the mountain has since enjoyed such anonymity that only an informally marked trail crosses its summit. A snowmobile trail circles both High Peak and Roundtop, providing access to High Peak's summit trail. (Roundtop is trailless.) Because the trail crossing High Peak from the snowmobile trail is remote, this should be regarded as a strenuous and challenging hike that requires solid direction-finding skills, a map and compass (and your GPS), and plenty of food and water. Allow plenty of time! The Kaaterskill Wild Forest is a very quiet piece of country, even when the neighboring trails to the south and north (the Devil's Path and Escarpment Trails, respectively) are busy.

At the entrance to the parking area you will see trailhead signs and orange snowmobile markers, an aqua-colored Long Path disc and/or blazes, and blue foot-trail markers. A sign denotes Junction with Loop Trail, 3.6 miles, your in-transit destination. Don't be confused by the curiously useless reference to Steenberg Road, a dirt road named for an early quarryman who lived in the vicinity of Huckleberry Point. It is not identified on maps or in the field.

Follow the snowmobile trail uphill through a dense forest of hardwood and hemlock, passing old stone walls and listening (in season) to a tumbling creek on your right. The trail follows a pleasing old dirt road that has eroded well below surface grade. Within 25 minutes you will reach a fork where arrows point to the right. Continue on the well-marked snowmobile trail, and in less than 10 minutes you reach another Y where you bear right, passing the Huckleberry Point Trail (Trip 46). Viburnum, yellow and purple violets, and trout lilies (it is the mottled leaf that resembles a trout) form a colorful understory. The trail is relatively level for the next 20 minutes until after you cross a pair of short timber bridges through a swampy area between two shallow creeks in a pretty spruce-fir swamp.

The trail then heads uphill and you begin to see beech trees and some remarkably large hemlocks and maples. Wildlife is abundant. Porcupines will scuttle away as you approach; owls will scrutinize you with haunting whispers as you rest. Here, amid the spring beauties, you can look south at Plattekill Mountain, and northwest at the shoulder of High Peak. After a fairly stiff ascent, the trail levels out into a birch forest with scattered evergreens and soon turns to a pure evergreen forest. Curiously, this pure spruce-fir forest is called the Pine Plains.

After 45 minutes of traversing this flat, swampy section of trail, wet and muddy in springtime, turn sharply left, still following the snowmobile markers, where the faint trail (the Long Path) to Palenville via Buttermilk Falls, Wildcat Ravine, and Poet's Ledge forks to the northwest in a beech wood, becoming a narrow foot trail. This sharp left (still the snowmobile trail) heads uphill now, and within 5 minutes you reach a T and the start of the loop around Kaaterskill High Peak and Roundtop. Turn right (west). There is no sign indicating a trail to High Peak's summit, and marking is poor, so at this time you must be very alert to spy it on your left. Within about 500 feet of turning, at elevation 2,933 feet, blue blazes can be seen off the trail heading in a southerly direction.

Kaaterskill High Peak and Roundtop were once thought to be the Catskills' highest.

(Hint: In spring, when water is running down the mountain and when seasonal streambed scars are visible, you'll find a capillary creek at the aforementioned junction. Shortly after this creek, you cross another one, and just

TANBARKING

The tanbark era in the Catskills ran from roughly 1830 to 1870, resulting in the near deforestation of the eastern or Canada hemlock (*Tsuga canadensis*) in the Catskills. The downfall of this romantic symbol of the north woods was its tannin-rich bark that was ground for use in the leather tanning process, mostly for the waterproofing of boots and equipment for Civil War soldiers. Trees could be peeled profitably only to the first branch, so much of the tree bark was wasted, and perhaps less than 1 percent of the lumber was used. Most of the trees were left to rot. Hides were easier to transport than bark, so these were shipped to the Catskills from as far away as Argentina for processing.

Tanning was a wasteful process in terms of the tree's utilization. In H.A. Haring's estimation, "From three to ten hemlocks were felled to obtain a cord of bark [128 cubic feet] . . . probably, in the life of the industry, one hemlock was cut down for each hide tanned into leather." Colonel Pratt, for whom Prattsville is named, turned out more than two million hides during the lifespan of his tannery. Tannersville (previously Edwardsville) was named for Colonel Edwards, one of the Catskills' most enduring "tanlords."

With at least 60 tanneries running for 40 years, you can get an idea of the vast number of trees involved. There are a few virgin tracts of hemlock in the Catskills, most of them positioned on upper elevation or steep slopes where oxen could not work. Chances are, some of these were in their vigorous youth as the industry waned. Aside from the tanner's hut foundations that can still be found in the hills, other evidence of the ruinous industry remains, including the old roads that many of today's marked trails follow.

In a 1984 interview the legendary forester Ed West (Mr. Catskill according to his Adirondack Mountain Club friends) remarked that twenty years earlier he had come across places where hemlock cut in barking days were still hard and firm, noting that "especially where it is damp it will stay like that [it is] one of the most durable and long lived of woods."

Hemlock is too slow-growing for plantations and was not considered a viable candidate for reforestation purposes.

before crossing a third, you see the blazes on your left. Take this with salt; conditions can change.) Look into the forest a couple of hundred feet if you don't see a blaze right away. Once you've found the marks, follow uphill, looking for blazes on rocks and trees, into an area of steep ledges and rock-strewn, moss-cloaked forest.

About an hour of strenuous hiking takes you across several ledges and through many tangled blowdowns as you gain the summit. You will get some views to the north of Kaaterskill Clove and the surrounding mountains, but mainly these are obscured by trees.

You will know you've achieved High Peak's summit when you reach a flat area among the evergreens, where benchmarks can be studied in the flat stones. Pieces of a wrecked aircraft are strewn about in the woods. Herd trails leading off to the east go nowhere in particular. Continue to Hurricane Ledge and its remarkable views by following the trail for another 15 minutes. This brings you to a large expanse of grassy, open terrain with an east-to-west, south-facing aspect. The view is rare, including a variety of topography from the Hudson River valley, the Shawangunks, the Hudson Highlands, and the immediate Catskills. The ledge is a fine place to snooze, snack, photograph, or bivouac.

High Peak and Roundtop are often present in Hudson River school paintings of the nineteenth century as background or subject matter, particularly in scenes from the Catskill Mountain House area. One of the finest representations of Kaaterskill High Peak appears in Thomas Cole's *Sunny Morning on the Hudson*, which depicts a highly romanticized version of High Peak from the vicinity of Roundtop. While it can be argued that the peak is not Kaaterskill, bushwhack up Roundtop someday with a photocopy of the painting, and you will have little doubt that it is.

Continue on blue markers now as you descend the mountain's southerly slopes. The trail is better marked now. There are a few steep spots, so watch your footing. Once again be on the lookout for a T, where a group of low cairns identifies the snowmobile trail loop again. Turn left (east), following the well-marked snowmobile trail for another 40 minutes. This will bring you back to the original loop intersection where you turn right, descend, and retrace your steps to the trailhead.

Return the way you came.

TRIP 45
POET'S LEDGE

RATING: Strenuous

DISTANCE: 3.4 miles

ELEVATION GAIN: 1,231 feet

ESTIMATED TIME: 4.5 hours

MAPS: USGS Kaaterskill; AMC Catskill Mountains; NY-NJTC Northeastern Catskills

A steep hike to a quiet ledge overlooking Kaaterskill Clove, the vantage for Sanford R. Gifford's *October in the Catskills* (1845).

DIRECTIONS

From Exit 20 of the NYS Thruway (I-87) in Saugerties, go north on NY 32 a distance of 6.0 miles and bear left at a light onto NY 32A. At 7.5 miles, bear left at a fork onto Malden Avenue. Proceed another 0.8 mile, crossing Woodstock Avenue, and find the Fernwood restaurant on your left. (You must ask permission to park here.) To park in the forest preserve access parking area, continue on NY 32A at the fork, go through Palenville, joining NY 23A at the light, bear left, and continue 0.5 mile. Park on the right and walk west on NY 23A to Malden Avenue (blocked to traffic from the west), and left again to the trailhead.

TRAIL DESCRIPTION

Only recently rediscovered after a very long period of anonymity (possibly 100 years), Poet's Ledge is now on the map with a signed and marked trail. The Ledge is identified on several very old maps, and was accessible by footpath from Haines Falls as early as 1840. It is likely that hunters and surveyors knew of it before then, for by 1820 preparations were being made just a short distance north across the Clove at Pine Orchard, to build the Catskill Mountain House (1823). Hikers will revel in the magical sense of isolation and removal of this historic destination, as they hover over the precipitous cleft and its adjoining, steep ravines, where almost 20,000 years of ice and running water has conspired to create the unforgettable landscape that is Kaaterskill Clove.

This is a strenuous climb. It may look very close to the road on the map, and it is; it's the elevation you need to consider. Although this can be a hard climb (don't use it as a season opener), finding parking near the trailhead could prove even harder. You may have to street park in Palenville, adding an-

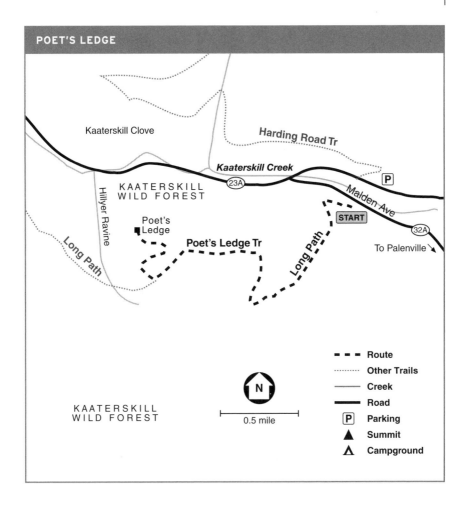

POET'S LEDGE

Kaaterskill Clove

Harding Road Tr

Kaaterskill Creek

P

KAATERSKILL
WILD FOREST

Hillyer Ravine

23A

Malden Ave

START

32A

Poet's
Ledge

Poet's Ledge Tr

Long Path

To Palenville

Long Path

KAATERSKILL
WILD FOREST

N

0.5 mile

- - - Route

·········· Other Trails

——— Creek

━━━ Road

P Parking

▲ Summit

⛺ Campground

other mile to the hike. You can also park at the forest preserve access parking area just west of Palenville on the north side of NY 23A, just before it enters the Catskill Park—but be careful, the traffic is very fast here. By all means drive to the trailhead first and inquire at the Fernwood restaurant if you can park in their lot, which they usually allow if the place isn't busy.

Assuming you've parked at the Fernwood, walk east back the way you came on Malden Avenue and look carefully for the trailhead about 200 feet east of the Fernwood. The trail is poorly identified, but you will see the trusty turquoise Long Path blazes on a telephone pole. Turn south on this little dirt road, and walk about 100 feet to a forest preserve access gate on your right, where you will see blue state trail discs. This is Red Gravel Hill Road. Follow it uphill as it rises behind the Fernwood and switches back once or twice before maintaining a long, fairly steep southerly ascent. The road's surface improves with elevation. By the time you reach the forest preserve boundary, identified by yellow paint blazes and wild forest signage, you'll have worked up a sweat.

Stay alert, as the trail turns off of the road to the right at a trail sign and disc, heading west and uphill, at a point where Red Gravel Hill Road continues into the south onto private property. Now you climb on a heavily washed out 1800s quarry road, hardly recognizable as a road anymore. As this section of trail switches north, it levels and improves. Look on the left now while the forest type changes markedly from second-growth hardwood to the typical oak and laurel cover of the mid-elevations and you'll see the remains of a quarry tucked into the undergrowth along the uphill edge of this terrace. Hand-dressed rubble may still be found along the trail.

The trail climbs, levels, climbs again, and rises through a series of ledges and natural stone steps to a point where a fine view upriver is encountered. Across the clove you will see Palenville Overlook and Indian Head, a pair of high ledges along the southerly flank of South Mountain. You also look out across the Hudson Valley to the vague blue-green hills of the Taconic Plateau and the Green Mountains, far beyond.

Back at it, you are soon pleased to see the forest type changing again, this time to hemlock, promising a boreal "summitlike" experience. A frail northern hardwood forest (beech, birch, and maple) has failed to invade this almost pure stand of conifers. Once again the trail flattens and begins to meander over a delightful and most welcomed stretch of flat ground at 1,700 feet. The trail is often wet here on the northern fringes of Deer Laurel Swamp.

Suddenly you come upon the Poet's Ledge Trail, a yellow-marked spur. The sign is wrapped in hardware cloth (wire) to protect it from porcupines. The distance is marked as 0.47 mile. Descend through an area of primordial texture, past huge boulders heaped with heavy clods of thick moss and detritus. The trail is self-guiding yet needlessly over-marked. Hemlock needles and cones blanket the trail. Patches of fern and laurel, an understory of vigorous red spruce, and maturing hemlocks make up a dense transition zone. Suddenly the trail flattens onto a bare bluestone "dance floor" hemmed in by pitch pines. Continue, bearing left and southwest, descending through ledgy terrain.

As you approach the open vista of Poet's Ledge, be alert to the existence of a substantial crevice dividing the ledge. Though narrow, this crack is deep enough to be of some consequence, especially if it is hidden by snow. It is large enough to fall into, and children should be carefully supervised.

From this small patch of rocks you can sit and muse over the deep abysmal clove and lose your thoughts in time, while gazing west at Onteora Mountain, the north draining ravines off Kaaterskill's shoulder, and the enviable, precariously perched houses of Twilight Park at the top of the Clove.

Although not documented, it is possible that William Cullen Bryant, whom together with Washington Irving created the first literary allusions to the Catskills, visited Poet's Ledge, thus engendering its namesake. More than likely a clever cartographer, familiar with the works of Cooper, Bryant, and Irving, and in tune with the romantic spirit of the times, made it up. Thomas Cole's paintings reveal that he ventured much farther afield than this spot. There is little doubt, however, that the errant walkers and artists of the time knew about Poet's Ledge. What seems hauntingly apparent (and is a subject of recent interest by the Clark Art Institute) is that the peripatetic Sanford R. Gifford painted his *October in the Catskills* from the vantage of Poet's Ledge (most likely from 1845 field sketches), where the Kaaterskill rises to the south and Haines Falls is seen due west. It was shown in the year of his death (1880, from malarial fever) and is now in a private collection.

Return the way you came.

TRIP 46
HUCKLEBERRY POINT

RATING: Moderate
DISTANCE: 3.5 miles
ELEVATION GAIN: 600 feet
ESTIMATED TIME: 3.5 hours
MAPS: USGS Kaaterskill; AMC Catskill Mountains; NY-NJTC Northeastern Catskills

A short walk through hemlock and pitch pine woods to a scenic overlook above Platte Clove and the Hudson Valley.

DIRECTIONS
The following directions will bring you up "the back way" over the rugged and scenic Platte Clove Road, a seasonal road that should not be attempted unless it is legally open and clear of ice and snow (April 15 through Nov 15). When it is closed or when the road conditions are questionable, follow the directions to the Codfish Point trailhead.

From Exit 20 of the NYS Thruway (I-87) in Saugerties (either northbound or southbound), bear left a short distance to the intersection of NY 32 and

NY 212. Set your odometer to zero and head west on NY 212 toward Wood-stock. At 2.0 miles, watch carefully on your right for CR 35 (Blue Mountain Road). Follow it, bearing left at a Y, through Blue Mountain. At 5.3 miles, pass Woodstock-Saugerties Road (to Woodstock and Bearsville) on your left. Pass Manorville Road on your right at 5.4 miles. Now you will head straight up the mountain on the infamously scenic Platte Clove Road. Use caution! As the road tops out, look on your right for the Kaaterskill Wild Forest parking area at 7.8 miles. Turn right into the lot. You'll see the trail register and trail signs here for Steenbergh Road (the trail follows this dirt road, named for an early bluestone quarry) and the blue trail. The trail begins on the northwest side of the lot. (For off-season directions to this trailhead, consult the Codfish Point hike, Trip 39).

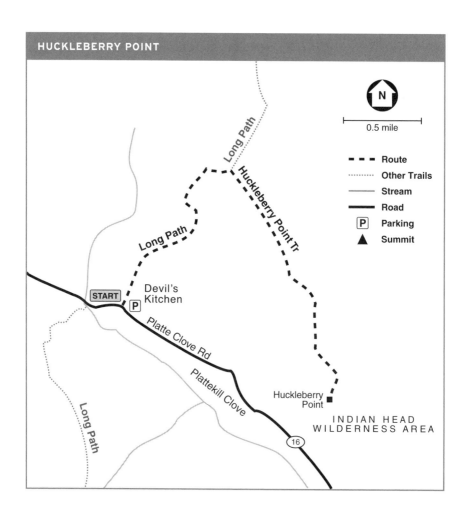

TRAIL DESCRIPTION

Huckleberry Point is an ideal picnicking spot, suitable for those sunny, clear days when an easy hike to its quiet, scenic ledges is the goal. However, especially on nice weekends, expect to see many other hikers. And it is no wonder—this pretty hike takes you to one of the Escarpment's most accessible and expansive southeasterly viewsheds on an easy trail with a minimum vertical rise.

The Huckleberry Point Trail is reached via the Kaaterskill High Peak snowmobile trail, which circles Kaaterskill High Peak and Roundtop, which you follow for 1.0 mile. From the Kaaterskill Wild Forest parking area, follow the blue foot-trail markers, red/orange snowmobile-trail markers, and aqua Long Path blazes (sparse). The first section of trail rises through a dense hemlock forest over a deeply eroded old quarry road, within audible range of Mossy Creek, lying downhill to the east. After 20 minutes of hiking uphill, the trail reaches a Y in the hardwoods where you bear right. Continue for 10 minutes to an arrow pointing to the right, following the blue footpath and snowmobile markers. Another 5 minutes along, you will leave the blue trail, bearing right (east) at the yellow-marked Huckleberry Point Trail (there's a sign and arrow).

Travel through a level hardwood forest with a developing hemlock understory, where you will see obscure signs of early settlement: stone piles, walls, and perhaps an old foundation or two, the remains of an early quarrying and subsistence-farming community. Within a few minutes you drop slightly downhill into an oak wood, crossing Mossy Brook, that's several feet deep during runoff. Ford cautiously and continue directly on the other side. Don't make the mistake of following one of the old overgrown quarry roads you may see at this point.

After the brook you begin to climb slightly into an oak and beech transitional forest. The trail undulates easily up and downhill, yielding

The vertical ledges of Huckleberry Point offer rare views of Platte Clove.

early spring views of the Devil's Path peaks, including Overlook, Indian Head, Twin, Sugarloaf, and Plateau. At this point you will enjoy the extensive "slicks" (shrub thickets) of mountain laurel (*Kalmia latifolia*) an evergreen named by Linnaeus for his researcher and student, Peter Kalm (1716–1779). These bright-leaved members of the heath family are sharply contrasted against a young overstory of paper birch. Laurel blooms in late spring with large, pink flower clusters. These vigorous but fragile trailside shrubs are easily killed or damaged by overzealous (or untrained) trail maintainers.

Within a half hour or less of the Huckleberry Point trailhead, you cross the southerly slope of a pitch pine hillock. In this area you may see the old white tin-can top markers of the Nature Friends Trail, a group which originated from German expatriates who liked to wander here and, in homage to that spirit, called themselves the Vanderverder or wandering birds.

This is the prettiest section of trail, where you begin to sense the abyss ahead. Your anticipation builds as the ledgy oak-pine terrain suddenly opens up like a curtain call onto the blueberry precipices of the Point. The views are expansive and the ledges are vertical, so be careful. You see the Devil's Path Mountains in the Indian Head Wilderness Area directly south, only a few miles away across the thousand-foot-deep Platte Clove (the hamlet of West Saugerties, below you, is 500 feet above sea level; you're at 2,200 feet). The north and east slopes are carved deeply by post-glacial parallel drainage ravines. Overlook (with the fire tower) and the Plattekill Ridge turns into the west to Indian Head, whose cigar-store Indian profile is very apparent, lying supine with its distinct chin, nose, and eyebrow. West of it is Twin, then Sugarloaf and Plateau. Going east from Overlook, dropping down its slopes to the small, near-vertical outcrop of Minister's Face, you look south over the east basin of the Ashokan Reservoir to the toothy hills of the Shawangunks. The left edge of the tooth is Sky Top; you can see the Albert K. Smiley Memorial Tower (a.k.a. Sky Top Tower) with binoculars at 203 degrees. To the right is Eagle Cliff. Hidden on the flat space between them are Mohonk Lake and the Mohonk Mountain House. Moving along the descending ridge of the northern Shawangunks is Guyot Hill, and finally, the last bump is Bonticou Crag. Moving east across the rolling expanse of valley above the flatlands of the Esopus and Rondout valleys, you may see the Fishkill Ridge dipping down into the Hudson at the Highlands, and coming north, you see the city of Kingston, then Saugerties. In the middle of the Hudson's southernmost visible bay is the Esopus Meadows lighthouse at 189 degrees. Above the marshes of Tivoli Bays, just north of the Kingston-Rhinecliff Bridge, are the buildings of Bard College.

With patience, you can find Stissing Mountain at 135 degrees. The long ridge in the east is the Southern Taconic Plateau.

The large birds you'll invariably see riding the thermals are not often hawks, but turkey vultures. Interestingly, you'll be looking down at their backs a good deal of the time as they scour the ledges for carrion.

Return the way you came.

TRIP 47
NORTH POINT

RATING: Moderate
DISTANCE: 7.0 miles
ELEVATION GAIN: 700 feet
ESTIMATED TIME: 4.5 hours
MAPS: USGS Kaaterskill; AMC Catskill Mountains; NY-NJTC Northeastern Catskills; North Lake Area

A popular outing along the Escarpment Trail's cliffs to the favorite haunts of the Hudson River school of landscape painters.

DIRECTIONS
From NY 23A in Haines Falls, turn north onto CR 18 (a.k.a. North Lake Road/ Mountain House Road) and travel 2.3 miles to the North/South Lake Public Campground's main gate.

TRAIL DESCRIPTION
This historic, scenic day hike begins along the legendary cliffs of Pine Orchard and reveals the best scenery of the Escarpment. This is the heart of the Catskills, the place that prompted the eloquence of James Fenimore Cooper, the fanciful pen of Washington Irving, and the romantic vision of Thomas Cole. If you have time for only one hike in the Catskills, make it this one.

The best way to approach this hike is from the beach and picnic area parking lot of the North/South Lake Public Campground and day-use area. This way you can conveniently combine the hike with a picnic or swim in spring-fed North Lake. Or you can bring your canoe and paddle North/South Lakes, reserve a campsite, and spend the night. Your other choices are to park outside

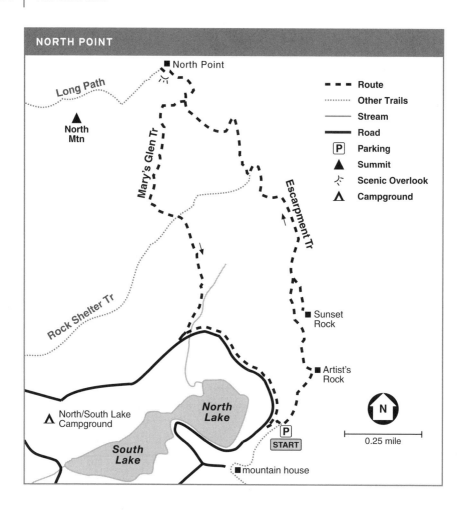

NORTH POINT

■ North Point

North Mtn ▲

Long Path

Mary's Glen Tr

Escarpment Tr

Rock Shelter Tr

■ Sunset Rock

■ Artist's Rock

North Lake

▲ North/South Lake Campground

South Lake

P

START

■ mountain house

- - - Route
········· Other Trails
——— Stream
▬▬▬ Road
P Parking
▲ Summit
⚡ Scenic Overlook
Δ Campground

N

0.25 mile

the campground's main gate and walk to the North Lake beach (a walk-in fee applies), or take the yellow-marked Rock Shelter Trail (no walk-in fee) to connect with the Mary's Glen Trail. To use the latter two options, park outside the main gate in the Scutt Road trailhead parking area. (Anticipate having an additional 2.0 miles of featureless, round-trip mileage using either option.)

Pay the day-use fee and drive through the main gate, bearing left at the Y to the North Lake beach and picnic area. As you approach the bathing beach and picnic area parking lot, note the North Mountain Trails sign on the left. Park, and backtrack along the road to the trailhead and follow the yellow spur east to the blue-marked Escarpment Trail (or from the picnic area simply walk east), toward Artist's and Sunset rocks, Newman's Ledge, and North Point. As you join the Escarpment Trail, turn left (north) and follow the edge of some vertical drops as the trail ascends easily in dense woods.

A series of historic lookouts begins as scenic vistas, opening up to the east across the Hudson Valley. The original locations of these lookouts as they were understood by Mountain House guests has been the subject of speculation among local toponymists, the most outspoken of whom is Robert A. Gildersleeve. If you'd like to square off in the debate, take a look at his recent *Catskill Mountain Trail Guide* (Black Dome Press). Very few of today's Escarpment placenames accurately match those of the nineteenth century, but for now, we'll stick to the most recent ones.

A snowshoer prepares to walk across North Lake.

Climb through broken ledges and along a rocky footway to the first signed lookout, Artist's Rock, among the well-loved and infamous field studios of Thomas Cole. Cole was fond of pointing out his home, Locust Grove, in Catskill from this spot, something you can still do today with the aid of binoculars; it's easier to spot Mount Everett and the long ridge of the Taconics across the Hudson River. Continue, and soon you arrive at Prospect Rock (2,280 feet), a more expansive version of Artist's Rock. Continue along, passing another little dimple of rock to the right of the trail, once known as Sunrise Rock, Sunset Rock, and Lake View Pinnacle, recognizable by its old initial carvings and more recent graffiti.

Continue along the trail, passing through pitch pine "orchards," so named for pure stands of the pine whose crooked limbs have some resemblance to a fruit tree. (This was the result of the romantic imagination at work, remember.) Soon, a large monolithic rock plateau appears to the right of the trail. This is Sunset Rock; a place that Mr. Gildersleeve points out was once the famous Bear's Den. As you reach the Sunset Rock Trail, bear right and follow the spur trail through the pitch pines to the rock, and you'll agree that the place-name works either way. The deep fissures and cracks make suitable bear habitat and you will want to be cautious not to slip. From here, the westerly views are magnificent. You see Kaaterskill High Point and Roundtop above the lakes, and the long line of the southerly Escarpment heading for Overlook Mountain. Farther south, you can make out the Shawangunk Ridge, with Sky Top jutting out to the left of Overlook's easterly slopes. Retrace your steps to the trail junction and continue north, climbing easily to Newman's Ledge, a fine, open vertical cliff looking northeast at 2,500 feet. Judging by its carvings, this was also a popular spot for Mountain House guests. Views expand to the north now, to include Albany on a good day, and the nearby valley of Rip Van Winkle Hollow (a.k.a. Sleepy Hollow). Look carefully and you might see the Old Mountain Road against the north face of the hollow. The trail continues north over a rocky surface, climbing terraces through hardwood and spruce thickets, walking the edge of a bog before meeting with the Rock Shelter Trail at the site of Badman Cave (2,650 feet). Climb to the right, remaining on the Escarpment Trail, walking the lip of a scenic, boreal ridge, and soon entering a flat hardwood forest. As you reach the junction with the Mary's Glen Trail (your return route), bear right on the Escarpment Trail to begin the only con- tinuously steep section of the trail. After 15 minutes of strenuous and aerobic effort, you pass through a white-birch stand that precedes the large, flat rocks and long views from North Point's summit. Investigate views from various parts of the ledge: Windham High Peak, Burnt Knob and Acra Point, Black- head and Roundtop to the north; the Hudson Valley toward Albany, to the east through the Taconics and Berkshires; and south across the Highlands and into the Escarpment, where North and South lakes lie like spilled quicksilver under the shadows of Kaaterskill High Peak and Roundtop.

Descend now, retracing your steps to the previous junction, and turn right on the yellow-marked Mary's Glen Trail. You'll walk through thick spruce-fir forests as you descend to cross the Rock Shelter Trail, continuing through a wet area to cross the top of Ashley's Falls before descending into the Glen.

This spot was a favorite of Mary Scribner's (wife of Ira Scribner, who op- erated a sawmill on Spruce Creek above Kaaterskill Falls). The Glen Mary Cottage was most likely where Henry David Thoreau, with William Ellery Channing, spoke of spending an evening in the early 1840s. Go left when you reach the bottom of Ashley's Falls (also called Mary's Glen Falls) on a spur trail to the stone rubble below the cascade. Turn around and follow the trail out to the campground road, turn left, and walk 0.5 mile back to the picnic area and bathing beach parking area.

TRIP 48
INSPIRATION POINT AND BOULDER ROCK

RATING: Moderate

DISTANCE: 8.0 miles

ELEVATION GAIN: 500 feet

ESTIMATED TIME: 4 hours

MAPS: USGS Kaaterskill; AMC Catskill Mountains; NY-NJTC, North Lake Area, Northeastern Catskills

A cliff-edge hike above Kaaterskill Clove to the North/South Lake Public Campsite, returning along the lakes.

DIRECTIONS

From NY 23A in Haines Falls, turn north onto CR 18 (a.k.a. North Lake Road/ Mountain House Road) and travel 2.3 miles to Scutt Road. Turn right on Scutt Road and within 300 feet turn right again into the Escarpment trailhead parking area (a.k.a. Scutt Road Corral).

TRAIL DESCRIPTION

The scenic lookouts and labyrinthine footpaths surrounding the old mountain houses of North Lake's Pine Orchard area have been destination hikes since the early 1800s. Detailed in the many guidebooks of the day, it could be said that the trail system around Pine Orchard had become America's first amusement park, and the great artworks of the Hudson River school of landscape painting that originated among them were the visual blockbusters serving as its first cinema.

Many of the trails emanating from the grounds of the Kaaterskill Hotel and the Catskill Mountain House have since disappeared, leaving only fanciful placenames such as Fairy Spring, Druid Rocks, and the Sphinx (Consult Robert A. Gildersleeve's *Catskill Mountain House Trail Guide* for details). But the scenery remains, and today's Escarpment Trail highlights the best of it. To visit the 175-year-old scenic destinations of Inspiration Point and Boulder Rock, walk the Escarpment's cliff edge between South Lake and the Catskill Mountain House.

Walk east across Scutt Road onto the Escarpment Trail, or ET (also the Sleepy Hollow Horse Trail at this point). Descend, soon crossing two old rail-

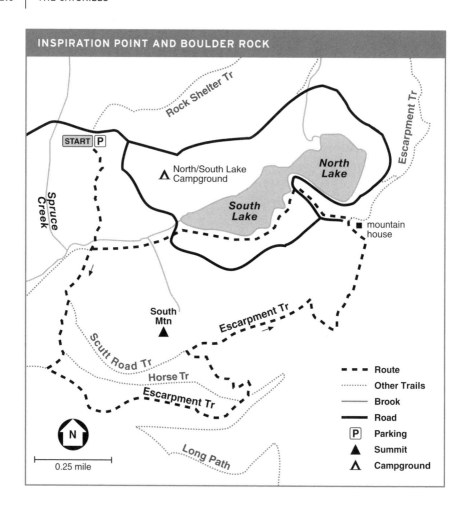

INSPIRATION POINT AND BOULDER ROCK

road beds, the first one belonging to the Catskill and Tannersville Railway, abandoned in 1915, the second to the Ulster and Delaware's Kaaterskill Branch that lasted to 1940. Cross Spruce Creek on a footbridge and ascend slightly, passing an unmarked woods road to the left, once the approach to the now derelict, but still interesting, stone laundry building of the Catskill Mountain House. This is the only extant structure remaining from the great hotel heydays.

Continue on the ET to the trail junction. Turn right, following signs for Layman's Monument. The trail passes a register and descends through laurels, arriving at the monument to the lost firefighter at 1.2 miles. Now the trail ascends, winding along the Escarpment's edge past steep drops. If you've timed your visit to coincide with the appearance of the pinxster blossoms (mid-May to mid-June), you'll also see swallow-tails, bronze coppers, and cabbage butterflies alighting on them and on the many-colored hawkweeds and wildflowers clinging to the weather-beaten cliffs along the way. Dodging in and out of oak and laurel woods over easy terrain, at 1.6 miles you pass the yellow-marked connector trail to the Scutt Road Trail to the left. Continue straight ahead on the ET, arriving at Sunset Rock at 1.7 miles. Views improve ahead at Inspiration Point (1.9 miles).

Inspiration Point is a long, vertical sandstone ledge with a southern exposure. From it you look across the deep canyon-like Kaaterskill Clove, at the precariously perched homes of Santa Cruz and Twilight Parks, and of the mountains immediately to the south, Kaaterskill High Peak and Roundtop. You can look west to Colonel's Chair (the section of Hunter Mountain where the ski trails can be seen). Over the top of Colonel's Chair is West Kill Mountain. Rusk and Ever-

The vertical precipice of Inspiration Point, high above Kaaterskill Clove.

green can be seen beyond. Fifteen hundred feet below you, Kaaterskill Creek flows toward the Hudson. At 304 degrees, Haines Falls can be seen. Without binoculars, a flume is not visible unless the water table is running high. The two mountains to the right of the Clove's head in Haines Falls are Onteora and Parker. Looking southeast and downhill from Kaaterskill High Peak, you can easily identify the otherwise elusive Poet's Ledge at 182 degrees (it is the higher of the two ledges on the slope's western side).

Continue through the forest for another 20 minutes of easy walking, passing views (and precipitous, dangerous ledges) to the south and east. Note Palenville Overlook, the ragged rock outcropping jutting from the Clove's northern flank, down to your right. Here the ET joins the horse trail at a level intersection, where you bear right. Two hundred feet farther is Shorey Point, named for an early DEC forester when the point was treeless. The Long Path joins the ET now, following the horse trail up from Palenville.

Bear left here on the ET/Long Path toward Boulder Rock (1.3 miles) and North Lake Campground (2.0 miles). The trail climbs a bit now, flattening as you approach the Hotel Kaaterskill site on South Mountain. Here there is another junction, where the red Scutt Road Trail goes left (west). The hotel site is neither marked nor obvious from the junction, but lies north of it and can be explored on the herd trails that circle and penetrate it. There are few remains, only a dump and some stone foundations to which the state has contributed its own debris. The hotel was built in 1881 and burned in 1924 as the result of a kitchen fire. In 1881, it was believed to be the largest wood-frame structure in the world.

Continue on the ET through a pretty oak and laurel forest dotted with single red spruce trees, (passing an unmarked trail that descends to the South Lake beach and picnic area road) and within 0.5 mile you reach a trail junction where the red-marked trail shortcuts off to the left toward the Catskill Mountain House site. Avoid this trail and continue following the blue markers, bearing right, and descending slightly. In a few moments you reach Split Rock, a large fractured megalith with a deep fissure lying close to the trail. Suddenly, you're at Boulder Rock, a large erratic that sits on a flat ledge with outstanding views. Old photos show an ornate gazebo perched on the rock.

Views of the Hudson Valley here are outstanding, giving an idea of what's to come over at Pine Orchard. You have fine, far-reaching views of the Shawangunks, Taconics, Berkshires, Stissing, the Hudson River and its sprawling lowlands. Continue on the trail, leaving boulder rock at your back, and ascending to pass the red trail on your left. Ledges—some of them dangerous— continue as you travel north along the Escarpment's edge. At Eagle Rock, where some carvings dating to 1850 are seen in the stone, bear slightly right to avoid dead-ending in a pitch pine orchard, drop downhill slightly, and after a switchback in the trail, arrive at the flat expanse where the Catskill Mountain House stood—the original Pine Orchard. Observe the stone carvings made by the guests of the Mountain House (and some lesser practitioners of late). When you've had enough of the views across the valley (similar to Boulder Rock's), head west with the ledge at your back and watch the blue markers. Shortly, the ET departs to the right (north) and drops downhill to an open area just east of North Lake (visible nearby) with its public beach, picnic grounds, and pavilions, and you're at the point where the Otis Elevated Railroad rose from the valley floor to the top of the Escarpment (you can see the cut in the mountain by exploring to the east a little here. It can be seen as far away as the Taconic Plateau). Leave the ET now and bear left, following the road that you can see ahead (also marked as a snowmobile trail) and walk along the south shore of North Lake. You will also see yellow foot-trail markers. Follow this road around the peninsula that juts into the narrows between North and South lakes, and at a point where the snowmobile trail turns east, follow the yellow foot trail into the hemlock woods as it goes south along the lake's edge. Skirt the edge of South Lake and walk past the bath house, keeping it to your left. The yellow trail continues along the edge of South Lake, re-entering the woods where the beach and the lake come together. (If you're feet are sore, you can follow the access road that appears to the left.) Follow the yellow trail into the woods. After 20 minutes, the trail ends on the South Lake access road (paved). As you rise to the road, you'll see the lake to your right. Bear left and across the road to the yellow-marked and well identified ski trail, a pleasant, flat trail that brings you 0.5 mile to the intersection of the ET and Scutt Road trails. From here, bear right on the ET to return to the trailhead parking area.

TRIP 49
KAATERSKILL FALLS

RATING: Easy
DISTANCE: 1.4 miles
ELEVATION GAIN: 200 feet
ESTIMATED TIME: 1.5 hours
MAPS: USGS Kaaterskill; AMC Catskill Mountains; NY-NJTC North Lake Area, Northeastern Catskills

The most popular short hike in the Catskills, to the state's highest waterfall, great for families.

DIRECTIONS
From Exit 20 of the NYS Thruway (I-87) in Saugerties, take NY 32 6.0 miles to NY 32A, bearing left into Palenville, and left at the light in Palenville at 8.0 miles onto NY 23A, ascending through Kaaterskill Clove. The trailhead is located at 11.2 miles, at the hairpin turn on NY 23A between the towns of Haines Falls and Palenville. Park at the designated area 0.2 mile west (uphill) of the trailhead.

TRAIL DESCRIPTION

By the mid-nineteenth century Romantic period, Kaaterskill Falls had become the most popular symbol of the American wilderness, when notions of the "picturesque" and "sublime" focused mainly on European scenery. The west was still a frontier by the time the Catskill Mountain House was built on the ledges of Pine Orchard in 1823, and Niagara Falls—discovered by travelers as early as 1683 was old news by 1778. One reason for Kaaterskill Falls' immense popularity was its proximity to the largest U.S. population center of the time—New York City—and to the fact that the rising upper and middle classes now had the time and means for destination travel. Another was the daunting realization that they are even higher than Niagara Falls, falling in two tiers for a total of 260 feet. By the late 1800s, the falls were averaging 100 visitors a day, most of them residents at the mountaintop hotels that were struggling

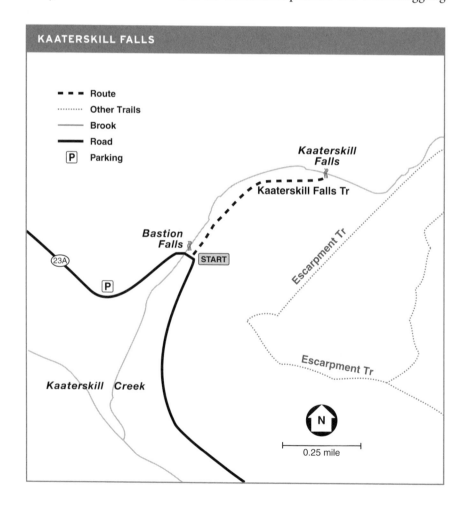

to accommodate more and more guests. At the time, people believed that nearby Roundtop Mountain (3,804 feet) was the highest of the Catskill peaks and therefore represented the heart of the Catskills, and they believed that the Catskills were the embodiment of a new national identity, making its definitive case in the art and literature of the times. Spearheading this new American Romantic movement was the singular image and symbol of Kaaterskill Falls.

Today the hotels are gone and the falls have enjoyed relative obscurity, but you won't believe it if you arrive on a sunny weekend, when the parking area is full, and hikers of all ages walk single file up the trail like strings of Sherpas.

From the parking lot, descend along the road (NY 23A) cautiously, keeping to the left, where the shoulder is wider. (For some reason, drivers do not show pedestrians the respect they deserve here, although new caution lights and signage have helped.) Supervise your children carefully for the 0.2 mile walk to the trailhead. Cross the highway bridge next to Bastion Falls, bear left, and go around the guardrail to begin the climb. There's a trail sign here, indicating the Falls at 0.5 mile on the dead-end spur trail. Follow yellow markers uphill steeply over stone and wooden steps to the trail register. Continue through a small grove of virgin hemlock (one of four such groves in the Kaaterskill Wild Forest) as the trail follows close along the shaded banks of Spruce Creek. Within 15 to 20 minutes you will arrive at the falls, hidden from view until you arrive at their base.

Try to time your visit to a period that is not too dry, and you'll be treated to the remarkable double-plumed fall; the uppermost, initial 175-foot drop is the most spectacular. The upper plume fills a huge basin (not seen from below) known as the Amphitheater, immortalized as the slumbering place of Rip Van Winkle.

Kaaterskill Falls' upper plume (the Amphitheater).

Many people scramble up the slope on the south side of the creek to scale the narrow herd trail leading behind the upper falls—a practice that has created sustained impact problems, and is the reason for the original Escarpment Trail's relocation to its present trailhead on Scutt Road. The DEC has long pondered the difficult management problems facing this area. Not only is the impact high, so are the dangers. Several people have died here, most of them in falls from the top. At least two people have (barely) survived falls from above. Several dogs are also among the deceased. The most memorable of them was Vite, a dog who, in the 1800s, had been trained to jump at his master's whistle. A thoughtless whistle caused Vite to jump over the falls. The bereaved master engaged a stone cutter to carve a lavish memorial to "Vite, the Bayard of Dogs" that can still be seen in the ledges on the steep slopes below the falls, where there was once a series of paths, ropes, and ladders leading to the Amphitheater.

The artists, writers, and poets who focused their creative genius on Kaaterskill Falls are legion. Thomas Cole is credited with the first and most influential painting, *The Falls of Cattskill, New York* (1825). Its impact in creating public interest about the Falls was immediate. Cole's protégés and imitators followed, among them Jaspar Cropsey (a late-generation Hudson River school painter), W.H. Bartlett, Winslow Homer, Harry Fenn, Currier and Ives, and countless engravers and illustrators. The poets featured William Cullen Bryant in particular ("Thanatopsis," "The Catterskill Falls"); even Thomas Cole was inspired to write poetry and essays about the Falls, as were many writers of the Knickerbocker Period—Washington Irving central among them. Thoreau visited the Scribners' cabin at Kaaterskill Falls in the summer of 1844, during a brief hiatus in the construction of his own cabin at Walden Pond, along with William Ellery Channing (recognized as a founder of Transcendentalism). However, Thoreau deleted references of his visit to the Catskills in the first draft of *Walden*.

John Bartram, the chief American horticulturalist of his time, and his son, the naturalist, explorer, and writer, William Bartram, visited Kaaterskill Falls in 1753. William's book dealing with his explorations, *The Travels of William Bartram* (1791), had a clear impact on both Wordsworth and Coleridge, who would in turn influence the American Romantic imagination. Timothy Dwight, president of Yale College in 1823, contributed his *Description of Kaaterskill Falls, September 28, 1815*. Listings in gazetteers, travel guides, magazines, geographical dictionaries, histories, sketch and art books, pictorial geographies, companion guides, and parlor books further assured the immortalization of Kaaterskill Falls as a household name.

But the most memorable of all the popular literary utterances comes from the American writer James Fenimore Cooper, in a passage that Alf Evers has called "one of the finest pieces of promotional writing to ornament the 19th Century." The reference is from Cooper's *The Pioneers*, published in the same year that the Catskill Mountain House opened for business (1823). The protagonist, Natty Bumppo (a.k.a. Leatherstocking and Hawkeye, Cooper's vision of the savviest woodsman alive), remarks on the Falls to his young companion, Edwards: "To my judgment, lad, it's the best piece of work that I have met with in the woods; and none know how often the hand of God is seen in a wilderness but them that rove it for a man's life."

Until you make the trip yourself, you'll have to take Natty's word for it. Return the way you came.

TRIP 50
BLACKHEAD MOUNTAIN

RATING: Strenuous

DISTANCE: 4.2 miles

ELEVATION GAIN: 1,550 feet

ESTIMATED TIME: 3 hours

MAP: USGS Freehold; USGS Hensonville; AMC Catskill Mountains; NY-NJTC Northeast Catskills

A steep climb into Lockwood Gap to the Escarpment Trail.

DIRECTIONS

From the corners of CR 40 and CR 56 in the village of Maplecrest, follow Big Hollow Road (CR 56) to the north and east, passing Peck Road on your left. Continue 4.5 miles to the end of CR 56 where you will see the red-marked Black Dome Range trailhead on the left. Park at the dead end (Batavia Kill/Black Dome trailhead) just ahead.

The short but scenic loop trail over Blackhead Mountain (3,940 feet) rewards you with the best scenery of the Windham Blackhead Range Wilderness without the extra work of traversing the entire "big three"—Blackhead, Black Dome, and Thomas Cole mountains. The west-lying two peaks of the range, with the exception of a small group of lookouts on the south and east of Black Dome's virgin fir summit (3,950 feet), have little to compare with Blackhead's enormous

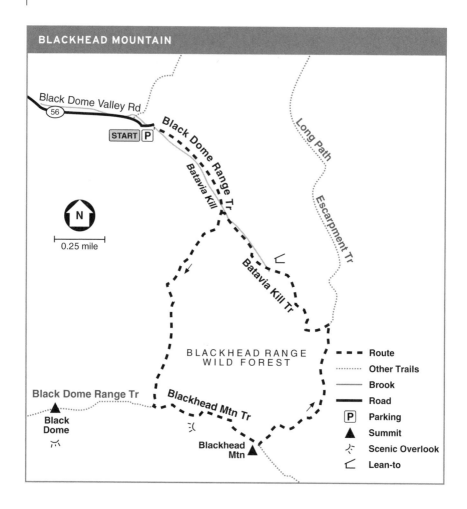

BLACKHEAD MOUNTAIN

Black Dome Valley Rd
56
START P
Black Dome Range Tr
Batavia Kill
Batavia Kill Tr
Long Path
Escarpment Tr

N
0.25 mile

BLACKHEAD RANGE
WILD FOREST

Black Dome Range Tr
Blackhead Mtn Tr
Black Dome

Blackhead Mtn

- - - Route
.... Other Trails
——— Brook
——— Road
P Parking
▲ Summit
Scenic Overlook
Lean-to

western viewshed, and still farther west, Thomas Cole Mountain—by a cruel twist of fate—is viewless. In spite of this, one of the nicest ledges in the Blackheads is the small lookout on Black Dome, so you may want to add a little extra time to diverge westward when you reach Lockwood Gap, bagging Blackhead on the way out.

Begin at the rustic Batavia Kill trailhead, and follow the route of both the yellow-marked Batavia Kill and red-marked Black Dome Range trails as they make their way southeast through dense mixed hemlock and hardwoods, crossing a pair of footbridges. The trail follows the washed-out imprint of an old road for 0.5 mile to the confluence of two creeks, at a trail junction where the Black Dome Range Trail bears southwest, and where your return route, the Batavia Kill Trail, continues east. Turn right on the Black Dome Range Trail, which soon climbs into the gap, becoming very steep. You will pass a

The Blackhead Range as it appears from the north.

reliable spring on the left, odd for this elevation in the Catskills and one of few near the Escarpment Trail, making an ideal resting spot. The ascent continues relentlessly through Lockwood Gap and levels in the saddle between Black Dome to the west and Blackhead to the east. (The very worthwhile, 0.5-mile ascent of 500 feet to Black Dome's pure fir summit will add another 1.5 hours to your hike, so weigh this side trip against your time and the weather.) The route to Blackhead is to the left (east), following the yellow-marked Blackhead Mountain Trail, a short connector between the Black Dome Range Trail and the Escarpment Trail. There is a poorly sited, legal campsite in Lockwood Gap to the northeast of the junction, with very little if any flat ground.

The Blackhead Mountain Trail ascends immediately into the east, climbing the long westerly slopes of Blackhead. A succession of increasingly scenic terraces leads to a grassy outcropping with broad and penetrating views southwest. These are the hike's best views. You see West Kill over Hunter Mountain's ski slopes, Hunter's fire tower, and the Catskill high peaks area, including Slide, Table, Cornell, and Wittenberg. East of Hunter is Stony Clove, Plateau, and the Devil's Path mountains to Overlook. Kaaterskill High Peak and Roundtop are due south. The trail climbs steeply ahead, easing up at 3,700 feet. The trail follows along through balsam and soon arrives at the summit, a bald but viewless dome enclosed in a fir thicket. The Escarpment Trail crosses the summit here. Follow it to the left (northeast), as it descends steeply, bending into the north and passing a scenic, east-facing overlook on the right. The trail terraces its way down through birch, beech, striped maple, and a ground cover of asters where the sun reaches through the canopy, and Canada violets, trout lilies, trillium, bunchberry, and oxalis are your regular companions along the trail.

The junction of the yellow-marked Batavia Kill Trail is reached at 2,850 feet in elevation. Bear left, following it downhill and northwest, leaving the only lean-to in the Windham Blackhead Range Wilderness to your right. The contours relax as you descend along the kill, and you'll find yourself back at the junction with the Black Dome Range Trail.

Continue straight ahead and you'll soon arrive at the trailhead parking area.

TRIP 51
WINDHAM HIGH PEAK

RATING: Strenuous
DISTANCE: 6.6 miles
ELEVATION GAIN: 1,475 feet
ESTIMATED TIME: 5 to 7 hours
MAPS: USGS Hensonville; AMC Catskill Mountains; NY-NJTC Northeastern Catskills

A charming, but strenuous, walk through mature spruce plantations to the northern escarpment with sweeping views to the north.

DIRECTIONS
From NY 23 turn south on CR 65 to Hensonville. From there go 2.0 miles into Maplecrest on CR 40. Turn left on CR 56 (Big Hollow Road) until you reach Peck Road at 1.8 miles on your left. The trail begins within a mile at the end of Peck Road.

TRAIL DESCRIPTION
This scenic hike follows the Escarpment's northern shoulder, where the long, western-sloping ridge of Windham High Peak (3,524 feet) reaches in a high

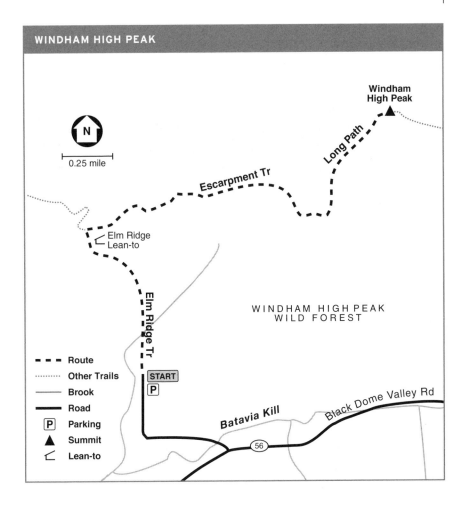

arch from Burnt Knob to Elm Ridge. Windham High Peak is the last mountain on the 23-mile Escarpment Trail beginning at Scutt Road Corral in Haines Falls. This 4,250-acre wild forest area was renamed the Windham Blackhead Range Wilderness in 2008.

Begin on the yellow-marked trail toward Elm Ridge Lean-to (1.0 mile), where you also see New York State snowmobile trail signs. Follow a dirt road through vestigial pasturelands, now grown into a forest of mixed hardwoods where stone walls mark the field divisions of early settlements. In 15 minutes you should reach the trail junction. Turn right, following the blue (Escarpment Trail, Long Path) markers indicating Windham High Peak, Burnt Knob, and Acra Point. The Elm Ridge Lean-to will appear on your right as you continue.

Windham High Peak.

The lean-to is nicely situated and frequently used. Nearby campsites are plentiful, however, if the lean-to is occupied and you are interested in spending the night.

After a half hour of hiking, you pass through dark, Norway-spruce forests that will spark your imagination. These trees (including the Norway pine) get their name from their nursery of origin in Norway, Maine. The trees were planted throughout the Catskills by the Civilian Conservation Corps in the 1920s and 1930s, mostly in the open fields of abandoned farmlands. Higher elevation lands in the Catskills were never very good for farming, and when they "ran out" as pasture lands, farmers often found it more profitable to sell to the state rather than to pay taxes. This stretch used to be very wet in the early season, until an Appalachian Mountain Club (AMC) trail crew improved it. The trail winds through these magnificent forests and then through hardwoods, gradually ascending. Most of the forest cover in this wild forest area falls within the northern hardwood types of beech, birch, and maple, with companion species of hemlock, basswood, red and white oak, and white ash.

Signs of early settlement are everywhere, some hidden and reclaimed by the forest, revealed by telltale, vagrant apple trees and runaway grape vines.

An extensive, pure sugar-maple forest follows as the trail gently ascends. Thick mats of grass cover the rich soils of the western slopes and you cross a seasonal creek. (The streams in the Windham Blackhead Range Wilderness area are high gradient tributaries of the Batavia Kill and Catskill Creeks and are dry most of the year.)

When you reach the southerly shoulder of the mountain at 3,000 feet in elevation, you get a look at the nearby Blackhead Range and the more westerly East Jewett Range. Blackhead and Black Dome are named for the dark balsam-fir growth you can see on their summits. At this point, you are about 3 miles into the walk; turn northeast for the 0.5-mile, 520-foot climb to the summit. During periods of scanty foliage in this birch, cherry, and maple forest, you will be able to look east at Burnt Knob and Acra Point and the long Escarpment ridge. The last (and steepest) incline will take you about 30 minutes. Once on the long, level summit, you discover a benchmark and the views that have made Windham such a popular destination hike.

The most imposing of these views will be into the Blackhead Range that feels remarkably close, only 3.0 miles south across the scenic Black Dome Valley. Down and to your right, southwest, you see the sister peaks of Round Hill and Van Loan Hill. Westerly views are available from northwest side of the summit, on a short spur to a rocky area that you will find easily. From this point you see a long line of lesser peaks disappearing into the Schoharie Valley, a flat stretch of open fields and farms, including Ginseng, Zoar, and Cave Mountain, and slightly to the north, Richmond and Huntersfield mountains with Ashland Pinnacle between them.

The most popular view is from beyond the summit (east), where a graffiti-inscribed outcrop hangs above the Hudson Valley. (These inscriptions are not of the same genre as the North Lake variety, and the few decent initials have been heavily eroded and defaced.) From here you can see the Helderberg Escarpment and, on a clear day, Albany's Empire Plaza (the Egg) and the State University buildings. It is also likely that you'll see Vermont's Green Mountains, the Berkshires, and the Taconic Range, including the Greylock massif, a geological member of the Taconics. Looking down over the ridge you see Burnt Knob (3,180 feet), the second knoll from Windham High Peak. The Escarpment Trail goes downhill at this point, to Burnt Knob, Acra Point, and points south.

The quiet town of Acra was the preferred hideout of the gangster Jack "Leggs" Diamond, whom many believe was murdered by rival mobster Dutch Schultz. According to Diamond's biographer, Gary Levine (*Anatomy of a*

Gangster), Leggs was pulling down over $16,000 a week in the Harlem numbers racket by the 1930s. This apparently annoyed Schultz, who supposedly buried a fortune in hard currency near Phoenicia (it was never found). Diamond was murdered in an Albany hotel room in 1931.

Some hikers prefer to make a large loop hike over Windham High Peak, returning via Burnt Knob and the Black Dome Range Trail, walking west along Black Dome Valley Road and back to the trailhead on Peck Road for a total distance of over 13 miles. Groups also can extend the hike by spotting a car at the end of Black Dome Valley Road (see Trip 52).

TRIP 52
ACRA POINT

RATING: Moderate

DISTANCE: 3.4 miles

ELEVATION GAIN: 800 feet

ESTIMATED TIME: 3 hours

MAPS: USGS Freehold; AMC Catskill Mountains; NY-NJTC Northeast Catskills

A short hike to an isolated lookout above the Black Dome Valley.

DIRECTIONS

From the corners of CR 40 and CR 56 in the village of Maplecrest, follow Big Hollow Road (CR 56) to the north and east, passing Peck Road on your left. Continue 4.5 miles to the end of CR 56 where you will see the red-marked Black Dome Range trailhead on the left, or park at the dead end (Batavia Kill trailhead) just ahead.

TRAIL DESCRIPTION

The route to Acra Point uses the northern portion of the Black Dome Range Trail, located at the eastern end of Big Hollow Road in Maplecrest. Don't be concerned if the road is washed out along the boisterous Batavia Kill—it often is in early spring. Since this is a dead end, you can park almost anywhere. The red-marked Black Dome Range Trail begins on the left (north) side of the road. It's the first trailhead you see; the next one, a few hundred feet ahead, is

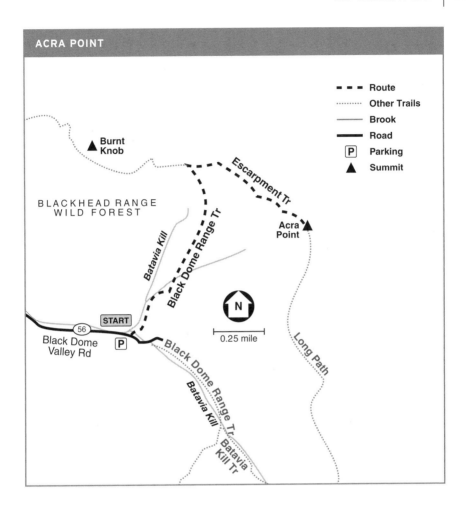

the Batavia Kill Trailhead (yellow markers). You can also use the Batavia Kill and Escarpment trails to reach Acra Point (or to return from it), more than doubling this hike's distance.

The Black Dome Range Trail has the advantage of providing the fastest and easiest approach to the top of the northern Catskill Escarpment, offering an ideal hike for days when you want a scenic outing that's not an overwhelming workout. This part of the Escarpment Trail is also less traveled than the North Lake area trails and the neighboring Windham High Peak or Blackhead Range trails, so you're likely to see fewer hikers. You may encounter thru-hikers, however. I enjoy meeting these trunk-trail hikers "going the distance" on the Escarpment Trail (also shared by the Long Path); in their floppy hats and rumpled bandanas, they come plodding along with their hiking staffs, blending in with the environment. If you meet one here in summertime, chances are they may try to yogi your food, especially your water, in exchange for tales of their adventures—for this part of the Catskills is notoriously dry.

Note that the Black Dome Range Trail sign alongside the road at 2,200 feet indicates Acra Point at a forgiving 1.7 miles (3,100 feet). Head north into the woods following the Black Dome Range Trail across the Batavia Kill on a wooden bridge. Sign in at the trail register on the north side of the Kill and bear hard right, fording a seasonal tributary. Marking is spotty here, but soon the trail is obvious and remains self-guiding. Climb easily through an attractive stand of large red spruce, some snapped in two by high winds. The trail follows the Batavia Kill, passing many pretty spots where the tiny trout stream flows over low, gray ledges into shallow pools. The trail soon crosses Batavia Kill again, turning sharply northwest and north again through a northern hardwood forest. The climb is consistent but never steep. As you gain elevation, there are small pockets of hemlock and a few large, isolated cherry trees, then oaks, providing a good combination of browse for deer, wild turkey, and ruffed grouse. At 2,700 feet, the trail levels out for the last 0.25 mile of the Black Dome Range Trail, into a shallow notch on the spine of the Escarpment Trail. There are trail signs here indicating that your direction of travel is to the right (south) to Acra Point, 0.7 mile distant. This and the neighboring Dutcher Notch Trail are re-supply stations for the college outing clubs and scout troops that regularly traverse the Escarpment Trail. Often they have drop points where you may see supplies, mostly gallon jugs of water brought in by their support staffs.

The following section of the Escarpment Trail is flat for a while then rises easily through the remaining 300 feet of ascent to Acra Point. As the trail gains the northwest-facing ridge, boreal forest takes over. Look to your right (west) for an established, unmarked spur trail, and follow it 75 feet to a flat sandstone outcropping. This is the place. Although you are not on Acra Point's summit (3,100 feet), this is the best lookout. The true "summit" lies near the next spur trail to the south, where, due to sustained impact on the thin soils, *No Camping* signs are posted.

The intimate views of the Black Dome/Batavia Kill Valley are the attraction here, where you can lie around on the warm, flat rocks off the trail and relax. Seldom are views of such magnitude attained with so little work on the part of the hiker! The Blackhead Range—from Blackhead, Thomas Cole, and Black Dome mountains—slopes downward in a massive ellipsis over Camel's Hump (the western-most little nub) into a semicolon of Round and Van Loan hills (named for the early Catskill writer and map maker, Walton Van Loan). To the right (north) of these is Cave Mountain. The large, distant peak with the dorsal profile lying due west (270 degrees magnetic) is Bearpen Mountain, a trailed peak outside the Catskill Park boundary in Delaware County. It is, however, still within the forest preserve, as is Vly, just south of it, recognizable by its long, flat top.

Looking north you have Burnt Knob directly in front of you, a sort of mirror point to Acra Point (with less interesting views from a small rock ledge on the trail's west side, and better ones in the north), and to the right of it, just over 2 miles distant, is Windham High Peak. Looking south past the immense shoulder of Blackhead Mountain (194 degrees), is Arizona Mountain, a high and dry plateau seldom named on maps. Farther south, the Escarpment winds away to Stoppel Point and North Mountain. Views of the Hudson Valley are limited from the east side of the Point.

Return the way you came. If you're tempted to add distance by returning on the longer route to the south (taking the Escarpment Trail to the Batavia Kill Trail), you're in for a relatively long and viewless slog.

THE ESCARPMENT TRAIL

While the Devil's Path Trail runs east to west, the Escarpment Trail travels south to north along the edge of the Catskill's eastern ledges, the high and sudden rise to plateau elevation known as the Escarpment. This 24-mile trail begins outside the gate of the North/South Lake public campground at Scutt Road Corral, and is most often hiked from south to north, since many hikers stage their hike from the North Lake camping area. The elevation change and gradient is a bit more forgiving than the Devil's Path (6,500 cumulative feet). There are fewer lean-tos on or near the trail. With the exception of the north and south extremes, the views are perhaps not as grand as the Devil's Path's because there are fewer peaks above 3,500 feet (Blackhead Mountain and Windham High Peak).

However, due to the relative lack of easy and convenient day hikes to this area (with the exception of the trails around North Lake), the sense of solitude is greater once the hiker passes North Point. The Long Path uses both the Devil's Path and the Escarpment Trail as it makes its way northward through the Catskills.

TRIP 53
HUNTER MOUNTAIN

RATING: Strenuous
DISTANCE: 7.2 miles
ELEVATION GAIN: 1,950 feet
ESTIMATED TIME: 7 hours
MAPS: USGS Hunter; USGS Lexington; AMC Catskill Mountains;
NY-NJTC Northeastern Catskills

**A long, gradual climb to the Catskills' second-highest peak and fire
tower, with a quiet westerly ledge viewpoint.**

DIRECTIONS

From Lexington, 8.0 miles west of Hunter on NY 23A, travel south on NY 42,
3.8 miles to turn left (east) onto CR 6 (Spruceton Road). Drive past the West
Kill Mountain trailhead, appearing on your right at 3.8 miles, and continue for
another 3.0 miles to the forest preserve access parking area on the left, where
there are trail signs for Hunter Mountain.

TRAIL DESCRIPTION

The most interesting and gradual climb to Hunter Mountain (4,040 feet—the
Catskills' second highest) is by way of the Spruceton Trail. The considerable
vertical rise of 1,950 feet is distributed evenly over this long western approach
beginning at the headwaters of the beautiful West Kill Creek. (Hunter can be
climbed in roughly half the time using the steeper Becker Hollow Trail from
Stony Clove. See end note.)

Locate the blue-marked Spruceton Trail on the north side of Spruceton
Road, which indicates the direction to the John Robb Lean-to and Hunter
Mountain. (There's an overflow parking area 0.2 mile ahead on Spruceton
Road; the Devil's Path Trail is another 0.2 mile past the overflow lot at the
dead-end of Spruceton Road.)

Setting out along a well-defined truck trail (also an equestrian trail), you
follow the old Jones Gap Turnpike (a.k.a. Old Hunter Road), built in 1880
and later improved to construct and maintain the present Hunter Mountain
fire tower. After 0.5 mile, the trail turns east and steepens gradually. About
50 minutes into the hike you arrive in the saddle between Rusk (trailless) and
Hunter Mountain, at 1.7 miles. You'll see an unmarked trail leading north and

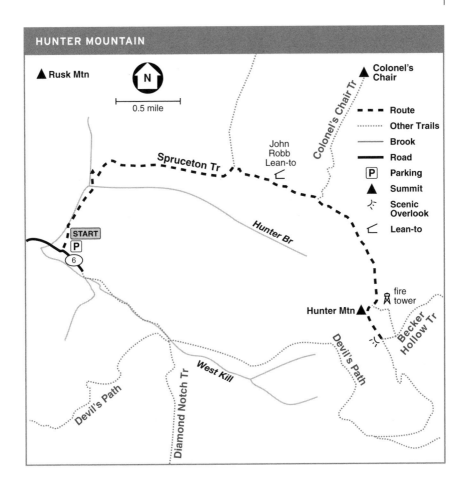

HUNTER MOUNTAIN

▲ Rusk Mtn

N

0.5 mile

Spruceton Tr

John Robb Lean-to

Colonel's Chair Tr

▲ Colonel's Chair

- - - Route
.... Other Trails
――― Brook
▬▬▬ Road
P Parking
▲ Summit
Scenic Overlook
Lean-to

START
P
6

Hunter Br

fire tower

Hunter Mtn ▲

Becker Hollow Tr

Devil's Path

West Kill

Diamond Notch Tr

Devil's Path

downhill onto private lands in Taylor Hollow.

The trail continues south southeast and ascends steeply, reaching a good spring on the right within 0.5 mile (Be careful, horses sometimes drink from the pool). Near the spring are views to the north and southwest with Rusk and West Kill in the foreground. Within 0.1 mile, you'll see the John Robb Lean-to on your left at the 3,500-foot mark.

Continue for another 0.1 mile into a flat area of thick evergreens, and you come upon the Colonel's Chair Trail, branching left (north, yellow markers, easily missed). This is part of the old Shanty Hollow Trail to Colonel's Chair; its last 0.5 mile has been erased by ski-trail construction. The mile-long side trip to Colonel's Chair and the ski lifts and summit lodge (open in summer) of the Hunter Mountain Ski Area is worthwhile if you've allowed the time, but the views are redundant to the fire tower's, and the elevation loss (500 feet) is significant. (See the AMC's *Catskill Mountain Guide* for details.)

Continue on the Spruceton Trail. The summit is 1.0 mile ahead and 450 feet in elevation above you. The heavily rutted, often wet trail leads you through a remarkably dense forest of spruce and fir with isolated ledges to the northeast. From the John Robb Lean-to, it will take you about 45 minutes to walk to the summit. Just before the final ascent at approximately 3 miles, a yellow spur trail (marked) leads 1,500 feet to a marginal spring.

Suddenly the fire tower and observer's cabin appear. Once you have enjoyed this rocky peak and the 360-degree view from the fire tower (this is the highest fire tower in the state; it is staffed seasonally, on weekends), continue on the blue-marked trail to the true summit, where the fire tower and a lean-to were previously located. This additional distance of 0.25 mile through a level spruce-fir wood takes only 10 minutes and is well worth the effort. When you reach the small clearing of the old tower site, at the junction where the Becker Hollow Trail rises from Stony Clove, you'll see a spur trail to the right (west), leading a short distance to a west-facing ledge with excellent views from the north northwest to the south southwest, including West Kill, North Dome, Sherrill, Balsam, Vly, Bearpen, and many other peaks in the southern Catskills and the Shawangunks. When the tower is busy, this is the place to head for.

In his 1918 classic, *The Catskills*, T. Morris Longstreth sums up Hunter's views: "Hunter is a climb-repaying mountain. From the steel tower on the top the entire Catskill mountainland is visible. Stony Clove . . . is but a gash in mother earth. The mass of the southern Catskills rises in ranged domes . . . dropped into gulfs made pearl gray by the mists of melting snow. Westward the chain that walls the valley toward Lexington wandered away until it grew soft with lilacs and lavendars [sic]." Longstreth suggests, "if you have your nerve with you, climb Hunter some forenoon that promises thunder . . . nowhere else can you find more beautiful concentrations of vapor."

Your shortest return route (from the Becker Hollow Trail junction) is the Spruceton Trail—the way you came (3.6 miles)—but consider that a loop can be completed, time allowing, by continuing ahead on the yellow-marked Hunter Mountain Trail to the Devil's Path Trail that turns west to join the blue-marked Diamond Notch Trail at West Kill Falls, and would bring you to a point about 1 mile east of the Spruceton Trail parking area (total mileage from Becker Hollow Trail junction, 4.6 miles, about 2.0 miles longer than returning the way you came).

Note: Hikers wishing the fastest ascent to Hunter's summit (2.05-mile, 2,220-foot ascent) and fire tower will find the Becker Hollow trailhead and hiker's parking area 1.3 miles south on NY 214 from NY 23A, between Hunter and Tannersville.

TRIP 54
DIAMOND NOTCH TO WEST KILL FALLS

RATING: Moderate

DISTANCE: 4.6 miles

ELEVATION GAIN: 1,500 feet

ESTIMATED TIME: 3.5 hours

MAPS: USGS Lexington; AMC Catskill Mountains; NY-NJTC
Northeastern Catskills

**A hike across the Schoharie-Esopus watershed divide to West Kill
Falls.**

DIRECTIONS

From Lanesville on NY 214, drive 5.0 miles north of Phoenicia, look for Diamond Notch Road on the left, where there are state trail signs. Go up Diamond
Notch Road 1.2 miles, and into the woods another 0.3 mile to the trailhead
parking area. Note that the last 0.5 mile is a rocky road that may be difficult for
all but four-wheel drive vehicles. A private landowner has posted the area, but
it is legal to park on the road as long as you are not blocking traffic. Coming
southeast from Hunter, take NY 214 (2.0 miles east of town), and you'll see the
trailhead signs 7.0 miles into Stony Clove (or 4.0 miles beyond Devil's Tombstone State Campground) on your right. Turn right onto Diamond Notch
Road and follow the above directions to the trailhead.

TRAIL DESCRIPTION

This is an easy-to-moderate hike that takes you into Diamond Notch via an
old turnpike converted in 1937 to a ski and hiking trail. Forest encroachment
and slides have reduced the trail's width considerably, but the footpath remains
intact. From the trailhead parking area, the trail is marked with blue state trail
markers and climbs next to Hollow Tree Brook. Soon you cross the brook on
a flight of stone steps. In spring you'll discover a wide variety of wildflowers:
Dutchman's breeches, Carolina spring beauties, yellow violets, and purple trillium. After 15 minutes of hiking, just beyond the bridge, you can make out
a high ridge to your left, which is part of West Kill Mountain, the ridge that
forms the west side of Diamond Notch in the Hunter West Kill Wilderness.
At this point some hemlock begin to appear, and the trail becomes heavily
eroded and gullied. Soon another bridge crosses Hollow Tree Brook, and the

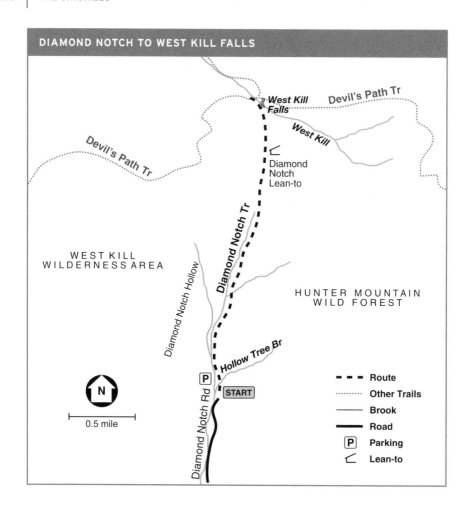

DIAMOND NOTCH TO WEST KILL FALLS

West Kill Falls

Devil's Path Tr

West Kill

Diamond Notch Tr

Diamond Notch Lean-to

Devil's Path Tr

WEST KILL WILDERNESS AREA

Diamond Notch Hollow

HUNTER MOUNTAIN WILD FOREST

N

0.5 mile

P

Diamond Notch Rd

START

Hollow Tree Br

- - - Route

.... Other Trails

——— Brook

▬▬ Road

P Parking

⌐ Lean-to

trail begins an even ascent, continuing due north into Diamond Notch Hollow. This is most likely the spot that suggested the development of a ski trail through the notch, but you'll probably opt for the novice slopes of a sanctioned ski area after you look down from above. Look up to your left (west), and you'll see the rocky, spruce-covered shoulder of West Kill's east ridge jutting out.

About 1.5 miles into the hollow, you come across a miniature waterfall on your right and another small kill just beyond it, both running straight down the mountain, crossing the trail. Some outcrops of thinly stratified sandstone lie ahead, hinting that the notch is not far beyond. Within 5 minutes, there are excellent views to the southwest, highlighting (from right to left) Slide, Table, Lone, Peekamoose, Cornell, Wittenberg, and Ashokan High Point. Up to the right is a long pile of landslide talus, with birch, cherry, and maple establishing themselves in its thin soil. Dr. Michael Kudish speculates in *Vegetational His-*

tory of the Catskill High Peaks that the slide "might date back to the 1890–1910 era when the area was logged and possibly burned."

An old road descends sharply into the ravine on the trail's west side. Now, 1.7 miles into the notch, you approach its highest point, where the mountains of West Kill and Southwest Hunter come so close together that you might touch them both at the same time. After you have enjoyed the notch and its fine view, follow the trail into an evergreen forest, descending gently to reach Diamond Notch Lean-to. The shelter has a wood floor; its site is cleaner than most; and it's in good shape as far as Catskill lean-tos go. Just below the lean-to is a small wetland that contributes to the upper reaches of West Kill Creek. Follow along on what can be a fairly wet trail, with a view of Rusk Mountain ahead and slightly left. To the west of Rusk Mountain is Evergreen Mountain, and to the east, Hunter Mountain, none of them visible. Within 15 minutes of the lean-to, you should reach the junction with the red-marked Devil's Path Trail and the bridge over

West Kill Falls along the Devil's Path.

West Kill Falls (a.k.a. Buttermilk Falls). Diamond Notch is back the way you came, about 2.3 miles away; the nearest road is ahead on the blue-marked trail, at 0.5 mile (Spruceton–Old Hunter Road).

The falls here are small but very attractive with a succession of large pools. The Devil's Path Trail (red markers) runs east and west past the falls. To the west lies West Kill Mountain. Straight ahead, the Diamond Notch Trail continues to the Spruceton Road trailhead to Hunter Mountain (Trip 53). Because of its proximity to Spruceton Road, this area was at one time subject to intensive overuse and unregulated camping, but it has since recovered and no camping is permitted.

You will find the falls an ideal place to spend a hot afternoon. Hike out the way you came in.

TRIP 55
WEST KILL MOUNTAIN TO BUCK RIDGE LOOKOUT

RATING: Strenuous

DISTANCE: 9.4 miles

ELEVATION GAIN: 2,030 feet

ESTIMATED TIME: 6.5 hours

MAPS: USGS Lexington; AMC Catskill Mountains; NY-NJTC Northeastern Catskills

A demanding hike across the elongated West Kill plateau, to the scenic Buck Ridge Lookout.

DIRECTIONS

To reach the trailhead, turn off NY 23A onto NY 42 south in Lexington, west of Hunter. Follow NY 42 toward Shandaken into West Kill. About 3.8 miles from NY 23A you see signs for Spruceton on CR 6. Turn left here, and go 3.8 miles to the Devil's Path on your right.

TRAIL DESCRIPTION

This is the longer but gentler approach to West Kill Mountain from Spruceton, with a slightly greater vertical rise than the approach from the eastern end of Spruceton Road (1,780-foot rise). This is the terminus of the red-marked Devil's Path Trail.

Go immediately uphill through a hardwood and pine forest. The trail levels out shortly, and after 10 minutes you find that you are walking the border of a forest transition, with hemlock on your right and hardwood on your left. To your right are Mink Hollow (not to be confused with the better-known Mink Hollow near Lake Hill) and its brook that joins the West Kill. Large, moss-clad boulders decorate the forest. Grouse may burst from dense cover as you walk along.

After 20 minutes or so, over rocky, root-covered footing, you meet the creek that runs into Mink Hollow. The trail then veers left, ascending into a rocky hardwood forest. In 10 minutes you hear a spring bubbling beneath the trail, as you look ahead into a gap or opening in the forest where a vernal pond sits between West Kill and North Dome. The gap runs south into the head of Broadstreet Hollow and the Timber Lake Camp. There are two signs at this pond section on the trail, one indicating West Kill Mountain summit; the

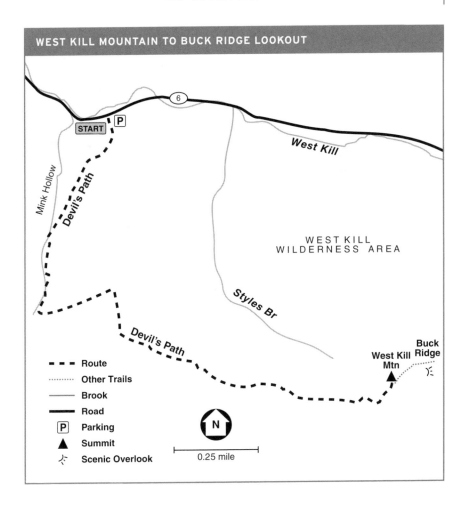

WEST KILL MOUNTAIN TO BUCK RIDGE LOOKOUT

other shows Spruceton Road as back the way you came.

Turn sharply uphill to the north. Continue climbing for 20 minutes or more, over the steepest section of trail you will encounter. The trail eases over grassy, fern-covered flats through ledges and undulating terrain where beech and cherry appear. This pattern continues for another 20 minutes until you descend steeply. But the drop is not severe or prolonged; it flattens out and the trail climbs again. Be very careful here while negotiating slanted slabs of bluestone that are slippery when wet.

As you ascend to a level walk again, it will take you 20 more minutes through winding flats to climb into alpine terrain where the trail narrows and balsam becomes prolific. A short spur to the north, just before you arrive at the summit, offers excellent views of the Blackhead Range, Huntersfield, Tower, and Cave mountains, and an extensive sprawl of lowlands where you have

West Kill Mountain.

a glimpse of the Schoharie Reservoir. A sign identifying West Kill's summit (3,880 feet) appears just ahead on your right.

Continue for another 3 to 5 minutes, to the ledge of Buck Ridge (3,740 feet). This is a view often on the favorites list of hikers, and it is impressive. There is enough room for a dozen people to rest here, poised in midair looking at a 180-degree collection of peaks. From left to right you can see Windham, Thomas Cole, Black Dome, Blackhead, Hunter West with its ski trails, Hunter and its fire tower, Southwest Hunter, Plateau, Overlook and its fire tower (for Hawkeyes only!), Slide, Table, Lone, Rocky, Wittenberg, Cornell, Friday, Balsam Cap, Ashokan High Point, the Mohonk Preserve's Sky Top, a piece of the Ashokan Reservoir, and down into Lanesville on NY 214. You can also see a widening in the Hudson River (Vanderberg Cove) as well as Olderbark, Little Rocky, Carl Mountain (in the foreground), and Mount Tremper to the right of the Ashokan Reservoir. See if you can find its fire tower.

Before you leave the summit, to retrace your steps, you may want to collect some balm of Gilead—the pitch of balsam fir—to save in a small container. This resin from the blisters of balsam is said to have medicinal value; it does keep bacteria and fungi to a minimum, at least in the tree's case. People once thought that it must also do that for them, recalling the prophet Jeremiah's reference to the balm that ancient Israelites found on Mount Gilead in the Holy Land. Native Americans called the healing balsam salve cho-koh-tung, or "blisters." The resin was used commercially to create adhesives for lenses and microscope slides until synthetics were found to be superior.

About the only thing you'll want to do with balm of Gilead is stash it with your Christmas ornaments or keep it in a desk drawer as a freshener. Use it to whiff that nostalgic thrill of the holidays or to return to West Kill Summit during times when life's requirements don't allow a personal visit. While you're wondering how to get the stuff off your hands, retrace your steps to your car.

TRIP 56
DRY BROOK RIDGE

RATING: Strenuous

DISTANCE: 10.6 miles

ELEVATION GAIN: 2,000 feet

ESTIMATED TIME: 5 hours

MAPS: USGS Margaretville; USGS Fleischmanns; USGS Seager; USGS Arena; AMC Catskill Mountains; NY-NJTC Central Catskills

A remote hike in the western Catskills in a first-growth forest little changed since the Ice Age.

DIRECTIONS

From NY 28, west of Margaretville, take South Side Road 2.0 miles to Hill Road. Bear left on Hill Road, and go an additional 1.3 miles to the Huckleberry Loop trailhead on the road's north side.

TRAIL DESCRIPTION

This interesting loop hike across the west-facing edge of Dry Brook Ridge has become more popular with organized groups in recent years. The ridge is fairly high (3,480 feet) and remote, offering a secluded and interesting vantage above Cold Spring Hollow from Penguin Rocks. The entire length of the loop trail across the top of the ridge is covered in first growth forest.

The suggested route begins from the north of Hill Road, using the Huckleberry Loop Trail. The trailhead lies at 1,900 feet. To save time or to maximize time spent on the ledges, some hikers choose to visit Penguin Rocks and return

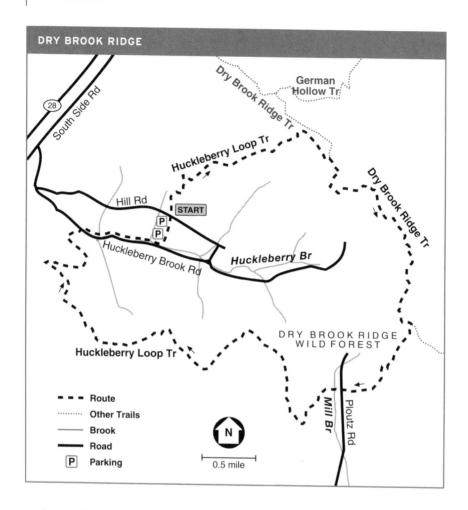

DRY BROOK RIDGE

to this trailhead, rather than completing the loop, thus saving some 500 feet in elevation and an additional 1.5 miles of hiking. But the forests and plantations of the southern end of the loop are well worth a look, so by all means plan to hike the entire route.

From the trailhead, travel uphill through several forest transitions of plantation Norway spruce and red pine, followed by native Carolinian hardwoods (you can see the plantations from the higher ridge elevations). The terrain flattens as the route turns east, soon crossing an old, disused woods road. Now the trail climbs again, until it intersects with the Dry Brook Ridge Trail at 1.7 miles. Turn right (south). You walk through a consistent distribution of beech, birch, and maple, with a corresponding appearance of moosewood, pin cherry, choke cherry, hop hornbeam, hobblebush, oxalis, wood fern, viburnum, blackberry, raspberry, and blueberry. Of course such a profusion of fruit attracts bears, but you will be very lucky to see one in these open hardwood areas.

The trail is flat for a stretch but rises shortly, and soon passes a high bog on the left at 3,100 feet. Dr. Mike Kudish calls this ridge "one of the most fascinating in the Catskills," owing to the presence of uninterrupted floral conditions since the Ice Age. Another reason, no doubt, has to do with his radio-carbon dating of the area's peat bogs. This first bog, he determined to be about 680 years old; the next one, near the junction ahead, "the middle summit bog," 3,450 years old. Still another he dated on the Huckleberry Brook Ridge is 6,908 years old. From peat macrofossil samples, he was able to construct the only comprehensive vegetation profiles of the area ever made.

After climbing another in a series of low ledges, you reach a boulder with limited views and, following it, weaving in and out of trees along the western ridgeline, you arrive at an unmarked spur to the 150-foot-long exposed outcrop of Penguin Rocks (3,300 feet; the placename origin is not known), covered in blueberry bushes and offering some fine views to the west. As you look straight out into the valley you see Cold Spring Hollow directly below you, with its Huckleberry Brook reaching for the Delaware. To the left, beyond Mill Brook Valley, is the long Mill Brook Ridge, running east-west from the vicinity of Woodpecker Ridge and the (unseen) Balsam Lake Mountain. You can see the Delaware's east branch as it flows from Margaretville and into the Pepacton Reservoir, a New York City water-supply reservoir that is known for producing record brown trout.

Continue south along the trail, passing another view from a point above a talus field and below the ridge's otherwise viewless summit. Descend through terracing terrain another 0.5 mile, as the Dry Brook Ridge Trail bends southeast at the junction with the red-marked Huckleberry Ridge Trail. Turn right (south southwest). The trail descends gradually through hardwoods to cross Ploutz Road at the site of an old settlement, probably that of a subsistence farmer. There's a trailhead parking area and register here, adjacent to Mill Brook. Signs of old settlements continue across Mill Brook, into an area where Norway spruce have been planted in old pasturelands. The trail rises along the grade of an old road, gradually steepening as it re-enters hardwood forest and following to the southwest of a wooded knoll (2,832 feet). The trail now works its way west, descending through ledgy hemlock woods to the edge of a large, open field where you have to keep a close watch on the trail markers. Cairns that guide the way across the open field may be obscured by high grass during summer. The trail enters the woods at the northerly edge of the field, ascends initially, and begins to switchback, downhill first into the northwest, then into the east. The extreme slope has resulted in sustained erosion here. The trail heads downhill steeply to a woods road that can wash out and descends again from red pine to hemlock woods, finally crossing Huckleberry Brook. Turn right on Huckleberry Road, following the trail markers east, crossing a small bridge and turning right, in front of the DEC storage facility (keeping the building to your left). The trail appears next to the storage building and climbs again, arriving at Hill Road in 0.3 mile. Turn left 150 feet to the trailhead parking area and your car.

Delaware County is a highly scenic and heavily farmed setting of low, gently sculpted hills spotted with rich, cultivated fields and long vistas. While in Arkville you should take advantage of the scenery by taking the Delaware and Ulster Rail Ride, running from Arkville to Fleischmanns and Highmount. Railroads came to the Arkville area in 1871, fostering the great resort boom that followed. Riding the Red Heifer (a combination diesel, mail, freight, and passenger car called a brill) through this scenic territory will give you appreciation for the easterly upper Delaware Valley that cannot be seen from the heights of Dry Brook Ridge.

TRIP 57
BALSAM LAKE MOUNTAIN

RATING: Strenous
DISTANCE: 6.0 miles
ELEVATION GAIN: 1,123 feet
ESTIMATED TIME: 4.5 hours
MAPS: USGS Seager; AMC Catskill Mountains; NY-NJTC Central Catskills

This spruce-fir summit would be viewless without its fire tower, which offers 360-degree views of the western Catskills.

DIRECTIONS
From NY 28 in Arkville, go south on CR 49 (Dry Brook Road) for 6.0 miles, through Mapledale. Turn right on Mill Brook Road; go 2.3 miles to the trailhead parking area on the right. Cross the road and locate the blue-marked Dry Brook Ridge Trail. Be sure you take this southerly section of the Dry Brook Ridge Trail, not the one on the north (or right) side of the road that crosses northerly Dry Brook Ridge.

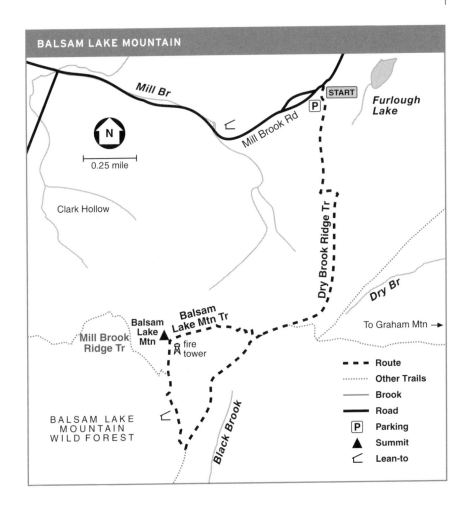

TRAIL DESCRIPTION

From the trailhead to Balsam Lake Mountain (3,723 feet) you enter a forest of beech, birch, maple, and cherry trees over cinnamon ferns, oxalis, and vibur-num. Pass the trail register on your left.

Follow along through a flat section of the trail to an ascent that allows occa-sional views across Mill Brook Hollow to the west. Climb gently through a few switchbacks, where jack-in-the-pulpit, Solomon's seal, wolf's claw club moss, and haircap moss appear. The upright, branched, and densely leaved stems of wolf's claw club moss are used commercially for Christmas decorations. (Pick-ing them in the forest preserve is prohibited.) The moss is widely distributed through the Catskills and northern North America. It can be confused with the similarly distributed tree club moss, or ground pine that is usually found in open pine woods and bogs.

In 10 minutes or so, you'll pass a spring to the right and downhill (indicated by a sign), among a series of sedimentary boulders, many of them covered with rock tripe. When soaked for several weeks in water, this lichen renders a purple dye that has some popularity among textile artisans. Rock tripe is also edible, but not at all "wholesome." The dried-up, curled disks of lichen resemble moldy potato chips.

In another 20 minutes, you pass a grass-covered trail on your left that leads to the summit of Graham Mountain (3,868 feet). (Although many hikers climb Graham along with Balsam Lake Mountain, there is no legal public easement.)

In a few moments, you encounter several trail signs. Take the red-marked Balsam Lake Mountain Trail to your right, heading for Balsam Lake Mountain fire tower (0.85 mile). Continue uphill over flat rocks with visible glacial scratches. The trail includes some vigorous ascents broken up by more moderate inclines, hedged in blackberry, bunchberry, and extremely dense spruce-fir thickets.

After 20 minutes of thinking that each rise will produce the summit you at last see the fire tower and observer's cabin. Climb to the top of the tower (without it, there would be no view), where you can see in all directions (staffed on weekends, seasonally). Below the tower, and running north, is the Dry Brook Ridge. To the northeast on a clear day, you can see as far as Bearpen Mountain, 15 miles away. Closer at hand is the ridge on the east side of the Dry Brook Valley and its series of peaks. From left to right are the masses of Belleayre, Balsam, Haynes, Eagle, and Big Indian. Between the latter two, the summit of Panther can be seen. Due east of you is the range that includes Slide and Table. The two neighboring peaks are Graham and Doubletop. To the south and west are the rolling, seemingly endless lower peaks of Delaware County. You can see Red Hill and its fire tower.

Just off the summit, in an impenetrable tangle of fallen trees, is a unique plant community: a bog. Researchers call this bog unique because it contains more sphagnum than other bogs in the Catskill region. A hurricane on November 25, 1950, caused extensive blowdown in the northeast half of the bog, followed by a heavy second growth of balsam fir. It has been hypothesized that this bog may never follow a bog's normal growth pattern because of the infiltration of acid rain, which acts to decompose peat. Water is retained, and the bog stage remains rather than progresses. Balsam Lake's summit has recently been the site of studies into acid rain, a phenomenon that has arisen in the Catskills, despite the profusion of limestone that acts to buffer acids.

The trail continues downhill past an outbuilding with signs indicating the lean-to at 0.45 mile. Follow downhill, passing the Mill Brook Ridge Trail that descends to the west, and farther on a spur trail to the right (west) that leads through a patch of broad-leaved cow parsnips to the Eleanor Leavitt Memorial Lean-to.

Descending, you intersect with the blue-marked Dry Brook Ridge Trail once again, within 20 minutes. Go left (north) and follow this pleasant, grassy road uphill for 20 minutes to the junction of the Balsam Lake Mountain Trail, which you'll recognize. Descend now, retracing your steps back to the trail-head parking area.

TRIP 58
PALENVILLE OVERLOOK

RATING: Strenuous

DISTANCE: 8.0 miles

ELEVATION GAIN: 1,300 feet

ESTIMATED TIME: 5 hours

MAPS: USGS Kaaterskill; AMC Catskill Mountains; NY-NJTC North Lake Area, Northeastern Catskills

An historic carriage road to a pair of peaceful lookouts over lower Kaaterskill Clove and the Hudson Valley.

DIRECTIONS
From NY 23A in Palenville, turn right onto Boggart Road, the first right after the light on NY 23A as you are driving west. Follow Boggart Road for 2.5 miles to a four-way intersection with Mountain Turnpike Road at Pelham's Four Corners (the portion to the right is dirt). There are horse trail signs here. Turn left and go 1.0 mile to the end of Mountain Turnpike Road, where you can legally park along the road.

TRAIL DESCRIPTION
To reach this quiet and isolated pair of overlooks, you hike the historic Old Mountain Road through Rip Van Winkle Hollow, which, notes Roland Van Zandt, became "the classic approach to the great scenic domain of the Catskill Mountain House for almost [all of] the nineteenth century." The road had its beginnings in 1823 as a tannery road and stagecoach route to the Catskill

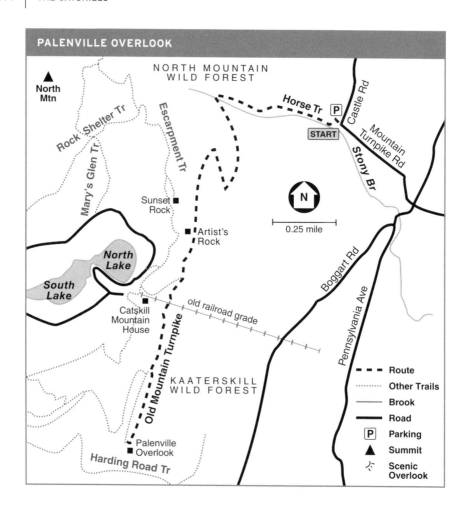

PALENVILLE OVERLOOK

NORTH MOUNTAIN
WILD FOREST

North
Mtn

Rock Shelter Tr

Mary's Glen Tr

Escarpment Tr

Horse Tr

P

Castle Rd

START

Mountain Turnpike Rd

Stony Br

N

0.25 mile

Sunset
Rock

Artist's
Rock

North
Lake

South
Lake

Catskill
Mountain
House

old railroad grade

Boggart Rd

Pennsylvania Ave

Old Mountain Turnpike

KAATERSKILL
WILD FOREST

Palenville
Overlook

Harding Road Tr

- - - Route

.... Other Trails

――――― Brook

――――― Road

P Parking

▲ Summit

Scenic
Overlook

Mountain House. It remained a stage route until the railroad came in the 1880s, causing its eventual abandonment. Yet, by 1931 H.A. Haring wrote in *Our Catskill Mountains* that the road "is impassable for any sort of vehicle, but is endlessly charming for the hiker who is equal to an ascent of 2,000 feet within a walking distance of 5 miles." The road has been repaired since, and new bridges are in place for equestrians, snowmobilers, and hikers.

Begin at the western end of the Mountain Turnpike Road. You will see the snowmobile trail markers as the road turns to dirt and curves uphill into Rip Van Winkle Hollow, with Stony Brook on the left. Continuing uphill you cross Black Snake Bridge within 0.5 mile. A hardwood forest slopes steeply up to your right toward the Escarpment, while a hemlock ravine pitches steeply down to your left. At the horseshoe turn in Sleepy Hollow, you can still see the old stone foundations of the Rip Van Winkle House, a "halfway" house and early boarding house and tavern. The 1.0 mile distance to this point will take you a half hour of uphill hiking, so you may enjoy a stop here at the traditional resting place for coach travelers to the Catskill Mountain House, who had already traveled 10 rough miles from the wharf at Catskill.

Every effort was made to assure Mountain House guests that this was the spot where Rip encountered the strange crew of Henry Hudson's Half Moon. Nearby was the rock upon which he took his famous slumber, and a tree could be pointed out beneath which the bones of his dog Wolf were "discovered." It's easy to imagine the romantics of the time accepting the story as fact. Haring recorded that "every summer visitors in hundreds scrambled up the perpendicular continuation of Sleepy Hollow in search of the 'flats' where Hendrick Hudson's gnomes thunderously rolled the balls in their game of ninepins." In fact, Washington Irving is not specific as to the location of the events in the legend, which appealed to the romantic mind for its very vagueness and mystery. He did not visit the Catskills until 1832, twelve years after the publication of the story—he only observed them from the decks of a Hudson River steamboat.

Continue from here on the 0.5-mile-long Dead Ox Hill, going steadily uphill through hardwoods toward Little Pine Orchard and Cape Horn. You reach Cape Horn within 30 minutes of Sleepy Hollow at the site of a stone fireplace and rough campsite. From Cape Horn, views to the east are fair, with the Taconics and the river valley visible. Make a 180-degree right turn here onto the Short Level that takes you up a moderate grade to another horseshoe bend in 0.3 mile, or 10 minutes.

Now you turn toward the north, and then switch back south to Featherbed Hill. This path is shown on Walton Van Loan's 1876 "Map of All Points of Interest Within Four Miles of the Catskill Mountain House." Van Loan's representation of this particular area, specifically from the Saxe Farm at the end of Mountain Turnpike Road to Palenville Overlook, while not entirely reliable for navigation, accurately shows this section of the trail.

From Featherbed Hill, you walk the next 1.5 miles uphill through a hardwood forest until you reach a Y in the trail. Take a left at this Y. This point is known as the Long Level, where the grade becomes flatter.

At the Y you follow a steep downhill grade left to the northeast that switches back almost immediately to the south. In a few minutes you cross the open gash that runs up the mountain—the abandoned Otis Elevated Railroad track. Opened in 1892, this incline railway saved from three to four hours' stage time for the trip to the Catskill Mountain House during the crucial period when other mountaintop resorts were challenging the supremacy of Charles L.

Beach's domain. Lack of patronage and the advent of automobile travel caused the railway to be closed in 1918, when its rails and cables were sold to the government for weapons manufacturing. The bare scrape it left in the Escarpment can be seen for miles.

After crossing the railway clearing, the trail narrows through a forest of mixed hardwoods and continues along, flat and featureless (except for limited views through the trees to the east), until you reach a fork within 20 minutes. Take the right fork. One hundred feet beyond is a posted trail junction with a sign to Halfway House Lookout (0.45 mile), another name for Palenville Overlook. Follow this trail about 10 or 15 minutes on level terrain, and suddenly you stand over the abyssal depth of Kaaterskill Clove, with the village of Palenville below and remarkable views of Kaaterskill High Peak and Roundtop to the south. To the west a short distance is Indian Head or Point of Rocks, reachable by following a faint herd trail along the cliff's edge. These grassy, open areas are ideal spots for picnicking, sketching, photographing, camping, or simply pondering. The vertical drops are extremely dangerous here, so be cautious.

Indian Head (not to be confused with the Devil's Path mountain of that name) was once a popular profile rock, and from More's Bridge in Kaaterskill Clove (just below Fawn's Leap) it does resemble a head if you use your imagination. As you face the south from Indian Head, the bridge is visible on your right, far below.

When you have enjoyed this place to your satisfaction, you can return the way you came. Before leaving, if you should wish to rest in the bewitching silence, high above the birthplace of Rip Van Winkle, be careful lest you too should sleep away a lifetime.

7

THE HELDERBERGS

THE HIKES IN THE HELDERBERGS EXPLORE two of the state's most striking geological formations. Here are found the accumulations of sand and lime-mud that have been compressed into rock, uplifted, and eroded to form the mountain bastions bordering the plains that much later became the Sea of Albany. These light gray-colored ramparts derive their name from the Dutch, helder (bright or light) and berg (mountain). The uplift of these hills in the early Tertiary Period and later glacial actions expose a long segment of the Earth's history. Views from the cliff face at Indian Ladder as well as Vroman's Nose are phenomenal. From Thacher Park the viewshed extends from the southern Adirondacks through Vermont's Green Mountains and across the Taconics. From Vroman's Nose, perched over the ancient Schoharie flood-plain, you look south and east from Grand Gorge to the northern Catskill Escarpment.

During the time of the great patroonships, most of the Helderbergs were owned by the family of Kiliaen Van Rensselaer, a major shareholder in the Dutch West India Company and one of the original patentees of the land grants of 1629. At the time, Fort Orange (Albany) was the center of the Dutch fur trade that ultimately proved to be much more profitable than the patroon system. The rich easterly bottom lands of the patroonship would later be popu-lated by the same Palatines who arrived in the New World at Germantown and were settled in East and West Camps in the failed attempt to produce naval stores. A hundred years passed before settlers began to arrive from the west to farm the rocky plateau of the Helderberg escarpment. Many settled along these rich alluvial flats of the Schoharie. Adam Vroman purchased the lands in this area from the Mohawks in 1711, but did not receive the official title to it until 1714. Vroman's Nose and the acreage surrounding it, now protected for public use, have been in the Vroman family ever since.

Thacher Park is open year-round from 8 A.M. to dusk. (Indian Ladder Trail is seasonal.) In season, weekend fees apply. Summer swimming pool season (June 25), daily fees apply. There is a one-hour free-parking limit at Cliff Edge Overlook. Thacher Park office: 518-872-1237.

THE LONG PATH

Originally conceived by Dr. Vincent Schaefer in 1931, the Long Path's purpose is the same today as then: to link the outstanding scenic, geologic, prehistoric, and historic features of the area traversed. Dr. Schaefer died in the summer of 1993. He will miss the completion of the Long Path as it forges its way north to the Adirondacks, but his memory is inextricably bound to it and to those who use the trail.

Beginning at the George Washington Bridge in New York City and ending in the northern Adirondacks at Whiteface Mountain (ultimately), the Long Path's founders originally intended to construct Adirondack-type lean-to shelters a day's hike apart along the trail, but these ambitious plans were interrupted by World War II. The Long Path still has its enthusiasts, however, whose mission it is to maintain and continue the trail to its planned destination.

Those who have walked sections of the Long Path may have been frustrated by the sparingly applied blue blazes that designate it. Unlike present hiking trails, the trail originally was meant to be unmarked except on topographic maps. "Thus," to quote Dr. Schaefer, "a hiker must know how to read a topographic map." Such a route eliminates most of the difficulties of trail maintenance and marking, over-use, litter, and the host of other problems that are inherent in the present trail systems. The Long Path is managed by the New York–New Jersey Trail Conference and its affiliate clubs.

TRIP 59
VROMAN'S NOSE

RATING: Moderate

DISTANCE: 2.0 miles

ELEVATION GAIN: 480 feet

ESTIMATED TIME: 2 hours

MAPS: USGS Middleburgh; Vroman's Nose Preservation Corporation handout map

A beautiful walk offering sweeping views of the Schoharie flood-plain and the northern Catskills. An ideal family outing.

DIRECTIONS

From the intersection of NY 30 and NY 145, just south of Middleburgh, go south on NY 30. Vroman's Nose is obvious; its vertical cliffs rise above NY 30 in front of you. At 0.6 mile, turn right onto Mill Valley Road. Go 0.6 mile on Mill Valley Road and park on your left in the designated lot.

TRAIL DESCRIPTION

Vroman's Nose is a trip to save for a lazy afternoon when you'd rather gaze out over the countryside than take a long hike. From this geologically unique, ice-gouged cliff, 600 feet above the Schoharie Valley, there are fine views of a vast alluvial farmlands floodplain, and the long ridge of the northern Catskills.

At the kiosk, help yourself to a map. A wagon road runs south through a hay field, then a pair of gates into a forest of large pine and hemlock, turning right as it leaves the field. This trail has been improved with waterbars and grading. Follow the green diamond markers. There are no state trail signs—this is private property belonging to the Vroman's Nose Preservation Corporation (VNPC). Formed in 1983, the goal of VNPC is to keep the area forever wild and open to the public. The path is self-guiding, and a steady climb over easy terrain (steep in places) continues through mixed hardwoods, pine, and juniper stands. At 1,100 feet or so, the trail turns from southwest to east where the Long Path joins the trail, then it swings north as it ascends, yielding fine views of the Schoharie Valley. Twenty-five minutes from the trailhead, you will arrive at the summit, a wooded plateau of roughly 10 acres. The area of flat stone near the precipice is known as the Dance Floor. Dances were actually

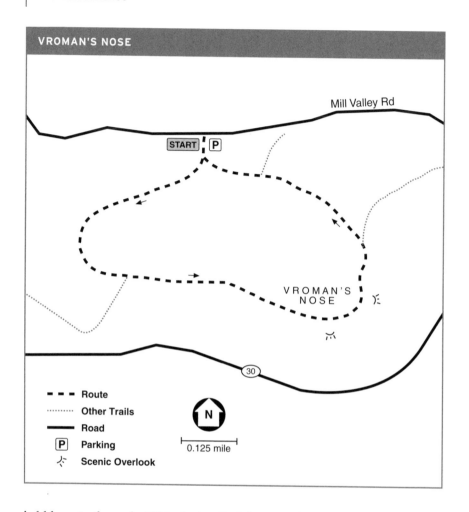

held here in the early 1900s during Prohibition. The eastern scarp is vertical and very high. Use caution.

The heavily scored summit of Hamilton sandstone shows evidence of its past in scratches (striae) and chatter marks of an advancing glacier that moved from the northeast beginning about 50,000 years ago, forming the present topography of the Schoharie Valley. The cliff is defaced with engravings and graffiti, to such a point that it has had an erosive effect. Several concrete fireplaces have been built to discourage the assembling of fire rings by visitors, and impact seems to be under control.

Trees such as oak, hickory, pine, and red cedar thrive on the plateau, covered in bearberry (called kinikinick by the Native Americans). The early spring flower, fringed polygala, also appears here.

Dr. Vincent J. Schaefer, founder of the Long Path, comments on the local

Vroman's Nose rises above the Schoharie Valley.

presence of brachiopods, pelycepods, and trilobites that characterize the Middle Devonian Period's thin sedimentary sheets of Hamilton sandstone. Flagstones from Vroman's Nose were used for sidewalks in cities such as Troy, Albany, and Schenectady. Early in 1942, Dr. Schaefer visited the Nose with an employee of the General Electric Research Laboratory to photograph the testing of artificial fog generators, ultimately used for the screening of ships, personnel, and cities from air attack during World War II. He pointed out a curious atmospheric phenomenon that generates a strong thermal updraft against the cliff, noting, "The dark-colored rocks of the cliffs of Hamilton shale and sandstone become quite warm whenever the sun is shining on them. This produces a massive upcurrent of heated air. Light objects such as grass, small twigs, and similar objects when thrown away from the cliff edge are carried upward and toward the north." You may notice birds, especially turkey vultures, taking advantage of this free ride.

The view of the Schoharie Creek is striking, and the ancient floodplain is remarkably well defined, with little farms and neatly arranged orchards fringing the creek. Beyond the valley to the east you see the Middleburgh Cliffs. Looking south you will have fine views of Windham High Peak and the Blackhead Range, beyond long esplanades of furrowed ground, a geographical contrast that is as unique as Vroman's Nose itself.

The long, open fields of farmland to the north, east, and south of Vroman's Nose were settled originally by Native Americans, who left evidence of campfires under its thin soils. It was a Schenectady farmer, Adam Vroman, who established the first farm here in 1713. He was followed by German palatines who originally settled in the lower Hudson River valley. Crops common to the valley today are corn and carrots. In the past, hops were grown successfully on the rich alluvial flats, where flooding regularly occurs, but normally this happens in early spring and has little affect on existing crops.

If it's icy underfoot, you'll be better off returning the way you came. Otherwise, walk north now, following the aqua Long Path blazes, passing a few more head-spinning cliffs to your right, and then descend steeply. At an intersection with an old woods road, continue on the yellow markers (don't follow right on the Long Path). The yellow trail comes out in the corner of the field where you began.

At the kiosk, you will find the Long Path North hiking club's "Hiker's Guide to the Schoharie Valley" as well as information about the Vroman's Nose Preservation Corporation.

For additional information visit www.nynjtc.org/clubpages/lpn.html and www.schoharie-conservation.org.

TRIP 60
THACHER PARK AND INDIAN LADDER

RATING: Easy
DISTANCE: 4.0 miles
ELEVATION GAIN: 200 feet
ESTIMATED TIME: 3 hours
MAPS: USGS Altamont; John Boyd Thacher State Park trail map

A narrow catwalk trail beneath the cliffs of the world's oldest exposed surface limestone, with extending trails along the Helderberg escarpment. Excellent for families.

DIRECTIONS

The park is 15 miles west of Albany on CR 157. From I-90, take Exit 4 and CR 85 west to CR 157. From the park's entrance sign on CR 157, continue 1.9 miles to the park office and park in the Indian Ladder parking area. A comfort station is located at the top of the trailhead. Be aware that weekends here can be very crowded. With some allowances made for conditions, the Indian Ladder Trail is open from May 1 through November 15.

TRAIL DESCRIPTION

Indian Ladder and the Thacher Park trail system offers a variety of short walks and activities, best enjoyed along with a picnic at one of the park's immaculate scenic recreation areas along the Helderberg Escarpment. By far the most interesting of these walks are the Indian Ladder Trail and its more recent extension to the north.

Verplanck Colvin, the surveyor who mapped the wilderness areas of northern New York, wrote about the Helderbergs in 1869, verifying the existence of the Indian Ladder that existed from about 1710, when Albany was "a frontier town, a trading post, a place where annuities were paid, and blankets exchanged with Indians for beaver pelts."

The Indian Ladder Colvin described once leaned against this cliff, but all that exists now are the heavy steel staircases that serve a curious public. This first section of trail follows what was originally the Indian Ladder Road, constructed in 1828 from Albany and westward into the Schoharie Valley for the conveyance of farm products. At the Indian Ladder trailhead, a second trail goes off to the north and circles around the northern escarpment, which you

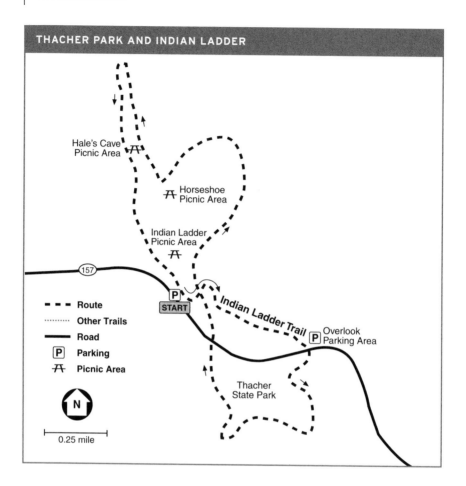

THACHER PARK AND INDIAN LADDER

Hale's Cave Picnic Area

Horseshoe Picnic Area

Indian Ladder Picnic Area

157

START

Indian Ladder Trail

Overlook Parking Area

Thacher State Park

- - - Route
········· Other Trails
—— Road
P Parking
Picnic Area

N

0.25 mile

can hike later. Descend the stairs and walk beneath the cliffs, heading south.

The upper layers of rock are the youngest, known to geologists as the Coeymans Limestone. That formation takes its name from the nearby town where it is well exposed. Of the two limestone formations in Thacher Park, the Coeymans is the thickest, averaging 50 feet from top to bottom. Look closely here and you may find the preserved remains of small sea creatures—crinoids, brachiopods, and tintaculites. These fossils date from the Late Silurian and Lower Devonian Periods, about 415 million years ago.

Continuing down the trail you notice thin layers (2 to 3 inches) of alternating light and dark beds of a "ribbon limestone," that is softer than the Coeymans and recedes beneath it as a result of erosion. This is Manlius Limestone, a formation used extensively in the manufacture of cement at Manlius near Syracuse. Those thin limestone ribbons form a 50-foot-thick layer that also contains the preserved remains of invertebrate sea creatures and algae. Part of the formation also contains a 2- to 3-inch layer of waterlime, used for making the Portland cement that will set up underwater. This forms a ledge known in the park as the Upper Bear Path. At the base of the Manlius formation is limey mudrock known as the Rondout Formation. It is a waterlime that is well exposed near the Ulster County town of Rondout. It was used to produce Rosendale, or natural cement—the invention that brought the Catskills' bluestone quarrying industry to a sudden end. This formation is less resistant to erosion but has eroded back to form the Lower Bear Path, the ledge you are standing on.

Limestone dissolves in rainwater and this causes such phenomena as disappearing streams, sinkholes, caves, and underground streams. The erosion below ground can form caves that occasionally collapse to form surface depressions, or sinkholes. The Karst topography is named after its frequent appearance in the Karst region of the Dalmatian Alps. Nearby Thompson's Lake is a sinkhole that drains through a subterranean cave at its south end.

Once in the large amphitheater, or Indian Ladder Gulf, you will see Outlet and Minelot creeks. Together they have been responsible for the erosion of this impressive embayment. When the water table is high, these two creeks form spectacular falls that you walk behind on the trail. The talus slope beneath the cliff consists of rock that has broken off and fallen from the cliff face. Along the Indian Ladder Walk, watch for the small, limestone-loving ferns, such as cliffbrakes and spleenworts. In the moist spring woods, purple trillium (wake robin) is profuse. Among the endangered species found in the park are the Indiana bat and the spotted salamander. Neo-tropical magnolia warblers, having wintered in the West Indies and Panama, nest in the park's coniferous woods.

At the south end of the Indian Ladder Trail, climb the stairs and turn left. (You will see turquoise Long Path markers along the way now. When the Indian Ladder Trail is open, the Long Path follows it: When it's closed, the path follows along the top, next to the fence.) Within 10 minutes you will arrive at the (auto-accessible) Cliff Edge Overlook. Take a minute to enjoy the views of the Green Mountains and the Adirondacks that are identified with the aid of a large viewshed map. Continue to the south entrance of the Overlook parking area, cross CR 157, and bear right on the paved Knowles Flat Picnic Area access road. Watch carefully to the left for the Long Path, which you'll see within 400 feet or so after crossing CR 157. Turn left and climb briefly to the Knowles Flat Picnic Area, bear left again (south) along the edge of a field, and enter the woods. Watch for the first junction, a Y, where the Long Path and the Red Trail go right (if you've reached the old rusty water tower, you've gone too far). Follow the trail through a dense, extensive hemlock woods for 15 minutes. At a T, take the Nature Trail (also marked with white discs) to your left, ascend, and turn right at a T where you'll see interpretive signpost 13 and signs that state To Red Trail. At a four-way junction, bear right at the Nature Trail sign. Follow the Red Trail downhill and cross Mine Lot Creek at the head of a tiny gorge. Bear right and descend into the beautiful Paint Mine Picnic Area. Go straight across CR 157, traverse the lawns, and turn left at the fence, following the dirt path back to the Indian Ladder trailhead.

You can finish the hike with a shorter (2.0 miles) loop on the Long Path along the recently designated northern Indian Ladder Trail that follows the escarpment from this point. From the Indian Ladder trailhead where you originally began, bear left now, and follow the trail along the high rim of the escarpment, passing through the Indian Ladder and Mine Lot picnic areas while threading your way through the woods on the Long Path, to the park's northerly boundary. Northeasterly views are excellent. Return on the Hailes Cave Picnic Area access road, passing a red pine plantation, arriving at the Indian Ladder trailhead and parking area in 10 or 15 minutes.

WEST NILE VIRUS

Many Hudson Valley hikers have expressed concern about the recent appearance of the West Nile Virus, a mosquito-borne infection that has been known to cause encephalitis. The chances of infection are small, but are greater in infants, the elderly, and people with weak or damaged immune systems. Symptoms include low-grade fevers and headaches, but more severe infections can result in high fever, head and body aches. There is no cure for viral infections—only the symptoms can be treated.

Of the 65 mosquito species in New York State, only the most common species, *Culex pipiens*, is associated with the virus. If you're concerned, you can protect yourself with insect repellant, long shirt sleeves and pant legs, and a hat or bug shirt during mornings and evenings when mosquitoes are most active. There is very little evidence of animals becoming infected, although the disease has been identified in horses. (Animals cannot transmit the virus to people.) Birds can contract encephalitis as well. Most of these have been crows, but infections have been confirmed in locally abundant birds such as gulls and kingfishers, ospreys, blue jays, broad-winged hawks, and eagles. Try to reduce your exposure if you are in an outbreak area. Consult the New York State Department of Health for more information.

Appendix A
HELPFUL INFORMATION

See New York State Department of Environmental Conservation (DEC) listings in the "Catskills" introduction.

TACONIC STATE PARK AND RECREATION COMMISSION

Mills–Norrie State Parks
Old Post Road, P.O. Box 893
Staatsburg, NY 12580
845-889-4646

The Taconic State Park and Recreation Commission manages land assigned to the Office of Parks and Recreation on the east side of the Hudson. It is responsible for state parks and historic sites there, including Hudson Highlands, South Taconic, and Fahnestock State parks.

PALISADES INTERSTATE PARK COMMISSION (PIPC)

Bear Mountain, NY 10911-0427
845-786-2701
www.nysparks.com
www.friendsofpalisades.org

The PIPC issues permits and trail information and supervises Harriman and Bear Mountain state parks and the state land of the Shawangunks.

APPALACHIAN MOUNTAIN CLUB (AMC)

Club Headquarters
5 Joy St.
Boston, MA 02108
617-523-0636
www.outdoors.org

New York–North Jersey Chapter
New York City Office
5 Tudor City Place
New York, NY 10017-6853
212-986-1430
office@amc-ny.org
www.amc-ny.org

Connecticut Chapter
www.ct-amc.org

The AMC, like most clubs, helps build and maintain trails in southern New York, including some sections of the Appalachian Trail and trails in Harriman, Hudson Highlands, and Catskill state parks. The AMC is also a leader in conservation, canoeing, and bicycling in the metro area. For the area covered by this book, they have a New York–North Jersey chapter, a Connecticut chapter, and a Western Massachusetts chapter.

The AMC publishes the *Catskill Mountain Guide* as part of its Mountain Guide Series (2002, featuring full-color maps), also by Peter Kick. The guide can be ordered from the AMC website or purchased in many local outdoor and bookstores.

THE SIERRA CLUB

Northeast Field Office
85 Washington St.
Saratoga Springs, NY 12866-4105
518-587-9166
E-mail: ne.field@sierraclub.org

The Sierra Club's grassroots advocacy has made it America's most influential hiking organization. Founded in 1892, the club has more than 700,000 members. The Catskills are included in the Mid-Hudson Chapter Area. The group conducts outings and speaker socials.

THE CATSKILL 3500 CLUB

www.catskill-3500-club.org

The Catskill 3500 Club is primarily a hiking organization. Candidate members receive notices of trips and outings. A membership patch is given for completing climbs of 35 summits more than 3,500 feet, four of which must be climbed a second time in winter.

NEW YORK-NEW JERSEY TRAIL CONFERENCE (NY-NJTC)

156 Ramapo Valley Rd.
Mahwah, NJ 07430
201-512-9348
E-mail: info@nynjtc.org
www.nynjtc.org

The NY-NJTC coordinates the construction and maintenance of some 1,100 miles of hiking trails, including the Appalachian Trail in New York and New Jersey and the Long Path, which connects the metropolitan area with the Catskills and beyond. They also publish regional maps of the Catskills, Northern New Jersey, West and East Hudson, Harriman State Park, the South Taconics, and the Shawangunks. They publish the "Catskills Trails" five-map set, the "East Hudson Trails" three-map set and the "Shawangunk Trails" four-map set. About 85 hiking clubs and conservation organizations belong to the conference, along with 10,000 individual members. Applications for individual membership are invited, and the annual fee includes, among other things, a subscription to the Trail Walker. This bimonthly publication describes the activities of the member clubs and features timely articles, book reviews, and trail updates. It is a reliable source of information on trail closings, relocations, and other potential problems associated with the hiking areas described in this book.

ADIRONDACK MOUNTAIN CLUB (ADK)

814 Goggins Rd.
Lake George, NY 12845-4117
518-668-4447
www.adk.org

The Adirondack Mountain Club (ADK) can supply information about their Ramapo, North Jersey, Mid-Hudson, Long Island, Knickerbocker, New York, Mohican, Albany, and Schenectady chapters, all of which schedule regular hikes in the area described in this guide. Membership is currently $35 a year.

THE CATSKILL CENTER FOR CONSERVATION AND DEVELOPMENT, INC. (CCCD)

P.O. Box 504

Arkville, NY 12406-0504

845-586-2611; catskillcenter.org

The Catskill Center for Conservation and Development (CCCD) is a regional advocate for land-use planning and environmental management, as well as an environmental "watchdog" and it is active in natural-area and historic preservation, community revitalization, and public review of regionally significant projects. The CCCD owns and manages the 200-acre Platte Clove Preserve, located at the top of Platte Clove in the town of Hunter. The Center publishes technical studies as well as a newsletter on conservation issues affecting the Catskills. The center also publishes a map entitled "The Catskill Region." Offices are in the Erpf House on Route 28 at Arkville, and applications for membership are welcome.

THE CATSKILL MOUNTAIN CLUB

www.catskillmountainclub.org

This club offers various hikes and outings for individuals of every ability level. Also conducts stewardship events and volunteer projects dedicated to the preservation of the Catskills.

THE NATURE CONSERVANCY, EASTERN NEW YORK CHAPTER

195 New Karner Road, Suite 201

Albany, NY 12205

518-690-7878; www.nature.org

The Nature Conservancy manages and protects natural areas throughout the United States. Two hikes in this guide are in Conservancy preserves.

USGS

Map Distribution Branch

U.S. Geological Survey

Box 25286, Federal Center

Denver, CO 80225

1-888-ASK-USGS

Many sporting-goods stores sell USGS maps, but for the occasional one that is unavailable, it is good to be able to order from the source using the appropriate online index. Hikers should be advised that most USGS topographic maps do not reliably show the trails described in this book.

Appendix B
LEAVE NO TRACE

THE APPALACHIAN MOUNTAIN CLUB is a national educational partner of Leave No Trace, a nonprofit organization dedicated to promoting and inspiring responsible outdoor recreation through education, research, and partnerships. The Leave No Trace Program seeks to develop wildland ethics—ways in which people think and act in the outdoors to minimize their impacts on the areas they visit and to protect our natural resources for future enjoyment. Leave No Trace unites four federal land management agencies—the U.S. Forest Service, National Park Service, Bureau of Land Management, and U.S. Fish and Wildlife Service—with manufacturers, outdoor retailers, user groups, educators, organizations such as the AMC and the National Outdoor Leadership School (NOLS), and individuals.

The Leave No Trace ethic is guided by these seven principles:

- Plan ahead and prepare
- Travel and camp on durable surfaces
- Dispose of waste properly
- Leave what you find
- Minimize campfire impacts
- Respect wildlife
- Be considerate of other visitors

The AMC has joined NOLS—a recognized leader in wilderness education and a founding partner of Leave No Trace—as a national provider of the Leave No Trace Master Educator course. The AMC offers this five-day course, designed especially for outdoor professionals and land managers, as well as the shorter two-day Leave No Trace Trainer course, at locations throughout the Northeast.

For Leave No Trace information and materials, contact: Leave No Trace Center for Outdoor Ethics, P.O. Box 997, Boulder, CO 80306; toll free: 800-332-4100, or locally, 303-442-8222; fax: 303-442-8217; www.lnt.org.

Appendix C
SELECTED BIBLIOGRAPHY

Adams, Arthur G. *The Hudson Through the Years*. Westwood, NJ: Lind Publications, 1983.

De Lisser, Richard Lionel. *Picturesque Ulster County*. Kingston, NY: Styles and Bruyn Publishing Co., 1896.

Evers, Alf. *The Catskills from Wilderness to Woodstock*. Reprint of 1972 Doubleday edition with additions. Woodstock, NY: The Overlook Press, 1982.

Goldring, Winifred. *Guide to the Geology of John Boyd Thacher Park (Indian Ladder Region) and Vicinity*. Albany: New York State Museum Handbook 14, 1933.

Gildersleeve, Robert A. *The Catskill Mountain House Trail Guide: In the Footsteps of the Hudson River School*. New York: Black Dome Press Corp., 2005.

Haring, H. A. *Our Catskill Mountains*. New York: G. P. Putnam's Sons, 1931.

The Hemlock (Catskill Center News). Cosponsored publication of the Catskill Center and Mountain Top Historical Society, Box 263, Haines Falls, NY, 1980.

Hoffer, Audrey, and Elizabeth Mikols. *Unique Natural Areas in the Catskill Region*. Arkville, NY: Catskill Center for Conservation and Development, Inc., 1974.

Hopkins, E. M. *The Sunk Mine. May 1887.* Copied by Olive Adams, Nelsonville, NY, June 1957, papers in the library of the Putnam County Historical Society.

Kick, Peter W. *Catskill Mountain Guide*, 2nd edition. Boston: Appalachian Mountain Club Books, 2009.

Kiviat, Eric. *The Northern Shawangunks: An Ecological Survey*. New York: Mohonk Preserve, Inc., 1988

Kudish, Michael. *The Catskill Forest: A History*. New York: Purple Mountain Press, Ltd., 2000.

————. *Vegetational History of the Catskill High Peaks*. Ph.D. diss., State University College of Forestry, Syracuse University, 1971.

Laird, J. R. Dunham. "Dunderberg." *South of the Mountain* (Tappan Zee Historical Society) 8, no. 4 (October–December, 1964).

Longstreth, T. Morris. *The Catskills*. New York: Black Dome Press Corp., 2003.

Lossing, Benson J. *The Hudson: From Wilderness to the Sea*. Facsimile of the 1866 edition. Somersworth, NH: New Hampshire Publishing Company, 1972.

MacCracken, Henry Noble. *Old Dutchess Forever!* New York: Hastings House Publishers, 1956.

Mack, Arthur C. *Enjoying the Catskills*. New York: Funk and Wagnalls Co., 1950.

Myles, William. *Harriman Trails: A Guide & History*. New York: New York–New Jersey Trail Conference, 1992.

New York–New Jersey Trail Conference. *New York Walk Book*. New York: Doubleday, 1984.

Newman, Joseph. "Recollections." *South of the Mountain* (Historical Society of Rockland County, NY) 13, no. 1 (January–March, 1969).

O'Brien, Raymond J. *American Sublime: Landscape and Scenery in the Lower Hudson Valley*. New York: Columbia University Press, 1981.

Posselt, Eric. *The Rip Van Winkle Trail, A Guide to the Catskills*. New York: Storm Publishers, 1952.

Putnam County Historical Society. *The Last 100 Years*. Third Workshop, 1957.

Quinn, Louise Hasbrouck, The Rev. A. Elwood Corning, Joseph W. Emsley, and Willet C. Jewell. *Southeastern New York: A History of Ulster, Dutchess, Orange, Rockland and Putnam*. Vol. 2. New York: Lewis County Publishing Company, Inc., 1946, p. 942 ff.

Ransom, James M. *Vanishing Ironworks of the Ramapos*. New Brunswick, NJ: Rutgers University Press, 1966.

Reed, John. *The Hudson Valley*. New York: Bonanza Books, 1960.

Rockwell, The Rev. Charles. *The Catskill Mountains and the Region Around*. New edition. Cornwall, NY: Hope Farm Press, 1973.

Snyder, Bradley. *The Shawangunk Mountains: A History of Nature and Man*. New York: The Mohonk Preserve, Inc., 1981.

Van Valkenburgh, Norman J., and Olney, Christopher W. *The Catskill Park: Inside the Blue Line*. New York: Black Dome Press Corp., 2004.

Van Zandt, Roland. *The Catskill Mountain House*. New Brunswick, NJ: Rutgers University Press, 1966.

———. *Chronicles of the Hudson: Three Centuries of Travelers' Accounts*. New Brunswick, NJ: Rutgers University Press, 1971.

INDEX

ABOUT THE AUTHOR

Peter Kick, a native of the Catskill Mountains, is a New York State–licensed canoeing and hiking guide and trip leader. The author of several hiking and mountain-biking guides, including AMC's *Catskill Mountain Guide*, his writing also has appeared in *Backpacker*, *Outdoor Traveler*, *Sailing*, and *Adirondack Life*. He lives in Saugerties, New York.

The Appalachian Mountain Club

Founded in 1876, the AMC is the nation's oldest outdoor recreation and conservation organization. The AMC promotes the protection, enjoyment, and wise use of the mountains, rivers, and trails of the Northeast outdoors.

People
We are nearly 90,000 members in 12 chapters, 20,000 volunteers, and over 450 full time and seasonal staff. Our chapters reach from Maine to Washington, D.C.

Outdoor Adventure and Fun
We offer more than 8,000 trips each year, from local chapter activities to major excursions worldwide, for every ability level and outdoor interest— from hiking and climbing to paddling, snowshoeing, and skiing.

Great Places to Stay
We host more than 135,000 guest nights each year at our AMC Lodges, Huts, Camps, Shelters, and Campgrounds. Each AMC Destination is a model for environmental education and stewardship.

Opportunities for Learning
We teach people the skills to be safe outdoors and to care for the natural world around us through programs for children, teens, and adults, as well as outdoor leadership training.

Caring for Trails
We maintain more than 1,400 miles of trails throughout the Northeast, including nearly 350 miles of the Appalachian Trail in five states.

Protecting Wild Places
We advocate for land and riverway conservation, monitor air quality, and work to protect alpine and forest ecosystems throughout the Northern Forest and Highlands regions.

Engaging the Public
We seek to educate and inform our own members and an additional 1.5 million people annually through AMC Books, our website, our White Mountain visitor centers, and AMC Destinations.

Join Us!
Members support our mission while enjoying great AMC programs, our award-winning AMC Outdoors magazine, and special discounts. Visit www.outdoors.org or call 617-523-0636 for more information.

THE APPALACHIAN MOUNTAIN CLUB
Recreation • Education • Conservation
www.outdoors.org

More Books from the Outdoor Experts

AMC's Best Day Hikes Near New York City

BY DANIEL CASE

This guidebook takes you to 50 of the best day hikes in New York, Connecticut, and northern New Jersey. Perfect for beginners, seasoned hikers, families, tourists, and even local residents, *AMC's Best Day Hikes Near New York City* will take you to hidden gems of the New York City metro area. (Coming Spring 2010)

ISBN: 978-1-934028-38-4
$18.95

Catskill Mountain Guide
2nd Edition

COMPILED AND EDITED BY PETER W. KICK

A must-have for every Catskills hiker, this revised and updated guide offers hikers comprehensive coverage of more than 300 miles of trails in the Catskill Mountains. Includes pull-out color paper trail map.

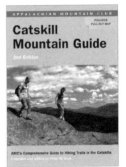

ISBN: 978-1-934028-19-3
$23.95

AMC's Best Day Hikes in the Berkshires

BY RENÉ LAUBACH

Discover 50 of the most impressive trails in the Berkshires region of Massachusetts. From short family nature walks to day-long adventures, this guide is an essential four-season reference for locals and visitors alike.

ISBN: 978-1-934028-21-6
$18.95

AMC's Best Day Hikes in Connecticut

BY RENÉ LAUBACH AND CHARLES W. G. SMITH

Explore 50 of Connecticut's most spectacular trails, from a riverside stroll along the Appalachian Trail to a more strenuous trek to the top of Bear Mountain.

ISBN: 978-1-929173-87-7
$16.95

AMC Books & Maps: Explore the Possibilities
Shop online at www.outdoors.org/amcstore or call 800-262-4455
Appalachian Mountain Club • 5 Joy Street • Boston, MA 02108

AMC BOOK UPDATES

AMC BOOKS STRIVES to keep our guidebooks as up-to-date as possible to help you plan safe and enjoyable adventures. If after publishing a book we learn that trails are relocated or route or contact information has changed, we will post the updated information online. Before you hit the trail, check for updates at www.outdoors.org/publications/books/updates.

While hiking or paddling, if you notice discrepancies with the trail description or map, or if you find any other errors in the book, please let us know by submitting them to amcbookupdates@outdoors.org or in writing to Books Editor, c/o AMC, 5 Joy Street, Boston, MA 02108. We will verify all submissions and post key updates each month.

AMC Books is dedicated to being a recognized leader in outdoor publishing. Thank you for your participation.

AMC BOOKS & MAPS

EXPLORE THE POSSIBILITIES